Irish Folk Music: A Fascinating Hobby

Francis O'Neill

In the interest of creating a more extensive selection of rare historical book reprints, we have chosen to reproduce this title even though it may possibly have occasional imperfections such as missing and blurred pages, missing text, poor pictures, markings, dark backgrounds and other reproduction issues beyond our control. Because this work is culturally important, we have made it available as a part of our commitment to protecting, preserving and promoting the world's literature. Thank you for your understanding.

IRISH FOLK MUSIC

A FASCINATING HOBBY

WITH SOME ACCOUNT OF ALLIED SUBJECTS
INCLUDING

O'FARRELL'S TREATISE ON THE IRISH OR UNION PIPES

AND

TOUHEY'S HINTS TO AMATEUR PIPERS

BY

CAPT. FRANCIS O'NEILL

COMPILER AND PUBLISHER OF
The Music of Ireland;
The Dance Music of Ireland;
O'Neill's Irish Music for the Piano or Violin.

ILLUSTRATED

"Music, miraculous rhetoric, that speakest sense,
Without a tongue, excelling eloquence;
With what ease might thy errors be excused,
Wert thou as truly lov'd as thou'rt abused.
Though dull souls neglect, and some reprove thee,
Thy sway I honor, because angels love thee."

CHICAGO
THE REGAN PRINTING HOUSE
1910
FOR SALE: LYON & HEALY, CHICAGO

487240

Copyright 1910.
BY
CAPT. FRANCIS O'NEILL

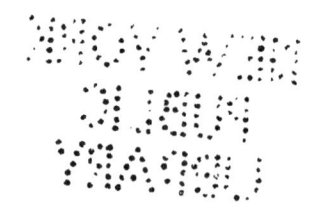

CAPT. FRANCIS O'NEILL.

PREFACE.

No alluring prospect of gain or glory prompted the preparation or publication of this series of sketches, dealing with the writer's research and experience while indulging in the fascinating hobby of collecting Irish Folk Music.

That much miscellaneous information of value to those interested in the subject had been acquired in the many years devoted to it is quite obvious, and it was not alone in response to the persuasion of men of prominence in the Irish Revival, but the desire to give publicity to certain features of the study of which the public had but a limited knowledge that the work was undertaken.

Originally written as a series of articles for a periodical of wide circulation; it was found that confining them within necessary limits would sacrifice to expediency, much of whatever interest the subject may possess, especially when extended over a period of fifteen months. Hence their appearance in book form.

In those days of astounding discovery and achievement when the irresistible attractions of the newspapers and the magazines compel attention, and ordinarily satisfy our literary longing, few books but those of uncommon brilliance or special merit, can be expected to arrest public attention or attain profitable circulation.

Believing that it is our duty to prove our faith by our works, this unique volume is contributed to a cherished cause in the hope that while it may not fill a long-felt want, it may at least stimulate an interest in the music of Erin, which though neglected, yet can excite the most tender and refined, as well as the most powerful emotions of which the human mind is susceptible.

Francis O'Neill

NOVEMBER, 1909.

CONTENTS.

CHAPTER I.

Home Influences and Experiences—Love of Music and the Faculty of Memorizing Tunes, a Source of Perennial Happiness 7

CHAPTER II.

Acquaintance With Musical Irishmen and Scotchmen in Chicago—Enlarged Opportunities for Acquiring Irish Folk Melodies — Reducing Them to Musical Notation Commenced 28

CHAPTER III.

How the Undertaking Developed, and Led to Important Results Not Originally Contemplated......................... 47

CHAPTER IV.

Stories of Tunes With a History—Airs..................... 65

CHAPTER V.

Stories of Tunes With a History—Dance Tunes............. 86

CHAPTER VI.

Stories of Tunes With a History—Dance Tunes—Continued.. 109

CHAPTER VII.

Diversity of Titles—Tunes With More Than One Name..... 128

CHAPTER VIII.

Duplication of Titles—Different Tunes With Same Name.... 145

CHAPTER IX.

Tunes of Disputed Origin—Claimed as Scotch or English.... 163

CONTENTS

CHAPTER X.
Curious and Incomprehensible Titles—Corrupt and Grotesque Irish Names.......... 187

CHAPTER XI.
Amusing Incidents and Experiences.......... 208

CHAPTER XII.
Sketches of Early Collections of Irish Music.......... 231

CHAPTER XIII.
Sketches of Collections of Irish Music Commencing With Moore's Irish Melodies; Also, Miscellaneous Collections Containing Irish Music.......... 246

CHAPTER XIV.
The Decline of Irish Music.......... 264

CHAPTER XV.
The Past and Future of Irish Music.......... 277

CHAPTER XVI.
Dr. P. W. Joyce's Estimate of the Total Number of Irish Airs Questioned.......... 293

CHAPTER XVII.
Remarks on Irish Dances.......... 296

CHAPTER XVIII.
Remarks on the Evolution of the Irish or Union Pipes.......... 308

APPENDIX A.
O'Farrell's Treatise and Instructions on the Irish or Union Pipes.......... 320

APPENDIX B.
Hints to Amateur Pipers, by Patrick J. Touhey.......... 332

APPENDIX C.
Illustrations of How Time, Taste and Development Have Varied Irish Folk Music.......... 338

IRISH FOLK MUSIC

CHAPTER I

HOME INFLUENCES AND EXPERIENCES—LOVE OF MUSIC AND
THE FACULTY OF MEMORIZING TUNES A SOURCE OF
PERENNIAL HAPPINESS

> "Music, how powerful is thy charm
> That can the fiercest rage disarm,
> Calm passions in the human breast,
> And bring new hope to a mind distrest;
> With amorous thoughts the soul inspire,
> Or kindle up a warlike fire,
>   So great is music's power.
>
> Inflamed by music soldiers fight,
> Inspired by music poets write;
> Music can heal the lovers' wounds,
> And calm fierce rage by gentle sounds;
> Philosophy attempts in vain,
> What music can with ease attain,
>   So great is music's power."

COLLECTING and preserving from oblivion the cherished melodies of one's native land must be regarded as a pleasure or pastime, and not an occupation, for none but those to whom music appeals instinctively and over whom it exercises an almost divine fascination would devote to it the time and talent which might be employed more profitably in gainful pursuits.

The music of Ireland is all that her oppressors have left her, and even that she is now losing by the indifference of her people. Our national music is a treasure, in the possession of which we should be justly proud, and as a writer in the *Dublin University Magazine* expressed it: there are few laborers in the service of Ireland to whom we should feel more grateful than to those who have devoted their talents and their time to its preservation. Believing as we do that the ancient melodies of a country afford us one of the most unerring criterions by which we can judge of the natural temperament and characteristic feelings of its people, we think it an object of the highest importance that as many examples of such strains as can be found in every country where they exist should be collected and be given to the public in a permanent form. Viewed in this way, the melodies of a country are of more value than they have been usually esteemed.

To posterity the zeal and self-sacrifice of the collector of Folk Music may be inestimable. For his reward, beyond the delights experienced in congenial studies, the collector must be content with the appreciation of those kindred spirits to whom music is the absorbing passion of their lives.

Impelled by a soulful desire to possess, for personal use, but more often for the purpose of preserving and disseminating the remnants which have survived of our musical heritage, a continuous chain of collectors and publishers of Irish melodies have, for nearly two hundred years, been engaged in this praiseworthy work, down to the present day, and it may be safely assumed that little of importance remains to be done in that line of effort by future enthusiasts.

Rarely, if ever, has the collection of Irish music been undertaken as a commercial enterprise, and owing to singularly unfortunate national, political and industrial conditions in Ireland, it is doubtful if any such undertaking ever justified the hopes of its promoters.

A later chapter, devoted to the enumeration and description of the many and various collections of Irish music published since early in the eighteenth century, will no doubt prove a revelation to the majority of readers; few having any conception of the extent to which that fascinating hobby has been pursued in the past.

From the accusation of having included in their lists, airs or tunes previously published, no collector is exempt. All, unless the first few, have perhaps unwittingly transgressed in this respect, and it is well that they did, for few airs obtained from different sources are identical. The influence of locality and individual preference constantly tend to vary original strains, and as musical compositions were preserved in the memory and mainly transmitted without notes from one generation to another, imperfect memorizing would account for the bewildering variety of strains traceable to a common origin.

A few generations ago, and down to the days of our grandparents, the harper, the union piper, the fiddler, and even the dancing-master, were cherished institutions. They met with cheerful welcome at the homes of the gentry and well-to-do peasantry throughout Ireland, and enjoyed the hospitality of their hosts as long as they cared to stay.

The pages of Carleton, Shelton Mackenzie, and other writers afford us many pleasant sketches of those characteristic features of Irish life in days gone by; and whatever causes may have led to the lamentable changes in rural life in Ireland in the nineteenth century, it is painful to note that little in the form of enjoyable entertainment is within the reach of the present generation.

Although the renowned harpers were rapidly diminishing in number at the end of the eighteenth century, the race did not become entirely extinct until early in the nineteenth century. The pipers, more popular even than the harpers, among the peasantry continued to thrive, and kept the national music alive and in vigorous circulation until the blighting famine years decimated both them and their patrons. For centuries music was the only means of livelihood available to the blind in Ireland; consequently, the afflicted practically monopolized the profession.

How the glad tidings flew far and wide when a piper or fiddler paid one of his periodical visits to a community, and with what delight did the simple, light-hearted people, young and old, boys and girls, look forward with thrills of anticipation to the evenings when they could call at the "Big house" and listen to the grand old inspiring music which finds a home in our hearts, and refuses to leave, go where we may, until life itself departs.

How often do we hear of Erin's exiles, whether on the sun-scorched plains of Hindustan, the snow-clad barrens of Alaska or beneath the Southern Cross, melted to tears or roused to unexampled valor, on hearing the strains of a cherished melody that recalled the sounds and scenes of their youth. Well has Hadow said: "Music, of all the arts, is the most universal in its appeal. From the heart it has come and to the heart it shall penetrate, and all true music shall take these words for its maxim."

The power of music over the soul is not to be defined; it appeals to every heart; it raises every latent feeling; so opposite are the sensations it inspires, that it will sometimes soothe the breast of misery, and sometimes plunge the arrow deeper; sometimes it draws the tears of sympathetic feeling even from the eye of happiness, or calms the rage of the unlettered savage.

To quote the words of an anonymous Irish writer of

Tom Carthy.
Who lived to the wonderful age of 105.
Irish Piper. Ballybunion, Co. Kerry.

one hundred years ago: "The power of music is arbitrary; it is unlimited; it requires not the aid of reason, justice or honor to protect it; it is delightful, though perhaps not useful; it is bewitching, though perhaps not needful. It delights all hearts; expands all minds; it animates all souls. It inspires devotion; it awakens love; it exalts valor; it rouses sympathy; it augments happiness; it soothes misery; and it has often been used as an instrument to lure us from innocence and peace."

When Ireland was a land of music and song, and fireside story, were the good old times in real earnest. In those days, life, seasoned with national and rational pastimes and pleasures, was more enjoyable and conducive to contented nationhood than in the first decade of the twentieth century, although the savings banks tell a tale of enhanced prosperity.

The Sunday afternoon "Patrons," which terminated the monotony of a weary week, and the flax "Mehil" dances and plays, which relieved the dreariness of the winter season, are gone and now but a memory to the aged and a tradition to the young.

With the discontinuance of those simple yet ancient diversions which the peasantry of every country but Ireland is permitted to enjoy, according to their taste and custom, the piper, the ballad-singer, and the fiddler also, it may be said, have followed the harper into extinction, so that virile and ambitious youth, unable longer to endure the intolerable dullness at home, is fleeing to the emigrant ship for relief.

This is merely voicing vain regrets which have but an indirect bearing on our subject of collecting Ireland's musical remains.

Realizing that few of the many tunes remembered from boyhood days, and others acquired in later years, were known to the galaxy of Irish musicians domiciled in Chicago, the writer decided to have them preserved in musical notation. This was the initial step in a congenial work which has filled in the interludes of a busy and eventful life.

Heedful of the dictum of the sociologist who proclaimed that the proper way to train a boy is to commence with his grandmother, the author of those sketches has deemed it advisable to begin with his grandfather.

O'Mahony *Mor*, or as he was generally called, "The *Cianach Mor*"—his clan title—kept open house in the old days in the glens of West Cork, not far from Castle Donovan, for the wandering minstrels of his time, who came that way, and it is owing to that characteristically Irish spirit of hospitality that the writer, his grandson, is now telling the story. Born and brought up in such a home, amid an environment of traditional music and song, it was to be expected that my mother—God rest her soul—would memorize much of the Folk Music of Munster and naturally transmit it orally by her lilting and singing to her children, inheriting a keen ear, a retentive memory, and an intense love of the haunting melodies of their race. Similarly gifted was our father, who, full of peace, and content, and occupying his accustomed chair beside the spacious fireplace, sung the old songs in English or Irish for his own pleasure, or the entertainment of those who cared to listen, of whom there were many not included in the family. Like the glens among the Ballyhoura Mountains, where Dr. P. W. Joyce imbibed and accumulated the hundreds of tunes which he has published, the glens and valleys in Southwest Cork were also storehouses of musical treasures unexplored by the great collectors of Irish melodies, Bunting and Petrie, whose work has won them undying fame.

Pipers, fluters and fiddlers were far from scarce in the early part of the nineteenth century, and between "Patrons" at the crossroads in summer and flax "Mehils" at the farmhouses in the winter, the tunes and songs were kept alive and in circulation, thereby adding zest and variety to an otherwise monotonous country life.

There were two pipers in our parish—Peter Hagerty, locally known as the *"Piobaire Ban,"* on account of his fair hair, and Charley Murphy, nicknamed *"Cormac na Paidireacha."* Murphy was a respectable farmer's son, who got a "blast from the fairies" one dark night, while engaged in catching blackbirds and thrushes among the furze hedges with the aid of straw torches. Becoming very lame as a result of the fairies' displeasure, he took to playing the pipes and soon acquired creditable proficiency, based on his previous skill as a flute player.

In those days succeeding the famine years, Irish was much spoken, and such children as did not get an education in English were obliged to learn their prayers and catechism from oral instruction in the Irish language. Our piper, being fluent in both languages and experienced in "Answering Mass," was chosen as instructor, and between his income from those sources and a prosperous "Patron" which he established at Tralibane Bridge, and playing at an occasional farmhouse dance, he managed to make a fair living.

With what wonder and curiosity we youngsters gazed on this musical wizard, as he disjointed his drones and regulators and tested the reeds and guills with his lips, over and over again, with exasperating deliberation. The impatience of the dancers never disconcerted him, for I really believe his actions were prompted by a desire to impress them by his seeming technical knowledge of his complicated instrument. One part of the tune was generally well rendered, but when he came to "turn it" or play the high strain his performance too frequently left much to be desired.

Peter "Bawn" or Hagerty, a tall dignified man, blind through smallpox since childhood, was an excellent piper, the best in West Cork. He had a "Patron" at Colomane Cross, was married, and maintained himself and wife in comparative comfort, until a new parish priest, unlike his predecessor, having no ear for music or appreciation of peasant pastimes, forbade "Patrons" and dances of all kinds in the parish.

The poor afflicted piper, thus deprived of his only means of making a livelihood, finally took refuge in the poorhouse —that last resource of helpless poverty and misfortune— and died there. To this day I remember a few of his tunes, picked up in early youth, but forgotten, it seems, by every one else in that part of the country.

On one occasion Peter "Bawn" was playing at a dance in a farmhouse separated only by a stone wall from my sister's dwelling. Being young and insignificant I was put to bed, out of the way, while the others went to enjoy the dance next door. It just chanced that the piper was seated close to the partition wall mentioned. Half asleep and awake the music hummed in my ears for hours, and the memory of the tunes is still vivid after the lapse of fifty years.

Many fine tunes were peculiar to certain localities in remote and isloated valleys in Ireland. Jerry Daly, a noted dancer now nearly ninety years of age, and living in Chicago, has no regard for musicians who can't play the tunes he knew when he gave exhibitions of his skill "dancing on the table" to Peter "Bawn's" music. Small blame to the musicians, for those tunes were unknown beyond a very limited circuit even then, and are entirely forgotten there now.

At another time, when a dance was given in my father's house, I was sent upstairs to be out of the way. The fascination of the music kept me awake, and young as I was, two of the tunes heard on that night still haunt my memory. John O'Neill, my father's namesake but no relative, played the German flute in grand style. He always carried with him, on such occasions, a light pair of dancing shoes, in which to display his Terpsichorean ability. He never married, and when he had grown too old to work, the sordid "strong farmer" in whose service he had spent his life, ungenerously carted him off to the poorhouse, where old age, reinforced by humiliation and grief, soon swept him into eternity "unwept, unhonored and unsung"—sad ending for a man who through life contributed so much to the happiness of others.

The rudiments of music on the flute were kindly taught me by Mr. Timothy Downing, a gentleman farmer in Tralibane, our townland. He was an accomplished performer on several instruments, but the violin was his favorite. He never played outside his own residence, and there only for a favored few. Humming a tune as he played it, was one of his peculiarities. How often since leaving home, at the age of sixteen, have I longed to get a glimpse of the chest full of music manuscript which he possessed, and from which he selected the tunes for my lessons. My wish has since been gratified, unexpectedly, for on a recent visit to Ireland I found some of it treasured by his daughter, Miss Jane, at the old homestead, and the rest of it in the possession of his son, T. A. Downing, at Bangor Wales. In addition to the tunes memorized from his playing in my boyhood there were found among his manuscripts several unpublished melodies—such as, "Open the Door for Three," "Three Halfpence a Day," and a rare setting of the hop jig, named "I have a Wife of My Own."

Except two tunes—"Far From Home," a reel, and "Off to California," a hornpipe, picked up in the San Joaquin Valley, California, in my nineteenth year, no Irish music was added to my repertory until I became a school teacher at Edina, Knox County, Missouri, where I attained my majority.

Music has had, at all stages of life, a strange influence on my destiny, not the least of which was the following instance.

The full-rigged ship Minnehaha, of Boston, on which I served "before the mast," was wrecked on Baker's Island, in the mid-Pacific. Our crew, numbering 28, were taken off this coral islet after eleven days of Robinson Crusoe experiences by the brig Zoe, manned by a white captain and a Kanaka crew. Rations were necessarily limited almost to starvation. One of the Kanakas had a fine flute, on which he played a simple one strain hymn with conscious pride almost every evening. Of course, this chance to show what could be done on the instrument was not to be overlooked. The result was most gratifying. As in the case of the Arkansas traveler, there was nothing too good for me. My dusky brother musician cheerfully shared his "poi" and canned salmon with me thereafter. When we arrived at Honolulu, the capital of the Hawaiian Islands, after a voyage of thirty-four days, all but three of the castaways were sent to the Marine Hospital. I was one of the three robust ones, thanks to my musical friend, and was therefore sent straight on to San Francisco. What became of my wrecked companions was never learned; but it can be seen how the trivial circumstance of a little musical skill exercised such an important influence on my future career.

Mr. Broderick, the school director with whom I boarded at Edina, was a native of Galway and a fine performer on the flute. Not a week passed during the winter months without a dance or two being held among the farmers. Such a motley crowd—fiddlers galore, and each with his instrument. Irish, Germans, French—types of their respective races—and the gigantic Kentuckians, whose heads were endangered by the low ceilings, crowded in, and never a misunderstanding or display of ill-nature marred those gatherings. Seated behind the fiddler, intent on picking up the tunes, was my accustomed post, but how much was memorized on those occasions cannot now be definitely stated. Three tunes, however, distinctly obtrude on my memory, viz.: A reel played by Ike Forrester, the "village blacksmith," which was named after him; "My Love is Fair and Handsome," Mr. Broderick's favorite reel; and a quickstep, which I named "Nolan, the Soldier." Nolan had been a fifer in the Confederate army during the Civil War. His son was an excellent drummer, and both gave free exhibitions of their skill on the public square at Edina to enliven the evenings while the weather was fine.

Residence in a large cosmopolitan city like Chicago affords opportunities in various lines of investigation and study not possible in other localities. Within the city limits, a territory comprising about two hundred square miles, exiles from all of Ireland's thirty-two counties can be found. Students in pursuit of any special line of inquiry will find but little difficulty in locating people whose friendship and acquaintance they may desire to cultivate.

Among Irish and Scotch music lovers, every new arrival having musical taste or talent is welcomed and introduced to the "Craft," to the mutual advantage of all concerned, and there is as much rejoicing on the discovery of a new expert as there is among astronomers on the announcement of a new asteroid or comet.

During the winter of 1875, James Moore, a young Limerick man, was in the habit of spending his evenings at my home on Poplar Avenue. His boarding-house across the street, although plastered, was yet without doors and far from comfortable, compared to a cosy seat on the woodbox back of our kitchen stove. Not having a flute of his own, he enjoyed playing on mine, and, being an expert on the instrument, it can well be imagined how welcome he was. While he had a wonderful assortment of good tunes, he seemed to regard names for them as of little consequence—a very common failing. Of the reels memorized from his playing, the "Flower of the Flock," "Jim Moore's Fancy," and the "New Policeman" were unpublished and unknown to our people except Mr. Cronin, who had variants of the two last named. The "Greencastle Hornpipe," one of the best traditional tunes in our collections, also came from Moore, as well as many others too numerous to mention. He went to New York in the spring and was never heard from after in Chicago.

Membership in the Metropolitan police force, which was joined in 1873, broadened the field of opportunity for indulging in the fascinating hobby of which I am still a willing victim. Transfer from the business district to the Deering Street station, was particularly fortunate. It was largely an Irish community, and of course traditional musicians and singers were delightfully numerous.

A magnificent specimen of Irish manhood and a charming fluter was Patrolman Patrick O'Mahony, commonly known as "Big Pat." His physique would almost justify Kitty Doherty's description of her lamented father, in her testimony before a Toronto magistrate: "He was the largest and finest looking man in the parish, and his shouldhers were so broad that Murty Delaney, the lame tailor, and Poll Kelly, could dance a *Moneen* jig on them, and lave room for the fiddler."

Born in West Clare, his repertory of rare tunes was

astonishing, the "swing" of his execution was perfect, but instead of "beating time" with his foot on the floor like most musicians he was never so much at ease as when seated in a chair tilted back against a wall, while both feet swung rhythmically like a double pendulum. Unlike many performers on the flute, whose "puffing" was so distressing and unpleasant, "Big Pat's" tones were clear and full, for his wind was inexhaustible.

From his playing I memorized the double jigs "Out on the Ocean," the "Fisherman's Widow," the "Cliffs of Moher," and several others. Among the reels learned from him were: "Big Pat's Reel," "Happy Days of Youth," "Miss Wallace," "Little Katie Kearney" and "Lady Mary Ramsey," or "The Queen's Shilling"; also "The Thunder Hornpipe" and "Bantry Bay," one of the most delightful traditional hornpipes in existence.

Many an impromptu concert in which the writer took part enlivened the old Deering Street Police Station about this time. An unique substitute for a drum was operated by Patrolman Michael Keating, who, forcing a broomhandle held rigidly against the maple floor at a certain angle, gave a passable imitation of a kettle drum. His ingenuity and execution never failed to evoke liberal applause.

It was soon learned that a local celebrity, John Conners, famed as a piper, lived in the district. When found, he proved to be an affable, accommodating business man whose musical talent was not in great demand at home. He was willing to play for me anywhere but in his own house when he had his instrument in order after long disuse. Being then unacquainted with the famous pipers residing in other parts of the city, I envied Mr. Conners his skill on a set of pipes which were neither Irish nor Scotch, but a combination of both. He kindly left them in my custody for months, so that by assiduous practice my former envy was transferred to him. Mr. Conners was a native of Dublin, and one of his juvenile pranks which he mentioned with pride was the capture and larceny of a patriarchal goat, whose hide was urgently needed to make a new bag and bellows for a set of Union pipes.

Before the Civil War he played on the Mississippi steamboats plying out of Memphis, Tennessee. While he prided himself on his fancied superiority in playing Irish airs, his memory will remain fresh and green longer on account of one particular jig, called "The Gudgeon of Maurice's Car," which he alone knew. The weird tale in connection with this now famous tune will be told in another chapter, so we will return for the present to the Deering Street Police District.

Within a few squares of the police station lived the Maloneys, a noted family of musicians—Denis, Dan, Tom and Mary—all good performers on the German flute. I believe all have passed away, except the first named, who resides in South Chicago, a hale, hearty old man and capable of holding his own yet with the best of them. He played with Delaney and Murnihan, piper and fiddler respectively, at the Gaelic Society entertainments and other occasions in recent years. Their father, a rather lively old man, was an agile dancer, but the rheumatism in one of his legs seriously handicapped him when dancing to the music of Jimmy O'Brien, a Mayo piper who spent a few months among us in the early seventies. While attempting to dance a certain jig, then to me unknown, he appealed to the piper, in strident tones, "Single it, single it; I can't double with the other foot." This concession granted, he continued for a time, amidst great applause. The jig alluded to I memorized, and, being without a name, it was christened "The Jolly Old Man," in honor of Mr. Maloney.

In later years a version of it, found in an old volume, was entitled "The Brisk Young Lad." It is also called "The Brisk Irish Lad." In a set of country dances, printed in London for the year 1798, and in Volume 1 of Aird's *"Selection of Scotch, English, Irish and Foreign Airs,"* published in Glasgow in 1782, a version of it is called "Bung Your Eye."

O'Brien was a neat, tasty Irish piper of the Connacht school of close players, and though his Union pipes were small, they were sweet and musical. To what extent I was indebted to him for tunes is a question not now easily determined, but there is no doubt that from his playing I picked up "Jimmy O'Brien's Jig" and the reels "Mary Grace," "The Woman of the House," "Jenny Picking Cockles" and "The Star of Munster," and several others. The first named reel was entirely unknown even to musicians from O'Brien's native county. In later years we found a fair version of it, as "Copey's Jigg," in an extremely rare volume of Irish music, called "The Bee," but undated. Under the same name it was also printed in Clinton's "Gems of Ireland," published in London in 1841. O'Briens style of it is much to be preferred. One of his peculiarities—and an unpleasant one, occasionally—was a habit of stopping the music in order to indulge in conversation. He could not be induced to play a tune in full, when under the influence of stimulants, as his loquacity was uncontrollable, and he never hesitated under such conditions to express a passing sentiment.

Amiable and harmless at all times, he died at a comparatively early age in Chicago, a victim to conviviality, his only weakness.

A musical star of great magnitude appeared in Chicago from the eastern cities in 1880. John Hicks, celebrated from Washington to Boston as a great Irish piper, accompanied by the no less renowned Irish dancer, Neill Conway, came to fill a theatrical engagement. They won immediate popularity, but, unfortunately, Conway had brought his eastern failings with him, and before Hicks knew it, his light-footed partner had squandered their joint salaries. As he had defrayed all traveling expenses from New York, even to the extent of paying for Conway's dancing shoes, Hicks found himself short of funds. This led to his playing in Conley's saloon, in Des Plaines Street, where he attracted a large and cosmopolitan audience. Differing from most pipers in many respects, he played modern airs, schottisches, waltzes, and polkas, to suit the most fastidious company. In short, he was a thorough musician, could read music on sight and transpose the key of any tune at pleasure, having been a protege of the "Sporting" Captain Kelly, of the Curragh of Kildare.

On one occasion he was encountered on State Street whistling from the sheet music displayed in the window of a music store. He inquired if I knew of any place where he could earn some money. Remembering James Rowan, a well-to-do property owner near the Bridgeport rolling mills, whom I had often heard remark that he would gladly give five dollars any time to hear a good reel on the Irish pipes, this appeared to be a fortunate opportunity to favor two interests at one time. So, together, we called on the liberal patron of pipe music without delay. We found this large-hearted man Rowan contentedly gossiping in O'Flaherty's tailor shop, and were received with every outward appearance of pleasure. Piper Hicks rolled out reel after reel in his best style for an hour or so, evoking only responsive grunts of approval from Rowan. Doubtless he remembered his boasts and my knowledge of them; hence the unsympathetic chill in his demeanor which betrayed his membership in the "Tightwad Club."

We withdrew with the best grace posible, but my humiliation was such that I borrowed five dollars from a friend and forced Hicks to take it, thus becoming eligible myself to full membership in the "Idiotic Order of E. Z. Marks."

An engagement of three weeks at St. Bridget's church fair was in striking contrast to our late disappointment. Such was the popularity and fame of Hicks' playing that a detail of police had no easy time in regulating the crowds which came from far and near to hear him and dance to his music. Whenever possible, the writer was on hand, charmed beyond expression by the precision, rhythm and melody of his execution. Of the many tunes picked up from his playing, one at least, is the double jig "Paddy in London," and another is "Hicks' Hornpipe," named for him, but never heard or found elsewhere. A delightful hornpipe of five strains, named "The Groves," was beyond my powers of memorizing completely in the limited opportunities presented, and its loss, with slight prospects of recovery, was much regretted.

Through Patrick Touhey, an even greater performer on the Union pipes in a younger generation, we obtained an excellent setting of this fine traditional tune, and it has since been printed in O'Neill's *Music of Ireland*. A good version of it was later published in Petrie's *Complete Collection of Irish Music*.

Hicks' wonderful music was the talk of the town. Old Mike Finucane, an ex-alderman and still a very important personage in the ward, was very anxious to hear him, but on account of his rheumatism was unable to attend the fair. The piper, always gracious, obligingly visited the great man at his residence, and entertained him for half an hour. Hicks was giving some extra flourishes to "Garryowen," by way of variations, when, relaxing his dignity, Mr. Finucane waved his hands in glee and shouted, approvingly, "That's all of it now—that's the whole of it—and it can't be bate; I often heard 'St. Patrick's Day' played before, but this is the first time I ever heard anyone play the whole of it." With sincere approval of his abilities from such a distinguished authority, the piper's smiles, on leaving, could not well be misunderstood.

I came near forgetting to mention that "Blind Murphy," whose eccentricities will be dealt with in a chapter on "Amusing Incidents," called on Mr. Hicks one morning to have his pipes put in order. "Put them on yourself, Mr. Murphy, as then I can tell best what is necessary," said Hicks, on learning Murphy's mission. The latter willingly complied, and wheezed out a few of his favorite tunes. "Play something," suggested Hicks, who evidently failed to realize that his visitor had already done his level best. This was too much for Murphy, who imagined he was doing wonders. In fact, his pride had been wounded and, unbuckling his instrument, he promptly departed, in no pleasant frame of mind.

This calls to mind another Murphy, a New York piper, who abandoned his occupation as coachman and came to Chicago to engage in business. He was a great romancer and professed his ability to play on all kinds of bagpipes equally well. His pretensions aroused some suspicion, so arrangements were made to put him to the test. Unexpectedly, and to his great confusion, after declaring his ability to finger the Scotch chanter like a Highlander, a nice set of Scotch pipes with drones arranged in a stock and blown with a bellows like the Irish or Union pipes, was handed to him. He endeavored to excuse himself on the plea of not feeling so well that evening, but he couldn't get out of it. He was fairly caught, and this fiasco punctured his pretensions.

The strains of a slashing but unfamiliar reel floating out

on the night air from the lowered windows of Finucane's Hall caught my eager ear one Saturday night, when Tommy Owens was playing for a party. Being on duty as Desk Sergeant at the time, and as the police station was just across the street, I had little difficulty in memorizing the tune. Although it had never been printed it soon gained wide circulation among experts, and it had become such a favorite with Inspector John D. Shea, that it has since been identified with his name. It is printed in O'Neill's *Music of Ireland*, under its original title, "The Ladies' Pantalettes."

While yet attached to the Deering Street Station as desk sergeant, I heard of John K. Beatty, a native of County Meath, who had quite a reputation as an Irish piper. He lived in an unfinished house into which altered fortunes obliged him to move from a pretentious mansion in Hyde Park, but his good humor and blinding egotism evidently had not suffered by the change. Nothing pleased him better than an audience, only they must be demonstrative in their appreciation in order to obtain the best results. This saved time, for if they relaxed at all in catering to his vanity he suspended the performance to tell how much superior he was to all other pipers. Yet withal he was the soul of geniality, and did not intend to reflect on anybody. It was not that they were poor or indifferent players, but that his superlative excellence put him in a class all by himself. Execution—too much of it—he had, but neither time nor rhythm. He was truly the dancer's despair, although an excellent dancer himself. In humming or lilting he was incomparable, but he couldn't for the life of him bring it that way out of the chanter. One call satisfied my curiosity, and besides, I felt unequal to the task of applauding a performance more amusing than edifying. Our friendship and mutual respect, however, remain unshaken to this day.

An American lady, of wealth and social distinction, proud of her Irish ancestry, once appealed to us for aid in getting out a suitable programme. The best Irish talent obtainable was engaged. But how about Mr. Beatty? It was contended that he could play "The Banks of Claudy" with trills and variations in an acceptable style, yet no one could guarantee that he would confine himself within limits. In any event he was the typical bard in appearance. His confident air and florid face, adorned with a heavy white mustache, and a head crowned with an abundance of long white hair, would naturally appeal to an Irish audience, so his name was placed on the programme, well towards the end, to minimize the effect of his possible disregard of instructions.

When his time came to execute "The Banks of Claudy," he met all expectations—and much more. Intoxicated by the applause, all was forgotten but the mad desire to get more of it, so he broke loose with rhapsodical jigs and reels, his head on high, nostrils distended like a race-horse on the home stretch, while both feet pounded the platform in unison. He evidently "had it in" for the regulators, for he clouted the keys unmercifully, regardless of concord or effect, and when he quit, from sheer exhaustion, it is safe to say that no such deafening laughter and handclapping ever greeted an Irish piper before or since.

He was sent home in a carriage, a circumstance which he proudly attributed to his personal distinction, but, strange to say, that was his last appearance on a public platform. "When I'm dead the last of the pipers are gone," he confided to me sadly one day. "There's none of 'em at all, not even Billy Taylor, of Philadelphia, could play the tunes the way I do."

In this I agreed with him, for none of them could—or would.

"Hail, music! sweet enchantment hail!
Like potent spells thy powers prevail;
On wings of rapture borne away,
All nature owns thy universal sway.
For what is beauty, what is grace,
But harmony of form and face;
What are the beauties of the mind,
Heav'n's rarest gifts, by harmony combined.''

CHAPTER II

ACQUAINTANCE WITH MUSICAL IRISHMEN AND SCOTCHMEN IN CHICAGO—ENLARGED OPPORTUNITIES FOR ACQUIRING IRISH FOLK MELODIES—REDUCING THEM TO MUSICAL NOTATION COMMENCED

> "Of all the arts beneath the heaven,
> That man has found or God has given,
> None draws the soul so sweet away,
> As Music's melting, mystic lay;
> Slight emblem of the bliss above
> It soothes the spirit all to love."

For several years subsequent to making the acquaintance of Mr. Conners, I circulated among the Highland pipers, such as William McLean, Joseph Cant, John Monroe, Neil McPhail, John Shearer and the Swanson brothers—all Highlanders. Patrick Noonan, Tom Bowlan, and the two Sullivans, were Irishmen. Only from the two first named did I derive any addition to my stock of tunes. McLean, who was an old man, claimed to have had no rival in Scotland in his early manhood, and I can well believe it. His style and execution were admirable, and he took great pleasure in playing such Irish tunes as were possible on the limited compass of a Highland chanter, while the majority of Scotch players confined themselves to the study of such tunes as were printed in books of pipe music.

Noonan was a character, suave and persuasive as a Donegal peddler in his commercial transactions. He was a fine performer on the Highland pipes, but his ruling passion

SERGT. JAMES O'NEILL.

was the acquisition of bagpipes of any kind and their equipments and disposing of them to amateurs at a profit. In effecting a trade, I am afraid he not infrequently disregarded a few obligations imposed by the Ten Commandments; but the sale once made, true to the traditional hospitality of his people, he would cheerfully spend the profits with the purchaser. Naturally enough, he died early and poor.

Joseph Cant, a Perthshire man, was a genial fellow who had the rare faculty of appreciating merit and good qualities in others. He wore a first prize medal won at an annual competition held at Buffalo, New York, between American and Canadian Highland pipers. It was through Mr. Cant that James O'Neill, who has been for years so intimately associated with me in collecting and popularizing the Folk Music of our race, was discovered.

A native of County Down, but long a resident of Belfast, James O'Neill was as familiar with Scottish music as Joe Cant himself, whose admiration he won by his airy style of playing flings and strathspeys on the violin. Quiet and unassuming in manner, his fine musical talent was unsuspected by his neighbors, and it was only by diligent inquiry that his address was learned. When found, he was all that our mutual friend Cant represented him to be, and much more, for his versatility in reducing to musical notation the playing, whistling, singing and humming of others, was truly phenomenal. None from the North Country possessed such a store of Ulster melodies as he, and it was chiefly because of his skill and unselfishness that the initial step in our joint work was undertaken.

Shortly after our acquaintance began, my transfer to Police Headquarters (an assignment which continued for nine years) was not conducive to successful co-operation. The acquisition of new tunes, however, suffered no abatement. According to the historian, Hume: "Almost every one has a predominant inclination, to which his other desires and affections submit, and which governs him, though perhaps with some intervals, through the whole course of his life." Irresistibly attracted by music, and particularly Irish Folk Music, no opportunity was overlooked to gratify this inborn desire; and while at this date it cannot be estimated how many fugitive melodies were thus promiscuously acquired, it is evident the influence of this persistent pursuit on final results cannot but be considerable.

One afternoon Sergeant James Cahill happened into the General Superintendent's office, and, knowing my interest in such matters, told me about a good Irish piper just arrived in town, who was playing in a saloon on Van Buren Street. Having been frequently disappointed in finding persons of that class not equal to their reputations, I was not prepared for the surprise in store. On reaching the building, and before entering, I knew at once that this was an exceptional instance where the musician's abilities were underestimated. Within we found Bernard Delaney, a comparatively young man, rolling out the grandest jigs, reels and hornpipes I ever heard, and in a style unequaled by any piper we previously had met, not excepting our accomplished friend, John Hicks. His instrument was not large, but, oh, my, what a torrent of melody it poured forth! What the Rev. Dr. Henebry in later years endeavored to describe with his comprehensive vocabulary, the writer will not attempt.

Here, indeed, was a prize—and what a repertory of unfamiliar tunes he had from Tullamore, King's County, his native place!

Without delay, Alderman Michael McNurney and Sergeant James Early, both good pipers, and a host of others

Bernard Delaney.

of similar taste in music, came to see and hear this star of the first magnitude. Before long Delaney's fame spread far and wide, and, being modest and unspoilt by flattery, he gained enduring friendship and prosperity. It is not to our purpose to enter into the details of what transpired about this time, except to mention that he soon had a pleasant engagement, and was accessible to all who desired to enjoy his music and learn his tunes. In the latter role the writer was by no means the least successful.

A few months had passed pleasantly for all concerned, when there came to Chicago, Power's delightful Irish play, *The Ivy Leaf*. Their piper, Eddie Joyce, a brilliant young musician, took sick and was sent to a hospital. Great failings are not infrequently the concomitants of great talents, and so this precocious genius, whose fame was nation-wide, passed away in his teens, sincerely mourned by a large circle of admirers. To take his place temporarily, Delaney reluctantly consented; but such were his success and popularity, that Powers insisted on keeping him permanently on an increased salary. While we could not help congratulating Delaney, we were by no means reconciled to our loss. Nothing but a more desirable position in Chicago could be expected to allure him to return. When that had been arranged for, the writer intercepted *The Ivy Leaf* company in New York city and returned to the western metropolis, accompanied by our piper, where he became and still is a member of the Chicago police force. The interest in the study and practice of traditional Irish Music was noticeably affected by the excellence of Delaney's execution, for he was in great demand as an attraction on festive and various public occasions.

Delaney, who had been traveling post for some in the Rolling Mill district, occasionally stepped into a saloon on

Ashland Avenue, where a near-blind piper named Kelly nightly entertained an appreciative audience. Kelly being but recently from the East, had no suspicion of Delaney's identity, and the latter, uncommonly mild and unassuming, gave no intimation that he knew anything about music. Of course, murder will out—Delaney was recognized, and, regardless of his remonstrance, he was carried bodily into the dining room, stripped of his uniform coat, and compelled to put on the astonished Kelly's pipes. What followed can be better imagined than described.

Two or three years later there came to my office at Police Headquarters a modest young man who introduced himself as Patrick Touhey and said he had been advised by the great piper, "Billy" Taylor, of Philadelphia, to call on me with a view of meeting Bernard Delaney. On our way to the latter's home I learned that Touhey had been playing for a troupe that got stranded down the state somewhere, on account of the country roads being impassable at that time of the year.

Playing together, Delaney and Touhey were a picturesque team, the former being right-handed and the latter left-handed. 'Twas a most enjoyable evening for those who were fortunate enough to be present. Touhey proved to be another surprise, who has since developed into a wonder. In the opinion of his admirers, he has no equal. As he has adopted the stage as his profession, the public has the opportunity to hear him; and if his qualities as an Irish piper fail to meet their expectations, I'm inclined to think they will be subject to disappointment to the end of their lives.

After many years of intercourse with all manner of Irish musicians, native and foreign born, who were addicted to playing popular Irish music with any degree of passable proficiency, I began to realize that there was yet much work left for the collectors of Irish Folk Music. Many, very many, of the airs, as well as the lilting jigs, reels and hornpipes which I had heard in West Cork in my youth, were new and unknown to the musicians of my acquaintance in cosmopolitan Chicago. Neither were those tunes to be found in any of the printed collections accessible.

The desire to preserve specially this precious heritage from both father and mother, for the benefit of their descendants at least, directed my footsteps to Brighton Park, where James O'Neill, the versatile northern representative of the great Irish clan, committed to paper all that I could remember from day to day and from month to month, as memory yielded up its stores. Many trips involving more than twenty miles travel were made at opportune times, and I remember an occasion when twelve tunes were dictated at one sitting.

Originally there was no intention of compiling more than a private manuscript collection of those rare tunes remembered from boyhood days, to which may be added some choice specimens picked up in later years, equally worthy of preservation. Drawing the line anywhere was found to be utterly impracticable, so we never knew when or where to stop.

Some difficulties were at first encountered in acquiring any tunes from some of our best traditional musicians, but curiosity in time awakened an interest in our work, and, as in the old story, those who came to scoff remained to pray, or rather play, and it was not long before the most selfish and secretive displayed a spirit of liberality and helpfulness truly commendable. Mutual exchange of tunes proved pleasant and profitable. Narrow, despicable meanness, the characteristic of the miser, whether in money or music, asserted itself in one case, however, where it was least expected or deserved, so that nothing was derived from that source except what had been already memorized from his playing.

At a wedding in the stock yards district in the winter of 1906 I formed the acquaintance of James Kennedy, a fiddler of uncommon merit. He was the smoothest jig and reel player encountered in Chicago so far. His tones were remarkably even and full, and his selection of tunes were all gems; in fact, he had none other. It is needless to say our chance acquaintance ripened into friendship. An exception in his class, he was modest, accommodating and, rarer still, entirely free from professional jealousy. His admiration for John McFadden, whom I had not yet met, was outspoken and sincere.

From another source we learned that Kennedy's father was a violinist of celebrity; in fact, "the daddy of them all" around Ballinamore, in the County of Leitrim. To him we are indebted for many fine unpublished tunes, such as the "Tenpenny Bit" and "My Brother Tom," double jigs; "Top the Candle," hop jig; and the reels "Silver Tip," the "New Demesne," the "Chorus Reel," the "Ewe Reel," the "Mountain Lark," "Colonel Rodney," the "Drogheda Lasses," the "Cashmere Shawl," "Green Garters," the "Cup of Tea," "Kiss the Maid behind the Barrel," and the "Reel of Mullinavat." The latter tune I am inclined to believe Kennedy picked up from Adam Tobin, for Mullinavat is in Kilkenny, Tobin's native county. Inferior settings of two others have appeared in different collections.

Notwithstanding Kennedy's opportunities, he did not play all of his father's tunes, it seems, for it turned out that his sister Nellie, over whom he had little advantage as a violinist, played three excellent tunes learned at home, which he did not know, namely, the jig called the "Ladies of Carrick," and the reels "Touch me if you dare" and "Peter Kennedy's Fancy."

Noting down tunes from dictation at his own home, or visiting those who could not conveniently call on him, kept my versatile collaborator, James O'Neill, decidedly busy. Nor was he at all slow in making discoveries by his own efforts. John Carcy, one of them, was a veritable treasure. Born and grown to manhood in County Limerick and brought up in the midst of a community where old ideas and customs prevailed, his memory was stored with traditional music. He numbered among his relatives many pipers and fiddlers, and being quite an expert on the violin himself in his younger days before that arch-enemy of musicians—rheumatism—stiffened his fingers, his settings were ideal. Gradually, from week to week, and extending into years, his slumbering memory surrendered gems of melody unknown to this generation, and not until within a few months of death did his contributions entirely cease. Even Mrs. Carey's memory yielded up a fine reel, the "Absent-minded Woman," which her husband did not play.

In the course of time, enthusiasts on the subject were frequent visitors to Brighton Park, the Mecca of all who enjoyed traditional Irish music. They came to hear James O'Neill play the grand old music of Erin which had been assiduously gathered from all available sources for years, and, pleased with the liberality displayed in giving everything so acquired circulation and publicity, they cheerfully entered into the spirit of the enterprise and contributed any music in their possession which was desired. Many pleasant evenings were thus spent, and those who enjoyed them will remember the occasions as among the most delightful of their lives.

To speak in praise of the ability of one whose work in

the arrangement of our collections should speak for itself, may be a violation of conventional ethics; yet I may be permitted to say that on more than one occasion, and without preparation, he has filled a place in an orchestra in the absence of a regular member, and that in rendering Irish airs on the violin he is so far without a successful rival.

Sergeant James Early, a very good Irish piper, and his friend, John McFadden, a phenomenal fiddler, both inheriting the music of David Quinn, the sergeant's instructor, posessed almost inexhaustible stores of traditional tunes. All that his admirer, James Kennedy, told me of McFadden's excellence, was more than realized. The best of them were inclined to take off their hat to "Mack," as he was familiarly called. Everything connected with his playing was original and defiant of all rules of modern musical ethics; yet the crispness of tone and rhythmic swing of his music were so thrilling that all other sentiments were stifled by admiration.

He came of a musical family, and it is quite certain that his attainments were due more to heredity than to training; but it does not appear that any connection existed, except the identity of surname, between the McFaddens of Mayo and the musical McFaddens of Rathfriland, County Down, from whom Dr. Hudson, editor of *The Dublin Monthly Magazine,* obtained some rare Irish melodies.

During successive years, strains almost forgotten kept coming from their stimulated memories and were deftly placed in score by our scribe, O'Neill. "Old Man" Quinn, as he was affectionately called, belonged to the Connacht school of pipers and had great renown as a jig player. He was much given to adding variations to his tunes, according to the custom of his time. As a wit he had a keen sense of the ridiculous, and his unlimited fund of humorous and oftentimes grotesque anecdotes derived from personal experience is even now as well remembered as his music. One frequently quoted was the case of a conceited fellow whose execution on the pipes was far from perfect. Fishing for compliments, he remarked to Mr. Quinn one day, "Most people say I'm the best piper in this part of the country, but I don't think myself that I am." "Faith, it is you I believe," was the old man's candid but uncomplimentary reply.

Not the least prolific of our contributors was Patrolman John Ennis, a native of County Kildare, who was both a fluter and a piper. His tunes were, as a rule, choice and tasty, and his interest in the success of our hobby was displayed in a curious way. Suspecting that several pet tunes were withheld from us by a couple of good players, he conceived the scheme of ingratiating himself with the musicians. Affecting unconcern, he contrived to memorize the treasured tunes, and then had them promptly transferred to James O'Neill's notebook. To him we are indebted for many good tunes, among them being the following: "Young Tom Ennis," "Bessy Murphy," "Ask My Father," "Child of My Heart," and "Will You Come Down to Limerick"—jigs; "Toss the Feathers," "Jennie Pippin," "Miss Monaghan," "Kitty Losty," "Trim the Velvet," "The Dogs Among the Bushes," "The Sligo Chorus," "College Grove," "Over the Bridge to Peggy," and the "Reel of Bogie." Two excellent hornpipes, "The Kildare Fancy" and "The Wicklow Hornpipe," were also contributed by Ennis. None of the above dance tunes, so far as the writer is aware, has ever been published in an Irish collection.

John Ennis was also a good entertainer, and many a Sunday afternoon was pleasantly passed at his hospitable home by a coterie of kindred spirits in those years. Besides, he possessed literary ability of no mean order, and contributed some able and interesting article on Irish music and dances to the press from time to time. His son Tom displays much musical talent and bids fair to rank high as an Irish piper.

"The Garden of Daisies," a famous set dance, was known to us all by name alone, and we had almost despaired of obtaining a setting of it, when, to our joy, we learned that O'Neill's next-door neighbor, Sergeant Michael Hartnett knew the tune as it was played where he lived. It varied but little from an air I heard my father sing. The old saying, "It never rains but it pours," was well exemplified in this case. While enjoying a steamboat excursion on the Drainage Canal a week or so later, what should I hear on the boat but another version of our long-lost tune, played in fine style by Early and McFadden! It had been sent them by Pat Touhey, who learned it from a fiddler recently arrived in Boston, and who in turn had picked it up from Stephenson, the great Kerry piper. The latter, whose execution on the Irish or Union pipes was remarkable, once accompanied Ludwig, the celebrated baritone, on one of his American tours. Two inferior versions of this tune have since appeared in Petrie's *Complete Collection of Irish Music*. The Stephenson setting, in O'Neill's *Music of Ireland,* is much to be preferred.

Another favorite, well known by name as "The Fox Chase," was obtained from the same source, and although I have since heard played and also found among the Hudson manuscripts other versions of it, none equals Stephenson's setting, which fills fifteen staffs.

According to Grattan Flood, "The Fox Chase" was composed by a famous Munster piper named Edward Keating Hyland, who had studied theory and harmony under Sir John Stevenson. He won the royal favor on the occasion of George the Fourth's visit to Dublin in 1821, and was rewarded with the King's order for a fifty-guinea set of pipes in appreciation of his fine performance.

In a large work entitled *Ireland,* by Mr. and Mrs. S. C. Hall, published about 1840, this composition is mentioned in connection with Gandsey, the "king of Kerry pipers." "To hear him play," they say, "was one of the richest and rarest treats of Killarney. Gandsey is old and blind, yet a finer or more expressive countenance we have rarely seen. His manners are, moreover, comparatively speaking, those of a gentleman. For many years he was the inmate of Lord Headley's mansion, and was known universally as 'Lord Headley's piper.' It would be difficult to find anywhere a means of enjoyment to surpass the music of Gandsey's pipes. No one who visits the lakes must omit to send for him. Those who return without hearing him will have lost half the attractions of Killarney. Above all, he must be required to play 'The Mothereen Rue,' or 'The Hunting of the Red Fox.' It is the most exciting tune we have ever heard, and exhibits the power of the Irish pipes in a manner of which we had previously had no conception. It is of considerable length, beginning with the first sight of the fox stealing the farmer's goose; passing through all the varied incidents of the chase—imitating the blowing of the horns, the calling of the hunters, the baying of the hounds, and terminates with 'the death' and the loud shouts over the victim. Gandsey accompanies the instrument with a sort of recitative which he introduces occasionally, commencing with a dialogue between the farmer and the fox,—

" 'Good morrow, fox.' 'Good morrow, sir.'
'Pray, fox, what are you ating?'
'A fine fat goose I stole from you,
Sir, will you come here and taste it?' "

This celebrated musician, who died in 1857, when ninety years old, was the son of an English soldier who won the love of a Killarney colleen and settled down in that romantic spot.

The following story, told me years ago in Chicago by a Kerryman, may be found not uninteresting:

An indifferent strolling piper happened along one day, and, after listening to Gandsey's music for a while, was induced to play a few tunes himself. The poorest performance rarely fails to evoke some recognition from an Irish audience, so the kindly Gandsey remarked, *"Ni holc e sinn"* ("That's not bad"). Not to be outdone in politeness, the stranger generously replied, *"Ni holc tusa fein a Gandsey"* ("You're not bad yourself, Gandsey").

Our placid neighbor, Sergeant Hartnett, born among the glens in northwest Cork, proved to be a rare "find." An excellent dancer of the Munster school, he remembered many old dance tunes beside "The Garden of Daisies," such as "The Ace and Deuce of Pipering," etc., as well as strange and haunting plaintive airs. What could be more characteristic in traditional Irish music than "The Fun at Donnybrook"? The text recited in Irish what a stranger saw at that noted fair, and of course the rhyming narrative extended to more than a dozen verses. This strain so charmed our kind and appreciative friend, Rev. Dr. Henebry, while on a visit to our city, that it was not without much persuasion he could be induced to lay down his violin, although dinner awaited him.

Rumors were afloat to the effect that a youthful prodigy on the fiddle lived somewhere in "Canaryville," a nicknamed settlement in the Stock Yards district. When located he proved to be a modest, good-looking young fellow, apparently about seventeen years old, named George West. Prosperity evidently overlooked him in the distribution of her favors; in fact, he had no fiddle. The five-dollar "Strad" his widowed mother bought him before she died had been crunched beyond repair by over two hundred pounds of femininity which inadvertently landed on its frame. A trip to Brighton Park demonstrated that his reputation had not been exaggerated. He was a wonder, all right, for his age, and a credit to any age. Such a bow hand and such facility in graces, trills and triplets, were indeed rare. 'Twas a revelation, truly, and it was little wonder that admiration of his gift was succeeded by jealousy occasionally. Everything was done to place him in some pleasant and profitable position. Work, however, was not to his taste. Ambition along that line held no lures for him. One solitary talent he possessed, and that uncultivated. Two lessons, aside from hearing and watching James Kennedy play, constituted his only musical training, yet he could memorize and play offhand any dance tune within a few minutes. I recollect one occasion when he picked up four from me in less than half an hour. Three good tunes were taken down from his playing—two double jigs, "The Boys of Ballinamore" and "The Miller of Glanmire," and a hornpipe called "The Boys of Bluehill." This latter tune, which West heard from a strolling fiddler named O'Brien, was entirely new to our Chicago musicians.

One evening I accompanied him to make the acquaintance of his friend O'Malley, who eked out a living by playing at house dances. A trip through a few dark passageways and up a rickety back stairs led us to his apartments. There was welcome for West, but his introduction of me as Captain of Police was very coldly received. With evident reluctance, O'Malley produced the fiddle, on West's request, while his wife and children viewed me as an interloper, with unconcealed misgiving. Calling the children to me in a friendly way, and giving them some coin, effected a sudden change in the atmosphere. Beer soon appeared on the table, and under its mollifying influence all indications of suspicion and distrust quickly disappeared. O'Malley, though handicapped with the loss of one finger from his left hand, played "like a house on fire" as long as we wanted to listen. His rapid yet correct execution was astonishing under the circumstances, but I learned afterwards that he was seldom capable of handling the bow after midnight if any kind of intoxicating liquor was within reach. In such emergencies, his understudy, Georgie West, completed the engagement. Thus lived the careless, improvident but talented Georgie, until an incident in his life rendered a trip to the far west advisable.

Attracted by the growing popularity of Brighton Park as a rendezvous for Irish music "cranks," and the publicity given to our meetings by the press, the number of visitors constantly increased. Among them were such desirables as Sergeants James Kerwin, James Cahill, Gerald Stark and Garrett Stack; also Patrolmen Timothy Dillon, William Walsh and John P. Ryan.

Sergeant Cahill, unassuming as he was, possessed many quaint tunes from the County Kildare, where he was born, and besides being an Irish piper, he was an expert woodturner. In a shop in the basement of his residence he made many chanters fully equal to Taylor's work in tone and finish. Even as a reed-maker he had few equals, and what was still better, his liberality and assistance were never appealed to in vain.

píobaiṙe Cloinne Néill ó Aṙdmacha.
(The O'Neill Pipers of Armagh in Gaelic Costume.)

Mr. Dillon, a veteran violinist and officer of the law, hailed from County Kerry, and any one at all acquainted with Irish geography and tradition knows what to expect of him. His tones and trills, weird as the banshee's wailing, realized the cherished ideals of our enthusiastic champion of traditional Irish music, the Rev. Dr. Henebry.

"Big" John Ryan, once champion "stone-thrower," and an amateur on several musical instruments, gave us the inimitable "Raking Paudheen Rue" and "The Fair Maid of Cavan," although he hails from historic Tramore, County Waterford.

"Willy" Walsh, a native of Connemara, County Galway, was and is a rare musical genius. Self-taught from printed music appropriate to the instrument, he became an accomplished "Highland" piper and toured the country with Sells Brothers' circus one season. He next turned his attention to the fiddle, but wind instruments being more to his liking, he chose the flute, on which difficult keyed instrument he became quite expert. For his own personal use he has compiled a large volume of selections, principally from O'Neill's *Music of Ireland,* but transposed to the Highland pipe scale, which, by the way, differs from that of all other musical instruments. Just a score of Irish tunes transcribed by him were forwarded to Francis Joseph Bigger, of Belfast, Ireland, in 1908, for the use of a band called "The O'Neill Pipers of Armagh."

In acknowledging the receipt of those prized tunes and marches, Mr. Bigger informed me that they were "just what were wanted," and he expressed the hope that we would favor "The O'Neill Pipers of Armagh" with more of them.

No words of mine could do justice to Sergeant Kerwin—the genial, hospitable "Jim" Kerwin, not as a fluter and a lover of the music of his ancestors, but as a host at his magnificent private residence on Wabash Avenue. On his invitation and that of his equally hospitable and charming wife, a select company, attracted and united by a common hobby, met monthly on Sunday afternoons at his house for years. They were all good fellows, unhampered by programme or formality. Pipers, fiddlers and fluters galore, with a galaxy of nimble dancers and an abundance of sweet-voiced singers, furnished diversified entertainment the like of which was never known on the shores of Lake Michigan before nor, unfortunately, since; but of this, more anon. "There is an emanation from the heart in genuine hospitality which cannot be described," says Washington Irving, "but is immediately felt, and puts the stranger at once at his ease"; and so it was at Kerwin's.

Not by any means the least distinguished of our number was Adam Tobin, a Kilkenny man, equally proficient as a piper or fiddler. Ordinarily genial and accommodating, he was easily aroused by opposition; yet he was universally popular, and year after year he has been engaged by one of the Scotch societies to play at their picnics. His repertory of tunes was both choice and extensive, and I am inclined to believe that a few of them escaped the vigilance of our scribe, Sergeant O'Neill.

The discovery of a new musical star of uncommon brilliancy by John McFadden, when announced, naturally aroused keen curiosity. When seen and heard at a select gathering at Lake View, a distant part of the city, the wonder was how an Irish violinist of such exceptional ability could have remained unknown to us all these years.

The new star was Edward Cronin, a Tipperary man from Limerick Junction. He was over sixty years of age, and his remarkably large and well-shaped head impressed one as being the seat of rare intellect. His features, set and expressionless as the Sphynx when playing, relaxed

EDWARD CRONIN.

into genial smiles in conversation at other times. Long, sweeping bowing, with its attendant slurs, gave marked individuality to his style which was both airy and graceful. In fact, he represented a distinct school in this respect, for among traditional Irish musicians nothing is so noticeable as the absence of uniformity of style or system. The pages of Grattan Flood's *History of Irish Music* afford us an insight to the causes which led to this result. When harpers and pipers were indiscriminately imprisoned by order of the government, Irish National Schools of Music could not be expected to prosper. Scotland had a College of Pipers, and still has schools of pipering, with an abundance of printed pipe music and books of instruction. The Irish aspirant for musical honors, outside of a few of the large cities, must learn as best he can from any one within reach who is willing or able to teach.

Returning to our friend Cronin, he was a mine of long-forgotten melody. Old tunes, some of them known to us by name only, he could reel off by the hour. Lacking congenial companionship, many of his traditional treasures were but faintly remembered; yet intercourse with music lovers gradually unlocked his memory until Irish Folk Music was enriched by scores of tunes through his instrumentality. They were all committed to the art preservative by our scribe, and it was fortunate for many reasons that such action was taken, one of which is that the majority of them entirely escaped the painstaking efforts of Dr. Petrie and Dr. Joyce.

Plucked from obscurity, Mr. Cronin became all at once famous and popular, and played at numerous public and private entertainments. As he was capable of writing music, this accomplishment enabled him to aid us materially by noting down the tunes of others, as well as his own. Scoring down ancient and composing new music became with him an absorbing passion, after many years of corroding apathy; but as Addison says, "Music is the only sensual gratification which mankind may indulge in to excess without injury to their moral or religious feelings."

> "Music has power to melt the soul,
> By beauty Nature's swayed;
> Each can the universe control,
> Without the other's aid.
> But when together both appear,
> And force united try;
> Music enchants the list'ning ear,
> And beauty charms the eye."

REV. JAMES K. FIELDING.

CHAPTER III

HOW THE UNDERTAKING DEVELOPED AND LED TO IMPORTANT RESULTS NOT ORIGINALLY CONTEMPLATED

"There is a charm, a power, that sways the breast;
Bids every passion revel or be still;
Inspires with rage, or all our cares dissolve;
Can soothe distraction and almost despair—
That Power is Music."

PRIOR to the organization of the celebrated "Irish Music Club," when our meetings were harmonious and altogether enjoyable at Sergeant Kerwin's hospitable home, a new and welcome element favored us with their appreciation and friendship. Although not a musician himself, we had the encouragement and moral support of Rev. John J. Carroll, an eminent Irish scholar, who is the author of *Fiorsgeul na n-Errione,* a history of Ireland in the old language of the Gael, and several other works, including a translation into Irish of the *Rubaiyat of Omar Khayyam.* Rev. James K. Fielding, an energetic worker in the cause of a regenerated Ireland, came among us, accompanied by Rev. William Dollard and the learned Rev. Richard Henebry, Ph. D., professor of Gaelic in the Catholic University at Washington, D. C. Earnest advocates of an Irish Ireland, they were all three musicians and interested in the preservation of traditional Irish music. Father Fielding's favorite instrument was the flute, on which he brought out the notes with a round, full tone. Dr. Henebry's execution on the violin was a revelation. Had his practice kept pace with his knowledge of the subject, our champions would be feeling uncomfortable. The amiable Father Dollard, who was an expert on both instruments, introduced to us several new tunes, among them being "Father Dollard's Hornpipe" and "The Mooncoin Reel."

Decidedly reactionary in his ideas concerning Irish music, Dr. Henebry strongly advocates a return to strictly bardic tones and traditions.

In a work entitled, *Irish Music—Being an examination of the matter of scales, modes and keys; with practical instructions and examples for players*, which he published in 1903, after his return to Ireland, Dr. Henebry very ingeniously and learnedly describes how he has discovered the lost scales and modes by the use of which the Irish harpers of old excelled all others in the art of musical expression.

Modern Irish music, including the world-wide favorite, "Killarney," according to our reverend author, is Irish in name only, and breathes not the true spirit of the Irish school, traces of which are to be found still surviving among the peasantry, uncontaminated by modern influences.

To his astonishment and joy, he found a healthy vein of it also among our best pipers and fiddlers, whom he heard play at a gathering convened for his edification at the writer's residence. From an article on Irish music printed in several periodicals, we quote his impression formed on that occasion: "Lovers of Irish music generally will be surprised and delighted as I was to discover that there exists in Chicago a lively activity in this matter and in the right direction. An influential and numerous body of experts devote their leisure time to the cultivation of traditional Irish music in this city. This happy condition is due to the interests and efforts of Mr. Francis O'Neill, General Superintendent of Police." Modesty forbids further quotation in relation to the writer, so we will pick up the thread of the reverend doctor's story further on. "I was astonished at the wonderful proficiency of the players and the inexhaustible extent of their repertoire. All the reels, hornpipes and doubles I had learned to fiddle as a boy, together with all the airs I had learned from my mother, were there, and a thousand others. I wish to say that I know nothing in art so grand, so thrilling, as the irresistible vigor and mighty onrush of some reels they played, filled with the hurry of flight, the majesty of battle strife, the languishment of retreat, and the sweep of a rallying charge, with a laugh at fate, though yet the whole was ever still accompanied by the complaining magic of a minor tone like the whisper of a faraway sorrow. I have heard much of the music of Ireland, and heard it often, but never yet better than that played by the Chicago pipers and fiddlers at Captain O'Neill's."

A slashing reel—"The Bank of Ireland," I believe—which Bernard Delaney was playing with great abandon on the Union pipes, caught his Reverence's fancy. Seizing a violin, he accompanied the piper with spirit. Not to be merely an onlooker, Father Fielding sailed in with his ever-willing flute. The humor of the situation seemed contagious, for Adam Tobin got into action with his pipes. To restore the balance, John McFadden with his fiddle reinforced Dr. Henebry. Of course, Sergeant Early could no longer remain inactive with his pipes on his lap, so he also helped to swell the concert. There being no apparent prejudice against odd numbers, "yours truly" lost no time in rallying to Father Fielding's aid with a second flute.

This impromptu concert, unique in its way, and prolonged by encouragement and applause, was thoroughly enjoyed by every one present.

At another such gathering at my house, arranged in

honor and for the benefit of the reverend professor, John K. Beatty, before mentioned, was present. The old man was certainly a picturesque figure, with his snow-white hair and mustache, while a magnificent set of Taylor's pipes, buckled on ready for business, gave him a rather formidable appearance.

At first he played naturally, until the courtesy of applause fired his brain. Regardless of tone, tune or time, he broke loose and, in an exuberance of enthusiasm, clouted the regulators, contorted his body, and beat time with both feet in unison, until exhausted.

After the deafening applause which followed this exhibition had subsided, Mr. Beatty announced himself as the "king of the pipers," a claim which no one seemed inclined to dispute.

From various sources we were favored with manuscript collections of Irish music, but in those much winnowing of chaff was necessary in order to find a few grains of wheat. By far the most important were those obtained from Father Fielding and Michael McNamara, originating in Counties Kilkenny and Tipperary, respectively. Both contained a surprising number of unpublished tunes. Another important manuscript collection was contributed by Philip J. O'Reilly, a native of County Cavan. It contained the "Two-penny Jig," which Dr. Hudson obtained from Paddy Coneely, the famous Galway piper, over seventy years ago.

A rather large collection, kindly forwarded from San Francisco, California, by a priest, seemed at first sight a treasure, but what were hastily believed to be rare and unpublished airs were later found to have been mainly copied from Bunting's first and second collections.

Another manuscript collection, the cherished property of Mr. John Gillan, contained not alone rare tunes, but uncommonly good florid settings of others, from County Longford and County Leitrim.

Meeting an Irish-American of prominence one day, who was quite in sympathy with our musical vagaries, he generously offered to send us an old book of music which from his conversation we took to be an heirloom in his family. His father, whom I had known for years, was a fine type of the Irish emigrant who attains substantial prosperity in America. Taking those circumstances into consideration, there were good reasons to anticipate the discovery of a rare volume in the possession of such people. When the carefully wrapped package arrived, Sergeant O'Neill, with a tenderness bordering on veneration, untied it and disclosed the precious treasure—soiled and tattered, of course, from the handling of generations, as we supposed.

What our feelings and remarks were can be better imagined than described, when we found that in his innocence of music our patriotic friend had sent us a modern copy of Moore's *Melodies,* which had evidently served many a day as a plaything for his children. That unsophisticated promoter of Irish music has since been elected and served as president of the "Irish Choral Society" of this city!

Occasional mention had been made of a large bound volume of music manuscripts in the possession of the widow Cantwell, but nobody believed that we could get more than a glance at it, under any circumstances. There was nothing to be lost by trying, so I called on the bereaved lady, wearing the full uniform of a Captain of Police, by way of introduction. Without hesitation the heirloom was produced, and, finding certain numbers suitable for our purpose, I asked permission for our scribe, Sergeant James O'Neill, to call and copy them. To my great delight, the obliging widow told me to take the book along, but to guard it carefully and return it, uninjured and undiminished, at my convenience.

She explained her reluctance in lending the volume to others. One seeker for hidden treasures, like the writer, to whom she had entrusted it, finding that copying music was tedious and tiresome, overcame the difficulty by just clipping out an odd leaf here and there, to save trouble.

In our social chat the identity of the late lamented Mr. Cantwell was disclosed.

At an Irish picnic at Willow Springs some years before, I recollected having seen him play a flute in the midst of a circle of admirers. Mosquitoes of the large gray timber variety were so numerous, ravenous and unafraid, that they perched on his quickly moving fingers in groups and tapped him assiduously for his blood. Mr. Cantwell, much as he loved music, could not endure this torture very long; so to give him a chance to resume the entertainment, one of the audience waved a handkerchief steadily over his hands while it continued.

Another sympathetic contributor was Mr. I. S. Dunning, former city engineer of Aurora, Illinois. Subsequent correspondence revealed him as an educated musician, particularly well versed in Scotch and Irish strains.

An instance of generous aid from an unexpected source was a call at my office at Police Headquarters, in 1901, from Edward Howard Mulligan, who brought with him a copy of Thomson's *Select Collection of Original Irish Airs,* harmonized by Beethoven—two volumes in one. Mr. Mulligan was a high official in a large corporation, and, being the grandson of an Irish exile, racial friendship prompted his unselfish act.

I came near forgetting that Sergeant James O'Neill

also possessed several volumes of manuscript music compiled by his father in Belfast and vicinity.

Notwithstanding the tendency to modernization in that great city of the North, the volumes were rich in characteristic Irish airs as truly traditional as those from the southern provinces. In his memory, also, as in the case of others of similar taste, the tender, plaintive songs of the crooning mother found tenacious lodgment.

Selections were made also from such scarce old printed collections as fell into our hands; and while many of our tunes had been previously printed, the settings obtained from our band of experts were preferable and not infrequently much superior to the printed versions.

The editor of Levey's *Dance Music of Ireland* announces in a footnote that he took the tunes without alteration from the street players of London, merely changing one sharp in one tune only. Monotonous and unattractive versions of many of the numbers in that work discredit the result of his conservatism. How much of the dance music originated will be explained later, so that it all depends on individual taste as to which version of a tune is the most meritorious; and as it has been transmitted orally, in most cases, from one generation to another, variants and diversity of settings have naturally multiplied.

Who, then, can lay claim to perfection; and why should palpably inferior versions or variants of traditional tunes be exempt from correction or alteration?

To compare, eliminate and revise the immense amount of material accumulated, became a question of such magnitude that it was deemed prudent to enlist the aid of an advisory committee. For this purpose Sergeant Early and Messrs. Delaney, McFadden, Cronin and Ennis were selected and a meeting arranged for at Sergeant James O'Neill's residence in Brighton Park.

Our scribe played from his manuscripts, but there was scarcely an air or tune that was satisfactory to all. Changes were suggested and opposed so frequently that little progress was made. The more modest, but by no means the less skilful, gradually subsided, not caring to be engaged in continuous debate, until one opinionated and domineering member had it all to himself. One meeting demonstrated plainly that our scheme of consultation was a failure, and the "inquest committee," as it came to be facetiously called, convened but once. The two O'Neills were obliged to exercise their own best judgment in continuing the work undertaken.

Ordinarily the music first noted down with pencil from the playing, singing, lilting, whistling or humming of the contributor, was played over by Sergeant O'Neill, and corrected or accepted, as the case might be. All strains considered worthy of preservation were subsequently copied in ink into books classified for convenience.

After over two thousand numbers had been so recorded there developed a general desire to have them printed. Then the question arose as to how comprehensive the work was to be. Were it to be confined to airs and tunes not generally known, leaving out those in common circulation, many music lovers would be disappointed—for every one realizes the inconvenience of being obliged to consult a number of books under such circumstances. And, again, how about such classics as "Kathleen Mavourneen" and "Killarney," and others of Balfe's composition, which are declared by some to be not Irish music at all? Besides, there were several of Moore's *Melodies,* which every lover of the music of Ireland would naturally expect to find included in any large printed collection of Irish music.

The consensus of opinion was in favor of a popular work

comprising such a variety as would be most likely to satisfy the preferences of all; and so that plan was adopted.

Then came the trying work of comparing various settings, eliminating the least desirable, and detecting duplicates. This may seem easy to some people, yet we found it a task of no ordinary difficulty. In some instances it was decided to print two and even three settings of the same tune, derived from different sources, each possessing some special merit.

Having listened to everything in our manuscripts played frequently, all strains were more or less familiar, new ones alone being easily detected, and it required great caution, aided by an acute ear and a retentive memory, to determine whether it was an hour or a month ago that a strain was heard among the hundreds played at a sitting, in quick succession. Duplicates, not infrequently written in different keys, are liable to pass undetected and add to the complexity of our problems.

Transcribing copy for the engraver was no small task; neither was proofreading, to persons burdened with the cares and importunities of official life all day, and occasionally all night. Exasperation hardly expresses one's feelings when engravers and printers ignore or overlook corrections, and in some cases aggravate an error instead of correcting it.

When published, O'Neill's *Music of Ireland*, financed and edited by the writer, was well received by the press and public, and the motives of its promoters justly appreciated. There was one discordant note, however, from an unexpected source, voiced by a clergyman of the city of Cork. His Reverence, of whose existence we were entirely ignorant, lectured on Irish Music in that famous city, warning his audience against the great danger to Irish music by the efforts of those who had not the advantage of being born and bred in the real traditional atmosphere, like himself.

Why, bless his simple soul! What could have led him to imagine that Watergrass Hill had a monopoly of the traditional atmosphere of County Cork, not to mention the rest of Ireland?

Although Petrie got as many as fifty notations of one melody, his Reverence dogmatically would tolerate no deviation from "old" settings. What strange patriotic fervor has awakened certain champions to almost deify Bunting and Petrie now, after more than half a century of silence and neglect! Their collections have to be sought, and are seldom found, in antiquarian bookshops, at almost prohibitive prices. Of what avail was it to the lover of his country's music to know that copies of such music still exist?

With an array of titled patrons, including six Right Honorables, Petrie undertook the harmonization and publication of his collection of *The Ancient Music of Ireland*. One volume reached the public in 1855, followed by a small supplement many years after his death, and the project was abandoned. Why? Perhaps our reverend critic can tell. It takes money as well as zeal and skill to publish Irish music. Strangely ignoring all mention of the dance music and marches, which constitute nearly two-thirds of the collection, he directs his batteries at the airs. "There were Scotch airs," he says, "such as 'Ye Banks and Braes o' Bonnie Doon,' included in the collection as Irish." But were they Scotch? Anyone who will take the trouble to read the footnotes on page 80 of Wood's *Songs of Scotland*, first edition, edited by George Farquhar Graham, will learn that the melody was claimed as being Irish long before Robert Burns appropriated it as an air for his verses. As a climax to dispose of the collection without benefit of clergy, he says: "All that was good in it was copied from Petrie, Bunting or Joyce"—a statement which would lead us to believe that the eighth commandment was suspended in Cork. The truth is that only the third volume of Bunting's collections and the first part of Petrie's were in the possession of the editor when O'Neill's *Music of Ireland* was being compiled. Many manuscript collections, as well as old collections printed in Edinburgh, London, and New York, were on hand, such as Smith's *Irish Minstrel,* Thomson's *Select Collection of Original Irish Airs,* Crosby's *Irish Musical Repository,* Forde's *Encyclopedia of Melody,* and Haverty's *Three Hundred Irish Airs.*

How, then, could airs derived from such sources be consistently credited to Petrie or Bunting, even though said airs were to be also found in their collections? Besides, more than one-half of the contents of O'Neill's *Music of Ireland* was noted down from the singing or playing of residents of Chicago, and varied more or less from the settings of Petrie or Bunting.

There is no dearth of skillful Irish musicians in Chicago who were nurtured in "an Irish musical atmosphere" as favorable to a true appreciation of Irish music as that inhaled by our Cork critic. What have the Irish in Ireland done for Irish music since Petrie's death? "By their fruits you shall know them." Now, when Irishmen in America have invaded a long-neglected field, lo! a guardian of "true Irish music" is aroused to warn the people of Cork that "Irish music was in great danger." It was, and is, in great danger—but from what source? The people who never do anything but criticize, or those who strive to keep Irish music alive by giving it publicity and prominence?

How peculiarly applicable to this case is the following

quotation from an American editorial: "It is a curious trait of human nature that sometimes leads workers in an important cause to criticize most vigorously the very co-workers who are accomplishing the most for it."

Every honest effort rightly directed deserves commendation and encouragement, even though the highest ideals may not be attained.

More and better Irish music can be heard in dozens of American cities than in Cork or even in Dublin. Why? Because it is encouraged, appreciated and *paid for,* and because the musician's calling is in no way suggestive of mendicancy.

The recollection of the delightful times we enjoyed at Sergeant Kerwin's hospitable home on Wabash Avenue will ever remain a milestone in our memories, and many are the vain regrets because they are no longer possible. In an evil moment an aggressive enthusiast conceived the idea of forming a permanent (?) organization, with monthly meetings in a rented hall, etc. Picnics and balls were to vary the anticipated pleasures and provide a revenue which was to be disbursed among the musicians.

The prospectus being reasonable, no outspoken opposition developed and it was not long before the "Irish Music Club" was born and christened. It would appear that the officers of the new organization had been already selected in private caucus, the wheels ran so smoothly and the election therefore was a mere formality. One prominent piper who had conspicuously flung his initiation fee to the treasurer, left the hall in high dudgeon, when he had not even been nominated for any office, and never returned.

The club prospered, however, and increased in membership. Many citizens with Irish sympathies, though not of Irish ancestry, attended the monthly meetings, and the free midsummer picnics at "Leafy Grove" and everything went along swimmingly for a time. The members of the Club, men and women, vied with one another in the sale of tickets for the grand ball. Tactless management caused several unpleasant incidents and defections at that entertainment, but the storm did not break out until after the distribution of the proceeds. The President was criticised by one of his most intimate friends, yet in justice to the former, it must be admitted that he followed the plan as announced and accepted long before.

Instead of calmly discussing a trivial misunderstanding, for such, in fact, it was, moderate counsel could not prevail against the intemperate zeal to expel the critic from membership in the Club. Violence was narrowly averted, but the rift enlarged and disclosed the beginning of the end. The musicians began to drop away from that forth. Still a few excellent ones maintained their membership with great pertinacity for a year or two, but there came a time when tactless and undiplomatic outbursts could no longer be endured and the "Irish Music Club" was left without musicians worthy of the name.

Acknowledged energy and zeal on the part of a presiding officer could not condone the fatal failing of temperamental infirmities. Even in this emasculated condition, new members, impelled by their unquenchable love of Irish music and dancing, continued to come in and replenish the treasury for a time.

After less than eight years of inharmonious existence, the most enjoyable, companionable and representative association of Irish musicians, singers and dancers ever organized in America degenerated into a mere shadow of its former prominence, until its disruption in 1909, following a clash of mercenary interests. A reorganization since effected has endowed it with a new lease of life but the absence of a staff of competent musicians from its membership, renders the Club's name an anomaly, and its potency for good not all that could be desired.

Irish music, however, is neither dead nor dying in this great western Metropolis, for a young generation of Irish-American musicians bids fair to rival their progenitors in the divine art "which gentler on the spirit lies, than tired eyelids upon tired eyes."

Pre-eminent among them is Miss Selena A. O'Neill, a prize-winner at the Chicago Musical College. A violinist of phenomenal talent, she is equally proficient as a pianist, and while her training has been exclusively in the classical courses, such is her instinctive grasp of the peculiarities and swing of all varieties of Irish music, that her astonishing ability in playing the most difficult dance music in perfect time and thrilling spirit has attracted wide-spread attention. From a prize-winner at sixteen, what may we not hope for at maturity?

In the language of the poet Brooke she was

> "Music to the tips of her fingers,
> And interpreting with reverence her music;
> She was touched from note to note.
> With momentary moods of her own nature,
> So that he that heard,
> Not only loved her music, but herself."

The seeds of revival sown by this pioneer club have germinated, however. An interest in Irish music and dancing had been awakened, and instead of one, there are now several correlated organizations conducted harmoniously in different parts of the city. To believe that an Irish piper would be the chief attraction at entertainments given by the "Chicago Athletic Association" and by a Presbyterian congregation would severely tax our credulity a few years ago, yet such is the fact in this year of our Lord, nineteen hundred and nine.

SELENA A. O'NEILL.

We must not forget, however, that success invites secession and rivalry. Whether prompted by egotism or mercenary motives, the desire to commercialize offshoots from a parent organization, betrays a sordid human frailty from which the Irish are by no means exempt. Such trivial devices as green ink, delusive letterheads, and whimsical stationery can never be as effective in arousing national sentiment or advancing the interests of a cause as unselfishness, co-operation, and singleness of purpose.

Dissensions in the "Irish Music Club" did not interfere with our work to any appreciable extent. Unpublished and forgotten melodies were sought with unabated persistence from year to year. While Sergt. O'Neill devoted his attention to one portion of the city, Mr. Cronin was equally industrious in another district. Including some forgotten tunes discovered by the writer in certain antiquarian publications of the 18th century, the result of our joint labors was highly gratifying. Nearly two hundred tunes, many of them both rare and valuable, were obtained since the publication of O'Neill's *Music of Ireland*.

Scarcely any attention had been paid by collectors and publishers of Irish music to the compilation and preservation of dance tunes. Bunting, the first great collector, almost entirely ignored them in his three consecutive volumes, and the few included in Moore's *Melodies* were, of course, vocalized and not intended for dancing. Dr. Petrie's *Ancient Music of Ireland*, containing 147 numbers and published under his personal supervision in 1855, includes but seventeen dance tunes, while less than one-fourth of the one hundred numbers in Dr. Joyce's *Ancient Irish Music* are of that class.

The first tangible result of our many years of incessant effort—O'Neill's *Music of Ireland*—includes over 1,100 dance tunes classified for convenience, an amount many times more than were supposed to be in existence altogether. The appearance of this surprising aggregation aroused much latent enthusiasm in the ranks of a certain class of Irish musicians. Letters of approval came pouring in, many suggesting the issuance of a smaller and less expensive volume devoted to dance music exclusively.

To satisfy this demand the preparation of a new work entitled *The Dance Music of Ireland—1,001 Gems*—was undertaken. It consisted of selections from *The Music of Ireland* and the additional tunes collected since that work was published.

Its only competitor was Levey's *Dance Music of Ireland*, consisting of 200 tunes collected and printed in London in two volumes in 1858-1873. In this work the tunes are printed promiscuously, with no attempt at classification, but it is worthy of remark that it was in England and in America and not in Ireland that practical efforts of this character were made to preserve and popularize the dance music of the Emerald Isle.

What influence such belated enterprise may exert in stemming the tide of decadence to which Irish dance music seemed fated, the future alone can determine.

The best settings, representing all varieties, had been selected to make up the contents of O'Neill's *Dance Music of Ireland* and it was gratifying to hear from all directions that in arrangement and comprehensiveness the collection exceeded all expectations.

Although much accumulated material yet remained unpublished we felt that our work was ended. Not so, however, for a demand for an edition arranged and harmonized for the piano was being voiced insistently. In the meantime I had discovered some rare and forgotten Irish melodies in a lately acquired volume of manuscript music formerly owned by H. Hudson of Stephens Green Dublin. The handwriting, much of which was in Irish script, was neat but almost microscopic and the notes and remarks showed that the 130 tunes contained therein had been collected prior to the year 1840.

A consignment of interesting music manuscript was kindly forwarded by Rev. Father J. T. Walsh, East Hampton, Connecticut, about this time. He was a violinist of ability, whose isolation in that part of New England had kept him out of touch with Irish musical affairs for a fourth of a century. Not finding in the index to O'Neill's *Music of Ireland* the names of certain tunes known to him in his boyhood days in County Waterford, his patriotism and love of the music of his native land prompted his generous act. That nice traditional dance tune entitled "Father Walsh's Hornpipe" in O'Neill's *Irish Music for the Violin or Piano* was contributed by him but without a name.

Too late for publication came a nice selection of dance tunes sent us by Mr. Patrick Dunn, of Thurles, Tipperary. Quite a few of them were unsuited to our purpose, being well-known English and American compositions, but his public spirit and generosity was none the less appreciated on that account. Mr. Dunn has been repeatedly a prize-winner at *Feisana* and some of his tunes hitherto unpublished will appear in our next Series.

McGoun's *Repository of Scots and Irish Airs*—an extremely rare work published about 1799—had also come into my possession. Many fine old Irish airs with variations, some of which are unknown to the present generation, were included in this splendid book.

From the sources named and from our previously published collections, a classified selection of 250 numbers, including Airs, Marches, Double jigs, Single jigs, Hop jigs, Reeels, Hornpipes and Long Dances, were harmonized and printed as the First Series of O'Neill's *Irish Music for the Piano or Violin*. To avoid conventional monotony none of Moore's *Melodies* are included in our selections. The rare setting of the "Coolin" with six variations, which is printed in this volume, obviously constitutes no exception.

The acquisition of a library of antiquarian musical works chiefly devoted to Irish music through Cork and London book agencies enriches us with an almost embarrassing wealth of excellent Irish airs and tunes so completely forgotten or unknown in this generation that none of even the old members of the "Irish Music Club" had any knowledge of them.

For the benefit of any and all who may feel interested in the revival of Irish music the second series of O'Neill's *Irish Music*, arranged for the piano or violin, will again bring to light some of the most charming specimens in the whole range of Ireland's renowned Melodies.

> "Melting airs soft joys inspire,
> Airs for drooping hope to hear;
> Melting as a lover's prayer,
> Joys to flatter dull despair,
> And softly soothe the am'rous fire."

CHAPTER IV

STORIES OF TUNES WITH A HISTORY
AIRS, ETC.

"There is a song, a simple song,
   I've heard in early youth,
When life to me seemed but to be
   All innocence and truth;
Nor wrong, nor guile, nor falsehood's wile,
   My merry heart had wrung,
When first I heard that simple strain—
   The song my Mother sung.

Oh, I have been through many a scene
   Of happiness and mirth,
In bower, and hall, and festival;
   But never upon earth
Such music sweet did ever greet
   Me yet where'er I roam,
As the song I heard, long years ago,
   My Mother sang at home."

To accord a full measure of appreciation and acknowledgment to everyone who contributed tunes to our collections had been our constant aim, and with that object in view the name of the contributor was printed with each tune so obtained. Where no names were appended their absence indicated that such tunes did not come into our possession from individuals.

This plan, while seemingly just, did not prove entirely satisfactory for several reasons. Many tunes credited to those from whom we obtained them were known to others, and had been memorized from the playing of some of our best musicians. A few of the latter quite naturally considered themselves entitled to recognition. For instance, quite a few of the tunes which the writer had dictated to Sergt. O'Neill had been picked up in years gone by from such noted players as Hicks, O'Brien and Delaney—long before the idea of compiling a collection of Irish Folk Music had been thought of.

It might be well to keep in mind that choice and rare tunes were regarded by not a few pipers and fiddlers as personal property and zealously guarded accordingly. Such musicians seldom or never played their "pet" tunes in the hearing of any one known to possess the happy faculty of a grasping ear and tenacious memory, but in spite of their utmost secretiveness the favorites leaked out eventually, and were promptly committed to musical notation for preservation and publicity.

Recording the sources from which tunes were derived as practiced generally by Bunting, Petrie, and Joyce, in Ireland could not fail to be of more historical and comparative value to the musical antiquary than similar notation made in England and America.

Irishmen from all parts of Ireland intermingle promiscuously in all countries to which they migrate and the man from Ulster soon learns the Munster man's music, and so on until the fact of obtaining an air or tune from a native of a certain county or province carries with it no assurance that the music was not learned from a stranger or chance acquaintance. Such firstclass players as Delaney, Touhey, Early, McFadden, O'Neill, Kennedy, Cronin and Carbray, picked up considerable of their repertory in different parts of the country and from people hailing from various locations. It can therefore be seen from the foregoing that printing contributors' names with their tunes served no useful purpose. On the contrary it not infrequently served to provoke jealousies and illwill instead.

Full acknowledgment is made in the introduction to the *Dance Music of Ireland*—the names and nativities of all who in any way aided in the enterprise being given in a manner which leaves no room for criticism.

What might be written concerning the incidental history of the large number of stray and rare melodies collected and published through our efforts would "fill a volume" but as time, space and patience must be respected, only a few can be mentioned at all, and those will be discussed briefly in the order in which they are published, commencing with

AIRS.

During the last week of a mission given at Bantry during my school days, the man who presided at a stall erected against the end of the schoolhouse for the sale of church wares, attracted trade by singing a rather depressing song to a fine melody which I memorized unconsciously and never forgot. Following is all I remember of the song,—

"Where sinful souls do mourn from whence they can't return
But there to weep and mourn bound in fiery chains."

No doubt this direful picture of perdition was intended to call attention to the impending departure of the missioners and the need of prompt repentance, so I named the Air "Fare you Well" or the "Sinners' Lament." This melody was unknown in that part of the country and no trace of it had ever been discovered in our experience until recently a version was found in the Complete Petrie Collection, under the title *"An garbh Cnoicin Fruoigh"* ("The rough little Heathy Hill").

"Cailin beag mo Chroidhe" or "The little Girl of my Heart" was a characteristic Folk Song which I frequently heard my parents sing in boyhood days near Bantry in W. Cork. It recited in Irish the appeals of an infatuated maiden to her unresponsive swain, and his evasive replies in alternate verses. Then as now it appears excuses to avoid incurring distasteful obligations were never wanting.

"Colleen beg machree, how can I marry you without a coat to my back?" the diplomatic deluder would say. To remove this obstacle the young woman supplied the deficiency only to be met with another shortage in wardrobe, and so on indefinitely. Nothing resembling this melody or song has been encountered in our researches. A previously unpublished air of great beauty which we named "The Fun at Donnybrook" was given us by Sergt. Mich'l Hartnett, a native of W. Cork. It consists of but one strain of ten bars. A lyric in five line verse was sung to this air. It recited the wonders witnessed at the fair by a stranger, on his return home. Nothing in O'Neill's *Music of Ireland* so captivated the fancy of Rev'd Dr. Henebry as this simple traditional strain.

"Bean Dubh an Gleanna" (pronounced "Ban dhuv an glanna"), or "The Dark Woman of the Glen," came to us through Patrick Touhey, the celebrated Irish piper from Daniel Sullivan, of Boston, a native of Millstreet, County Cork. In the florid execution of Irish airs, Mr. Sullivan had no superiors on the violin. Even now in his advanced old age his tones, trills and graces breathe the very soul of tradition and it is cheering to know that his son and namesake is already famous as the composer of the music of the opera, *Pocahontas*. The airs called "The Maiden" and "The Dark Maiden of the Valley" in O'Neill's *Music of Ireland* are but simpler versions of Sullivan's melody.

Among the many unpublished airs which I learned at the

old homestead were "The Friars' Hill," "My Love is a Bandboy," "The Colleen Rue," "My Darling, I am fond of you," and "Teige Maire's Daughter." The latter is an exceptionally fine traditional melody to which was sung a song beginning

> "Johnny bought a beaver hat,
> Then Johnny bought a new cravat;
> Johnny bought more things than that,
> To coax Teige Maire's daughter."

A rollicking chorus ending in the phrase "I wish you were my darling" followed each verse. The song remembered only in a fragmentary way was not very edifying in sentiment. The subject dealt with ordinary escapades of merely local interest.

"Farmer Hayes" and "Raking Paudheen Rue" are plainly derived from a common origin. Those airs known in South Munster at least, combined with typical Folk Songs, seem to have been overlooked by Bunting, Petrie, and other collectors. The airs were also known by other names such as "The Bold Undaunted Fox," "Raking Red-haired Pat," and "McKenna's Dream." In his recent work, *"Old Irish Folk Music and Songs,"* Dr. Joyce prints a version under the latter name.

"The Woods of Kilmurry" is a restoration of an ancient air partly forgotten, which my mother sang. How far we have been successful in reproducing it is left to the reader to judge.

One of the best remembered airs memorized from my father's singing is "Rodney's Glory." The song dates from the naval success of an English admiral of that name, who died in 1792, but the air is doubtless much older. Other names by which it was known are "My Name is Moll Mackey" and "The Praises of Limerick." The tune "Rodney's Glory" is also a favorite Long-Dance and is included in a list of such tunes printed in O'Keeffe and O'Brien's *Handbook of Irish Dance.*

"Fair Mary Mulholland" is the air of a Folk song in the County Down, which Sergt. James O'Neill learned from his mother. It had not been previously published and the original title being unknown it was named for the woman who sang it.

Versions of *"Seaghan O Duibhir an Gleanna"* or "John O'Dwyer of the Glen" are almost as numerous as the singers of that fine old air. Sergt. O'Neill endeavored to note down the melody as played on the violin with trills and graces by Mich'l G. Enright, a native of County Limerick.

It would be difficult, indeed, to do justice in musical notation to his inimitable execution of that ancient strain, which differs considerably from the setting in John O'Daly's *Poets and Poetry of Munster.*

The great popularity of the air in the southern province was well illustrated at the Munster *Feis* which I attended in 1906. Variants of it could be easily recognized in the airs to which different songs were sung by half a dozen at least of the local competitors.

One of the numbers in Bunting's third collection entitled "A Little Hour before Day" is unquestionably a version of the original melody. It was obtained from Byrne, the harper, in 1806, and in his remarks Bunting says that it is "Ancient author and date unknown." In O'Keeffe and O'Brien's *Handbook of Irish Dance "Seaghan O' Duibhir an Gleanna"* is listed among the Long-Dances. A setting of it obtained from Edw. Cronin, who alone knew it in this style, is printed in the *Dance Music of Ireland.* It is peculiar in having but six bars in each strain.

An extremely plaintive Lamentation air was sent us

by mail from Sault Ste. Marie, Northern Michigan. The sender, whose name I believe was Dwyer, stated that his grandmother, from whom he learned it, used to tell of a Gen'l Munroe in the rebellion of '98 in connection with the song. Reference to a volume of Irish biography verifies the story. The martyr was Gen'l Henry Munroe of the County Down, who was betrayed, tried by court-martial, hung, and beheaded, within a few hours.

We are indebted to a gentleman of wide musical knowledge, I. S. Dunning, former city engineer of Aurora, Illinois, for "Rory Dall's Sister's Lament," a decidedly ancient strain. The great harper and composer was known in his native Ireland as Rory Dall O'Cahan or "Blind Rory." Like many others of his class he wandered into Scotland, where, in time, his "ports" or compositions, as well as himself, were claimed as belonging to that country. Four of the ten specimens of ancient socalled Scotch melodies for the harp, printed in a modern publication, entitled *Irish and Scots Harps,* are Rory Dall's compositions. How he came to be known as Rory Dall Morison in that country is not explained even in Brown and Stratton's *British Musical Biography.* The harper and poet is mentioned by both names but his birthplace is given as the Island of Lewis, Scotland.

To Sergt. James O'Neill's elaboration of an old Irish strain we are indebted for "Thanskgiving." As one of the grandest airs in the whole range of Irish melody it certainly deserves the wide popularity which it has already gained.

There was an industrious weaver and poetaster in Bantry named John Sullivan in the sixties whose prolific muse was never at a loss for a theme. Margaret Sheehan, a likely young girl, who attracted his fancy, was done into verse as follows, attuned to an unpublished local melody, which my memory preserved.

> "M-a was placed the first, with an r before the rest,
> G-a-r is the next, and e-t has it proved;
> S-h then follows after, with double e in right good order,
> And h-a-n is the latter of my Darling Colleen Fune."

Johnny Sullivan, "the poet," as he was best known, has long since ceased to sing, and what is worse, was remembered only by a few of the oldest inhabitants when I visited Bantry in 1906. Such is fame.

"Hugh O'Neill's Lament" is another of those fine melodies from the North of Ireland contributed by Sergt. O'Neill. Judging by the inquiries concerning its origin it has attracted much attention.

A good illustration of the many versions and variants developed in the course of time from a popular composition transmitted by ear throughout the country from one generation to another is *An Seanduine*, or "The Old Man." The first setting in O'Neill's *Music of Ireland* is that learned from my mother as she sung the song in the Irish language. The second and third settings are those printed in O'Daly's *Poets and Poetry of Munster*. All three may be played in regular order as one piece, so varied are they, while yet preserving the fundamental melody. "The Campbells are Coming," better known than either, is the Scotch version of this ancient air.

In my boyhood days I heard my sisters chant a song commencing "Holland is a fine place where many a fine thing grows" and ending with "The low, low lands of Holland between my love and me." This air, characteristically Irish, bears little resemblance to the "Lowlands of Holland," printed in Dr. Joyce's *Ancient Irish Music*. The Scotch also have an air, or rather airs of that name for which many claimants contend, according to the editor of Wood's *Songs of Scotland*. Our melody appears to be unknown beyond a limited district in W. Cork, where I'm sorry to say, as a result of the suppression of the "Patrons" and farmhouse dances, most of the music and melodies of half a century ago, are now forgotten.

An unpublished old Irish air of quaint cadences, to which was sung some verses reciting the adventures and heroism of the "Cumberland's Crew," was known as "Cahirciveen" around Northwest Cork, according to Sergt. Mich'l Hartnett. The setting printed in O'Neill's *Music of Ireland* was mine, but when or where it was acquired has escaped my memory.

"The Barley Grain," as sung in W. Cork in my youth, is an entirely different air from that published in the Petrie and Joyce collections—both the latter being obtained from the same source. The song as I heard it commenced,—

"There were three farmers from the North;
As they were passing by
They swore an oath—and a mighty oath—
The barley grain would die.

Chorus:
"With my right faladidy ldy O, etc., etc."

The cereal did not have any too easy a time of it, the song goes on to explain, but finally fortune favored it and

"The barley grain stuck out its nose
And then belied them all,"

which goes to show that even the wisest are sometimes mistaken.

A delightful, though simple air, was that of a song in common circulation among the peasantry of W. Cork, fifty years ago. Each verse began with the hypothetical phrase

—"If all the Young Maidens"—varying the situation ad finitum until the singer's muse was exhausted. In songs of this character every singer was privileged to extemporize, and no end of fun was possible under such unrestrained freedom. A few samples of the verses may not be found uninteresting to the general reader,—

" If all the young maidens were blackbirds and thrushes,
If all the young maidens were blackbirds and thrushes;
How soon the young men would get sticks and beat bushes,
Fal the daw, fal the day, fal the didy o-dee.

If all the young maidens were swans on the water,
If all the young maidens were swans on the water;
How soon the young men would strip off and swim after,
Fal the daw, fal the day—etc., etc.

If all the young maidens were birds on the mountain,
If all the young maidens were birds on the mountain;
How soon the young men would get guns and go fowling,
Fal the daw, fal the day"—etc., etc.

Bunting says this peculiar species of chant having a frequently recurring chorus or catchword is called a *Loobeen*. It is sung at merrymakings, and assemblages of young women, when they meet at spinnings or quiltings, and is accompanied by extemporaneous verses of which each singer successively furnishes a line. In Scotland, particularly in the Highlands, and the Isles off the west coast, tunes of this class were known by the name of *Luinigs* or *Luinniochs,* signifying cheerful chorus music.

Some years ago a letter from a resident of British Columbia making inquiry for an old Irish air entitled "The County Mayo" plunged me into many a fit of thinking. This air bore no relationship except in name to the modern favorite called the "Lass from the County

Mayo." Many indexes were consulted in vain, yet memory assured me I had seen that name among my books. But where? After a tiresome search a song named "The County of Mayo" was found in Alfred Perceval Graves' *Irish Song Book,* commencing "On the deck of Patrick Lynch's boat I sit in woeful plight." It was to be sung to the beautiful air "Billy Byrne of Ballymanus." This information readily solved our problem, for an excellent setting of this melody was printed in O'Neill's *Music of Ireland.*

"When a Man's in Love he Feels no Cold" is a melody from the province of Ulster heretofore unpublished and so is "The old Plaid Shawl." To Sergt. James O'Neill we are indebted for both, which he learned from his mother in the County Down. "The old Plaid Shawl," a fine traditional strain, is much superior to the music of the modern song of that name, which owes its popularity chiefly to its catchy title.

"The Proposal," or "He asked me name the Day," is an air of much beauty when sung or played with expression. Forgotten since early youth, it came to me like a flash one afternoon. For fear of again losing it I grasped Sergt. O'Neill's bow-hand, lest his strains unhinge my memory. This unpublished melody, which possesses marked individuality, came dangerously near passing into oblivion.

An air so universally known as the "Blackbird" would find no mention in a cursory sketch of this kind except that we desire to invite attention to Sergt. O'Neill's unique traditional version which he learned from his father. It has been often remarked and I believe not without justice, that the song could not very well be sung to the music of it as commonly printed. A setting of the "Blackbird" appropriate for a Long-Dance is printed in the *Dance Music of Ireland.*

Of the various old melodies which my father soothingly sang after the daily routine of farm work was over, none is better remembered than *"Mo Muirnin na gruaige baine"* (Mavoureen na gruiga bauna), or "My Fairhaired Darling." I do not recollect having found this grand old air in any collection of Irish music except as "Dobbin's Flowery Vale" in Joyce's *Ancient Irish Music.*

It is mentioned frequently by its Irish name in Hardiman's *Irish Minstrelsy.* The song in full in the Irish language is printed in the first volume of that rare work. The words of John Bernard Trotter in his *Walks through Ireland*—1812 to 1817, are particularly applicable to this fine strain. "I heard an old Irish air sung with Irish words by an Irish woman," he says; "it was mournfully and remarkably melodious, sung very slow, and with astonishing and true pathos. It appealed powerfully to the heart."

A correspondent who evidently was familiar with old airs, especially those found in Scottish collections, informed us that our fine melody entitled "There's an End to my Sorrow" was the Scotch air called "There'll never be peace 'till Jamie comes hame." True enough a song of that name was written by Robert Burns to a modification of the tune, "There are few good fellows when Jamie's awa." The Scotch air is quite simple and resembles but slightly the florid setting full of Irish tonality, printed in O'Neill's *Music of Ireland.* Notwithstanding the superiority of the melody to which we gave publicity as Irish, a feeling of having trespassed on the preserves of our Caledonian kin lingered in my mind. To our great relief and joy, we find the air included in Dr. Joyce's *Old Irish Folk Music and Songs,* just fresh from the press.

under the name "My sorrow is greater than I can tell." The learned editor tells us that it was noted down from James Keane, an old man in his 83rd year, living in Kilkee on the Atlantic coast of the County of Clare. Thus were we vindicated unexpectedly. No doubt the tune had been learned in Scotland from the wandering Irish harpers.

It is a strange coincidence that two versions of an unpublished air—one from County Antrim and the other from W. Cork—should be known only to Sergt. O'Neill and myself.

As "The Croppy Tailor" in Ulster, the song told of the humiliating adventures of a tailor whose domestic relations had been invaded by a dragoon. The Munster song, "White Bread and Butter," recites the not altogether pleasant experiences of a "spalpeen" or laborer among the farmers in harvest time.

A violinist of the old school—I. S. Dunning, before mentioned—took a keen interest in our work since its inception; and besides contributing rare unpublished airs and dance tunes his critical but kindly comment served a useful purpose. In reviewing the *Music of Ireland* he tells us that the melody which captivated his fancy and that of his family above all others in the collection is "Tralibane Bridge." The fact that its haunting plaintiveness had made it also my choice is more than a mere coincidence. When affliction beyond the power of pen to describe cast its withering blight on our home, this weird and fascinating air obsessed my waking hours for days unnumbered. To me no other strains in the whole range of wailing dirges so deeply touches the heart or so feelingly voices the language of sadness and despair.

Two versions of this air—one from Mayo and the other from Armagh—are to be found in the *Complete Petrie*

Collection lately issued in London. They are named "The Little Red Lark of the Mountain."

Trailbane Bridge, ivyclad and ancient, spans a rocky, brawling river named on the maps *Owennashingaun,* in West Cork. Three townlands meet at this bridge, a significant circumstance to at least one disciple of the "black art," who one May morning at sunrise stood knee deep in the rushing current and performed certain mystic ceremonies. One consisted in dividing the waters with a scissors along the imaginary lines of the townland boundaries under the centre of the main arch. Whatever songs may have been sung to this touching air are lost as far as the writer has been able to ascertain.

While visiting at Mr. Cronin's house in Lake View one evening there came to mind a verse of a song called *"An Peacadh 'sa Bas,"* which I had often heard my father sing. It was a dialogue between "Death and the Sinner," of which I remember a quatrain from the latter's statement:

> "The night of my wake there will be pipes and tobacco,
> With snuff on a plate on a table for fashion's sake;
> Mold candles in rows like torches watching me,
> And I cold in my coffin by the dawn of the day."

To what I could recall of the air Mr. Cronin supplied additional bars from his memory, but we were not at all sanguine of ever recovering the full measure. To our great delight Mrs. Cronin had a better recollection of the air than either of us, so with her assistance we succeeded beyond our expectations. Mr. Cronin's style of playing it, which differs from Sergt. O'Neill's arrangement, is a revelation as an example of the traditional, which some doubting Thomases pretend to believe does not exist. Comparatively few of the Irish musicians of this generation can produce the traditional expression, which baffles my powers of description, but when heard is easily recognized.

As in other instances, this elusive air was no sooner committed to notation than another setting of it was obtained from Sergt. Mich'l Hartnett, whose mind was a storehouse of rare tunes. The constant intercourse among our musical people in those years stimulated their dormant memories. Strains heard after the lapse of years brought to mind tunes long forgotten, that, had they not been promptly noted down, may never again be recalled.

Another of my father's favorite songs was *"Beidmaoid ag ol,"* or "Let us be drinking," song to a very spirited air of that name. The burden of the song described the accomplishments of a so-called "classical teacher" in his own words. In the first line he introduces himself with confidence:

"My name is O'Sullivan; I'm an eminent teacher."

What follows this egotistical announcement I have forgotten, but in listing his questionable accomplishments, he says,—

"I can write a fine letter on paper or parchment,
Construe an author and give the due sense;
I court the fair maidens unknown to their parents
And thresh in their barns without evidence."

Then follows a chorus in Irish after each verse,—

"*Beidmaoid ag ol,*" etc., etc.

Our setting of this rare air is much superior to Petrie's, which he obtained in County Kerry. It is not to be found in other collections.

In the year 1874, official duties brought me in contact with George Gubbins, one of the superannuated officers detailed as lockup keeper at the famous Harrison Street Police Station. He was a native of County Limerick and amused himself during the night-watches in playing the fiddle. Contrary to the almost universal practice of his countrymen, he played all his tunes, including jigs and reels, in slow or singing time. One quaint air, new to me, I contrived to memorize, but as he was inclined to be unsociable on such occasions I failed to learn the name of it. For identification I christened it "Geo. Gubbins' Delight," and nothing even suggestive of its strains was since discovered until we found a version of it named "The Wedding Ring" in Dr. Joyce's *Old Irish Folk Music and Songs,* just out of press.

Only a few miles intervened between Hospital, Gubbins' birthplace, and Coolfree, where Dr. Joyce obtained his air. The melody, evidently of local origin, had not penetrated beyond a limited district.

At an auction sale of an English library held at Chicago, after fierce competition I fortunately succeeded in getting possession of *Cock's and Co.'s Encyclopedia of Melody,* arranged by William Forde and commonly called *Forde's Encyclopedia,* dating from the first half of the 19th century. Finding therein a number of Balfe's Compositions, I was much pleased with the discovery and selected five of them, including "Killarney," for reprinting in the *Music of Ireland.* The fact that Balfe was a native born Irishman did not save me from the petulant criticism of some of my best friends for being so deficient in musical discernment. Balfe's music, they contended, was not Irish at all, even if he was.

Few born in Ireland who have not heard of the song named "Rocking the Cradle," or, as it is sometimes called,

"Rocking a Baby that's none of my Own." Both song and air are now almost entirely forgotten, and it was a matter of no little difficulty to get a setting of the music. In preference to an unsatisfactory version of my own, we selected a setting found in an American publication of over fifty years ago. A fair version was also printed in Smith's *Irish Minstrel*, published in 1825 at Edinburgh.

It was quite a trick to play this piece to suit the old Irish standard of excellence, in which the baby's crying had to be imitated on the fiddle. To bring out the tones approaching human expression, the fiddle was lowered much below concert pitch. The performer held firmly between the teeth one end of a long old-fashioned door key with which at appropriate passages the fiddle bridge was touched. This contact of the key produced tones closely imitating a baby's wailing. Miss Ellen Kennedy, who learned the art from her father, a famous fiddler of Ballinamore, County Leitrim, was very expert in the execution of this difficult performance.

An air remembered from my boyhood days to which my father sung a song entitled "Castle Hyde" was printed in good faith under that name in O'Neill's *Music of Ireland*. As the "Groves of Blarney" and "Castle Hyde" are in the same metre, the former being a parody on the latter, a growing belief that I must have been in error became a settled conviction when I found the strains of the "Groves of Blarney" printed under the name "Castle Hyde" in Fitzsimon's *Irish Minstrelsy*, published in 1814.

From the sense of humiliation resulting from this discovery there has come eventually welcome relief. In the descriptive text relating to "Castle Hyde" in Dr. Joyce's *"Old Irish Folk Music and Songs,"* he says, "I find by an entry in the Forde MSS. that it was also sometimes sung to 'Youghal Harbor.' "

This information vindicates my memory, for the air we printed is a version of "Youghal Harbor," of which there are quite a few.

So many of the great bard Turlough O'Carolan's compositions were met with in both ancient and modern publications that they were given separate classification. Most of them were designated Planxty—a name which is not easily defined. The term cannot be very old, as the word in any form does not appear in O'Reilly's *Irish-English Dictionary* or in others which have been consulted. That it signifies lively music is the generally accepted opinion. Dr. Hudson, musical editor of *The Citizen,* and *The Dublin Monthly Magazine,* 1841-42, says it is hard to assign an exact origin or meaning to either name *Pleid raca* or *Plaing stigh,* which seem to be interchangeable. Dr. Douglas Hyde is authority for the statement that O'Carolan composed over 200 airs, many of them lively and full of curious turns and twists of metre. Many of his airs and nearly all his poetry, with the exception of about thirty pieces, are lost.

Certain peculiar cadences identify most of O'Carolan's compositions, and from internal evidence, in the absence of any claim to the contrary, we have ventured to include under this classification a few airs believed to be his. On that theory the "Lamentation of Owen Roe O'Neill" was printed as the first number. When I read in Grattan Flood's *History of Irish Music* that "Owen Roe O'Neill's Lament" was composed soon after his death, which occurred in 1649—twenty-one years before O'Carolan was born—you can imagine my embarrassment.

From that state of mind partial relief, at least, has come through finding it listed by Hardiman in *Irish Minstrelsy* as one of O'Carolan's compositions and discovering the affecting air in Bunting's *General Collection of the*

Ancient Irish Music, published in 1796, and also in Clinton's *Gems of Ireland,* published in 1841—and in both credited to O'Carolan. If we are in error, then, we may derive some satisfaction from being in such distinguished company. As an instance of fugitive pieces not listed by Irish writers among the bard's compositions, we mention "Blind Mary," attributed to him in the *Encyclopedia of Melody* before referred to.

Very naturally we were elated on getting an unlisted tune called "Planxty Dobbins" from John McFadden, whose store of gems was well nigh inexhaustible. The first strain consisted of eight bars, the second sixteen, and a third twenty-four bars in three-four time, a truly novel arrangement. Our delight was somewhat modified, however, in finding a version of it as "Planxty Reilly" in Bunting's first and second collections, published in 1796 and 1809 respectively. Bunting's settings consisted of twelve bars repeated in each of only two strains and they were not as pleasing to the ear in three sharps as McFadden's version with one. I may add that he learned the tune from David Quinn, the famous Mayo piper.

The stimulation of Edward Cronin's memory yielded up from time to time many a forgotten gem, among them being an air known to him as "Tom Judge." A limp in the metre caused by a missing bar was easily supplied, but the air which to me was fascinating excited nothing but dislike in my Ulster namesake, our talented scribe. Like "Planxty Dobbins," it proved not to be a new one entirely, for a version of it named "Thomas McJudge" was later discovered in Bunting's second collection.

Besides the version of the airs just discussed, a better example of the mutations which time and tradition have effected in old strains can be studied in the case of "Planxty Toby Peyton." The first setting in O'Neill's

Music of Ireland was taken from Bunting's third collection. Our second setting was a nameless vagrant air from County Clare, easily identified as a version of "Planxty Toby Peyton," while our third setting, as played by James O'Neill of County Down and John McFadden of County Mayo, is a striking instance of what skilful violinists can accomplish in the embellishment and modernization of old Irish strains. Both learned the air from their fathers, and, considering the distance between their native homes, it is evident the florid modern version gained immediate popularity. It is worthy of notice that the first and third settings have twelve bars to each strain, while the County Clare version has but ten.

"O'Carolan's Farewell" and "O'Carolan's Farewell to Music" end our collections of the renowned bard's compositions. Those plaintive strains expressive of the aged and dying composer's sorrow deserve to be better known. Of all the players of traditional Irish music who ever happened into Chicago, Turlough McSwiney, the Donegal piper who came to play at Lady Aberdeen's Irish Village at the World's Fair in 1893, was the only one who had any knowledge of those laments. Unexpectedly both were found printed in Mooney's *History of Ireland.* "O'Carolan's Farewell," I faintly remember having seen elsewhere, but not in the Bunting or Petrie collections. This Lament commemorated the bard's departure from the hospitable home of his great friend Robert Maguire, of Tempo, County Fermanagh. Realizing that his life was drawing to a close, O'Carolan paid hasty visits to several cherished friends in Leitrim and Roscommon, on his way to Alderford House, the residence of Mrs. McDermott, his lifelong friend. After he had rested a little on reaching his destination, he called for his harp, and with feeble fingers wandering among the strings, produced his last composition, the weirdly plaintive "Farewell to Music," his dying wail.

To obtain a copy of a rare book requires zeal, patience and persistence, not to speak of the cost of indulging in such expensive antiquarian hobbies. To criticise those who through honorable motives trace and reprint Irish airs and dance tunes found in such works for the benefit of this and future generations, betrays a narrowness of spirit, which too often discourages commendable effort. Such strains, even if previously printed in volumes long out of print and obtainable only through special research, are practically lost to the public; and there is every reason for asserting that if such old traditional airs or tunes are found to possess merit, they should be given publicity, instead of being embalmed in museums for the exclusive benefit of musical archaeologists.

> "Oh, surely melody from heaven was sent
> To cheer the sad when tired of human strife;
> To soothe the wayward heart by sorrow rent,
> And soften down the rugged road of life."

CHAPTER V

STORIES OF TUNES WITH A HISTORY
DANCE MUSIC

"God's Blessing be on you, old Erin,
　　Our own land of frolic and fun;
For all sorts of mirth and diversion,
　　Your like was not under the sun.
Bohemia may boast of her polka,
　　And Spain of her waltzes talk big;
Sure they're all nothing but limping,
　　Compared with our old Irish Jig.''

THE classification of Irish melodies is to a certain extent arbitrary, as dance tunes are not infrequently used as airs for songs and marches, and vice versa.

Among the thousands of Irish melodies which have survived through centuries of adversity, the dance tunes are relatively few. The strains of the older airs and marches from which they have been evolved are plainly traceable in much of the popular Irish dance music of the present day. Even the most rapid Irish tune, when played in slow time, will be found to contain some lurking shade of pathos, and even to possess something of that melancholy luxury of sound which characterizes our most ancient melodies.

Not every tune has a story which would justify its telling in this article, therefore only those about which something is known likely to interest the average reader, will receive more than casual mention.

When Edward Cronin, an excellent fiddler of the traditional school, was brought into the limelight from obscurity, little did we suspect the wealth of rare folk music which lay stored in his retentive memory. Generous as the sunlight, he dictated without hesitation musical treasures known only to himself. In every variety of dance music he was a liberal and prolific contributor, and not only that, but a capable reader and writer of music also.

No double jig ever introduced in Chicago met with such immediate popularity among musicians and dancers as "Shandon Bells." Mr. Cronin learned it in his youth at Limerick Junction, Tipperary, but it was entirely unknown, it seems, except in that locality. It has also been called "Punch for the Ladies" and "Ronayne's Jig," I learned during our investigations.

"Hartigan's Fancy," "The Walls of Liscarroll," "The Pipe on the Hob," "Guiry's Favorite," "Castletown Conners," "Martin's One-horned Cow," "The Foot of the Mountain" and the "Maids of Ballinacarty," all unpublished tunes and new to us, were obtained from John Carey, a native of Limerick, who died at an advanced age since then. Another jig which he called the "Jolly Corkonian" is the original of the march which the Scotch call "The Hills of Glenorchy." In Dr. Joyce's recently published work, *Old Irish Folk Music and Songs,* the jig named "Green Sleeves" is a variant of "Hartigan's Fancy," while "The House of Clonelphin" is Carey's "Jolly Corkonian," and so is "Mrs. Martin's Favorite" as well.

"Kitty's Rambles," or "The Rambles of Kitty," is by no means a new tune, but my setting of it with four strains instead of two deserves special mention. In a simpler form it was also known as "Dan the Cobbler" and "The

Lady's Triumph." A setting of it in two strains is to be found in Dr. Joyce's *Old Irish Folk Music and Songs,* entitled "I'm a man in myself like Oliver's Bull."

"Doctor O'Neill" and "The King of the Pipers" created a sensation when first introduced by Mr. Cronin. None among his audience had heard them before. Each tune consisted of five strains and it is quite probable that they had originally been clan marches. As nothing resembling those ancient tunes have been encountered in our researches, we are fortunate in being the means of their preservation. Insipid settings of the "Templehouse Jig" have heretofore been printed in America, but none to compare with Mr. Cronin's version, which is the real thing from the glens. Another of his good ones is "Banish Misfortune," a version in three strains, which is much superior to the two-strain setting in the Petrie Collection.

Once when he was playing a characteristic old Irish jig then heard for the first time by his audience, Sergt. Early remarked with evident appreciation, "Ah, that's well covered with moss"—alluding to its ancient strains. Its original title being unknown even to Mr. Cronin, it was promptly christened "All Covered with Moss." This jig is printed as an unpublished tune under the name "Roger the Weaver" in Dr. Joyce's *Old Irish Folk Music and Songs,* just out of press.

After years of playing since our first acquaintance and at a time when his dormant repertory was supposed to be exhausted, an unfamiliar jig tune caught my ear. "Everything comes to him who waits," thought I, when Mr. Cronin told us the tune was known to the oldtimers as "O'Sullivan's March." This name had been met with in my studies, but nothing purporting to be the air in question was ever discovered until recently, when it was found printed in Lynch's *Melodies of Ireland,* published in 1845.

JOHN McFADDEN, SERGT. JAMES EARLY.

The arrangement is unattractive in that volume and much inferior to Mr. Cronin's version. In its present form, like many original marches, it is a jig and printed as such in the *Dance Music of Ireland*. The identity of the name "O'Sullivan's March" alone appears to have been lost, for the strains may be recognized as resembling those of the "Old Woman tossed up in a blanket seventeen times as high as the moon," a very ancient Folk Song.

"The Gold Ring," one of Pat Touhey's favorite jigs, came to us through John Ennis. It consists of seven strains, although the "Pharroh or War March" from which it has been evolved contains nine. Bunting states that the latter is "Very ancient—author and date unknown." Other excellent traditional double jigs contributed by Ennis are "Malowney's Wife," "Bessy Murphy" and "Nancy Hynes." A version of the latter as *Maire ni h-Eiden* is printed in the Petrie Collection.

In all matters relating to music, Sergt. James Early and John McFadden are inseparable. They are natives of adjoining counties in the province of Connacht and, aside from their long association with the noted Irish piper, David Quinn, from the same province, who died in this city at an advanced age in 1888, they have played together in public and private for so many years that they have come to be regarded as a musical unit.

Nowhere in Chicago are Irish musicians, whether old residents or new arrivals, more welcome than in Sergeant Early's hospitable home. Centrally located, it had been at all times and still is a meeting place for a choice circle of music-lovers, and no one has been so unselfishly and unobtrusively helpful in all that relates to the well-being of new comers and strangers as the resourceful sergeant himself.

That a vein of subdued sadness pervades our animated

measures as well as our slow airs is well exemplified in "The Cook in the Kitchen" and *"Cailleach an t-airgid,"* or "The Hag with the Money." Those plaintive jigs contributed by Early and McFadden are not included in any previous collection of Irish music. Even the indefatigable Dr. Petrie missed them.

Among the many florid and varied settings of jigs popular in bygone years is "Galway Tom," in five strains. In O'Farrell's *Pocket Companion for the Irish or Union Pipes,* volume 3, published in 1804, we find a different setting of "Galloway Tom" (as it is given) with but four strains. In pencil some former owner of this rare volume noted phonetically "Boughaleen Buee" after the English name. Similar notes over other tunes evinced a creditable knowledge of the subject on the part of the critic. An air entitled *An Buacaillin buidhe,* in common time, in the Petrie collections bears no resemblance to either version of "Galway Tom" above mentioned. Many other fine double jigs were obtained from Early and McFadden, such as "The Piper's Picnic," "Saddle the Pony," "I Know What You Like," "Sergt. Early's Dream," "Stagger the Buck," "Scatter the Mud," "The Miners of Wicklow," "The Man in the Moon" and "The Queen of the Fair." In Bunting's third volume, *The Ancient Music of Ireland,* "The Miners of Wicklow" is included as an air. Dance versions of it, however, were printed in Aird's *Selection of Scotch, English, Irish and Foreign Airs,* 1782, and in McGoun's *Repository of Scots and Irish Airs, circa* 1800.

"The Queen of the Fair," a composition of uncommon excellence by the adroit and versatile Mac. himself, gives an idea of the originality and talent possesed not by him alone but others such as James O'Neill and Edward Cronin, who under more favorable circumstances would be not unknown to fame in the world of music.

No one contributed more to the success of the efforts of the American Irish of Chicago to preserve and perpetuate the music of the Emerald Isle than our scribe, Sergeant James O'Neill himself. Tireless and patient in noting down vagrant strains from others, often traveling long distances for the purpose, he also possessed treasures in his father's manuscripts and his own memory. Those he arranged according to his personal judgment, consequently the writer knows little of any stories connected with most of them. Not the least appreciated was the unfailing welcome and hospitality which made his home the Mecca for all interested in Irish music. Some came to increase our aggregation of melodies, while others came only to enjoy good music or learn tunes new to them and not elsewhere obtainable. All were equally welcome, and the "Evenings at O'Neill's" were among the most enjoyable of our lives.

The story of that splendid double jig, "The Old Grey Goose," is exceptional and not uninteresting. One of the tunes picked up by the writer from John Hicks, the great Irish piper before mentioned, consisted of the first and third strains of our printed setting. Many years later I heard James Kennedy, a fine fiddler from County Leitrim, play another version of it, being the first and second strains of our tune, which he called "The Geese in the Bog." While noting down from my dictation the three strains referred to, Sergt. O'Neill's memory was aroused to the fact that he had a version of this jig among his father's manuscripts. A slight rearrangement resulted in a jig with six distinct strains which will compare favorably with any tune of that class in existence. But about the name—a different jig known to a limited extent and printed in an American publication was called "The Geese in the Bogs." A somewhat similar tune under the same name is also printed in the Petrie collections. Even though Kennedy was possibly right, and there be some who say he was, a change of name was deemed advisable. To preserve to some extent the connection of the historic and popular fowl with our prize, it was christened "The Old Grey Goose." In O'Farrell's *National Irish Music for the Union Pipes,* published in 1797-1800, a version of it resembling Kennedy's is printed under the name "We'll all Take a Coach and Trip it Away." To add to the confusion D'arcy McGee has written a song for the melody entitled "I would not give my Irish wife for all the dames of Saxon land." A variant of our jig and named "The Rakes of Kinsale," can be found in Dr. Joyce's new work, *Old Irish Folk Music and Songs.* It has but four strains, one of them being a duplicate of the first an octave higher.

So much for the perplexities incidental to the study and collection of Irish Folk Music at this late day.

"Doherty's Fancy," a jig so named for the musician from whom Sergeant O'Neill learned it, is a characteristic Ulster tune. It differs noticeably in its decisive ringing tones from the soft and affecting plaintiveness of the tunes belonging to the West and South of Ireland.

Less distinct is "Wellington's Advance," a jig or march unknown in the Southern provinces.

Few names are more universally known than "Morgan Rattler," yet few tunes are more rare. In Aird's *Selection of Scotch, Irish, English and Foreign Airs,* Vol. 3, 1788, the tune appears as "Jackson's Bouner Bougher" (whatever that may mean) and consists of but two strains. Jackson was a famous Irish piper and fiddler, who composed enough dance tunes, mostly jigs, to fill a volume, which actually appeared in 1774 as Jackson's *Celebrated Tunes.* His name, almost invariably connected with the titles of his compositions, indicated their origin, although in course of time many of them came to be known by other titles. Elsewhere in *Aird's Selection,* etc., etc., "The Morgan Rattler" in four strains meets the eye. This identical version is to be found in McGoun's *Repository of Scots and Irish Airs,* before alluded to, and in McFadyen's *Selection,* etc., etc., printed in 1797. "Morgan Rattler," with three strains, is included in the contents of Wilson's *Companion to the Ballroom,* published in London in 1816.

Sergeant O'Neill's setting, copied from his father's music books, is much superior to all, having been embellished by a skillful hand, according to the custom prevailing a century ago, until a total of ten strains display his versatility.

Many fine dance tunes came into our collection through the liberality of John Gillan, a retired business man, whose interest in Irish music and musicians has been perhaps the leading feature of his life. Among his manuscripts formerly in the possession of prominent musicians in Longford, his native country, and the adjoining county of Leitrim, were several elaborate settings of very ancient tunes, such as "Biddy Maloney," a double jig of seven strains. Another unpublished jig is one named by us, "Gillan's Apples." On the manuscript it was called "Apples in Winter," but as another jig of that name was to be found already published a slight change was made in the title to avoid confusion. The two first strains of this tune were played by John Hicks. Whoever added the two additional strains was no novice in composition.

"Paudeen O'Rafferty," or "Paddy O'Rafferty," as Bunting calls it, is another of those ancient tunes which has been the subject of embellishments or variations about the end of the eighteenth century. It is said to have been composed by O'Carolan in honor of a little boy of that name who won immortality by obligingly opening the gate for the bard while paying a visit to his first love, Bridget Cruise.

What is probably the original setting in two strains was printed in Aird's *Selection of Scotch, English, Irish and Foreign Airs,* Vol. 3, 1789, as "Paddeen O'Rafardie, Irish." Bunting's version, which he obtained in County Antrim in 1795, and printed in 1840, consists of five strains, but the author and date of composition he notes are unknown.

Our setting of that rare old jig, "Cherish the Ladies," in six strains, was obtained from the Gillan manuscripts. Versions of it in three strains are to be found in the Petrie and Ryan collections. Dr. Petrie refers to it as a Munster jig, yet none whom the writer heard play it in any style were natives of that province. In its original form of two strains it was one of Jackson's jigs, and Dr. Petrie's opinion receives corroboration by finding a simple version of the tune in Dr. Joyce's *Old Irish Folk Airs and Songs,* just published.

"Be Easy, You Rogue," which is a free translation of the Irish title, *"Stadh a Rogaire Stadh!"* also from the Gillan manuscripts, is a florid setting of an old jig or march in four strains. Its relationship to "The Priest with the Collar" in the Petrie collections is plainly evident. "The Monaghan Jig" is another of Mr. Gillan's contributions, but "Katie's Fancy" has the most interesting history of any.

Peter Kennedy, a farmer living near Ballinamore, County Leitrim, and a fiddler of more than local reputation, from whom Mr. Gillan obtained this tune, told in an amused way how he had followed a fluter around the streets of that town in order to learn a new jig he was playing. Failing to memorize it to his satisfaction, Kennedy was obliged to trace out the fluter's lodgings and pay four pence for his services in dictating "Katie's Fancy," as he called it to his visitor. The tune was regarded by Mr. Gillan as a rare prize, and he safely guarded it on his return to Chicago. Miss Nellie, his daughter, with her characteristic good nature, surreptitiously wrote me a copy. As soon as I could whistle it, the jig was given general circulation.

The mention of her name suggests this as an auspicious opportunity to say that Miss Gillan is a pianist of rare accomplishment and phenomenal execution. It is entirely beyond the descriptive powers of the writer to do her justice in this respect. In the playing of Irish dance music of all varieties she was simply in a class by herself.

Perhaps no dance tune of such marked individuality as the "Lark in the Morning" can be found in the whole range of Irish music. It was furnished us through Sergeant Early from an Edison record made by James Carbray in Quebec, Canada. Nothing but hearing it played, on the violin particularly, would give an adequate idea of its originality and beauty. Mr. Carbray, now a resident of Chicago, tells us he picked up the tune from a Kerry fiddler named Courtney. Nothing even suggestive of this rare strain has been encountered in our researches, but I have a recollection of hearing it alluded to as an old Set-Dance.

Other tunes sent us on Edison records by Mr. Carbray were a double jig named "Courtney's Favorite" and a single jig, which for want of a title, we named "Carbray's Frolics." Since the publication of O'Neill's *Music of Ireland* Mr. Carbray has become a resident of Chicago, and, being an excellent musician and maker of musical instruments, as well as a kindly, courteous gentleman, it goes without saying that his welcome was warm and his companionship appreciated.

We are all more or less indebted to Bernard Delaney for the introduction of many fine tunes to our community. His well deserved reputation as an Irish piper did much to spread the knowledge of his music among local musicians, as well as to promote the popularity of Irish music in general. To give him due credit at this date in that respect would be no easy task for much that was noted down by Sergeant O'Neill from the dictation of others was no doubt memorized from Delaney's playing. As a matter of fact, his repertory was so comprehensive and his memory so retentive that discrimination is now almost out of the question. Like all pipers of our acquaintance, he entertained a decided preference for reels. So fertile in imagination and deft in execution was he, as well as Patrick Touhey, that their graces, trills and deviations were endless in variety. While their style and skill entranced the listener, both were the despair of the music writer.

It was Bernard Delaney, I believe, who introduced to the Chicago pipers and fiddlers an unpublished jig of rare traditional flavor known as *"An Bean Do Bhi Ceadna Agam,"* or "My Former Wife." The sudden popularity which it achieved became a source of no little embarrassment to its sponsor. It was one of the "pet" jigs which he liked to play at public entertainments. When Early and McFadden happened to be on the same programme and came on the stage ahead of Delaney, the mischievous pair never failed to play his favorite tune.

Incidents of this nature influence not a few good musicians to keep from circulation their best tunes, and which they do not choose to remember except on special occasions. What can be more amusing, if not provoking, than to hear a fine performer roll out a string of "chestnuts" to the exclusion of all rare tunes when one understands the motive for this tantalizing practice?

Being an audience of one, on a certain occasion in the home of one of our most eminent pipers, he, seeing no necessity for restraint, played in grand style half a dozen reels and jigs entirely new to me, although we had been more than intimate friends for years. Very civilly he agreed to give us the tunes whenever Sergeant O'Neill was prepared to note them down. Together we called a few evenings later ready for business, but, alas—in the meantime our piper's memory had suffered a relapse, and neither name nor suggestion could arouse it. He couldn't remember any of the tunes, and, judging from prior experience, I am inclined to believe that, like others formerly heard from his facile fingers, those tunes are forgotten in real earnest now.

One of Delaney's best jigs was the "Frieze Breeches," which in some form is known all throughout Munster. A strain remembered from my mother's singing of it was added to Delaney's version, making a total of six in our printed setting. A ridiculous, although typical, folk song, called "I Buried My Wife and Danced on Top of Her," used to be sung to this air, which bears a close resemblance to our version of "O'Gallagher's Frolics."

Dr. Joyce in his new and most important work prints two versions of "Gallagher's Frolic" as unpublished tunes, and unconsciously perhaps a third version under the name, "Breestheen Mira." This latter title, it will be observed, preserves the word "Breestheen" or "Breeches" as in the name of our tune.

Another great favorite of Delaney's was the "Rakes of Clonmel," which the writer memorized and dictated to our scribe. The latter, remembering a third strain from an Ulster setting, called the "Boys of the Lough," annexed it.

How certain airs and strains more or less diversified

can be traced all over Ireland is indeed remarkable, while others plainly traditional remained unknown beyond a limited district in which they apparently had originated.

The following instance well illustrates this limitation: Abram Sweetman Beamish, of Chicago, from whom we obtained the *Buachaillin Ban,* or the "Fairhaired Boy," "My Darling Asleep," and the "Knee-buckle" jigs, also the "Skibbereen Lasses," "Tie the Bonnet," "Dandy Denny Cronin" and the "Humors of Schull" reels, was a native of a parish adjoining the parish of Caheragh, in which the writer was born. Our ages are equal and we left Ireland about the same time, yet I never heard in my youth any of the tunes above named. The first and fifth only were known to the local musicians. Similarly most of my tunes were unfamiliar to Mr. Beamish.

Such is its decadence now in that part of Ireland that none of the rising generation, including amateur musicians, have any but the most fragmentary knowledge of the wealth of Folk Music in common circulation fifty years ago.

Through Edward Cronin's efforts we obtained from John Mulvihill, a native of Limerick, an unpublished jig named the "Stolen Purse," which in its quaint tonality indicates its evolution from some traditional lament. A good reel, named "Bunker Hill," was also noted from his playing. The name was suspiciously modern, but upon investigation I find that Bunker Hill is Dr. Henebry's address in or near the city of Waterford, Ireland. Were the writer to tell what is remembered of his personal experiences and contributions, being naturally familiar with a mass of details, the reader would be justified in thinking that personality was being given entirely too much prominence in those notes. Such is not the intention, however, because the constant aim has been to confine those discursive sketches within the narrowest possible limits.

The avoidance of duplicates, and the inclusion of all that deserved a place in our collections, has at all times been the subject of our greatest concern, still with all our care in the vast amount of material to be considered, complete success has not been attained. One of my earliest boyhood recollections was an air or jig called "Get Up Old Woman and Shake Yourself," which, by the way, is not to be confounded with "Go to the Devil and Shake Yourself," although it has been so misnamed in Alday's *Pocket Volume of Airs, Duets, Songs, Marches, etc.*, Dublin, 1800, and in Haverty's *Three Hundred Irish Airs*, published in New York in the year 1858. Neither title appears in the Bunting or Petrie collections. Under the head of *Diversity of Titles* this complication will be more fully discussed.

The "Humors of Bantry" is a sprightly double jig, which escaped Dr. Petrie and other collectors, although known to several of our musicians in a simpler form than our setting, which has a second finish of great spirit to its second strain. "Fire on the Mountain," the name under which Dr. Joyce prints it as an unpublished tune in his late work, *Old Irish Folk Music and Songs*, is also the name by which it was known to Early and McFadden, and it is also a supplementary name in the index to O'Neill's *Dance Music of Ireland*.

Who has not heard of the humorous classic, "Nell Flaherty's Drake"? But how many knew the air of it? It is scored in O'Neill's *Music of Ireland*, as I heard it sung in the old homestead. Fluent and melodious as it is simple, the air was never before printed. A verse of a still older song sung to it ran as follows:

"My name is Poll Doodle, I work with my needle,
And if I had money 'tis apples I'd buy;
I'd go down in the garden and stay there till morning,
And whistle for Johnny, the gooseberry boy."

One often wonders why a popular tune passes current for years without a name among non-professional Irish musicians. Nothing is more common than to be told on making inquiry, "I never heard the name of it," and seemingly nothing concerned them less than the name as long as they could play a tune to suit their fancy. Such was the case with the fine old traditional tune, the "Merry Old Woman." None of our best performers had any name for this favorite jig, so it could not be permitted to remain nameless any longer. By dint of persistent investigation we eventually learned that it was known as the "Walls of Enniscorthy." Few double jigs equal it. None excel it, and I'm inclined to believe that it is one of "Old Man" Quinn's tunes preserved to us by Sergeant Early. A variant of this jig I find appears in Dr. Joyce's late work under the name, "Rakes of Newcastle-West," but in a much simpler setting.

While traveling on post, one summer evening in 1875, the strains of a fiddle coming through the shutters of an old dilapidated house on Cologne street attracted my attention. The musician was an old man named Dillon, who lived alone, and whom I had seen daily wielding a long-handled shovel on the streets. His only solace in his solitary life besides his "dhudeen" was "Jenny," as he affectionately called his fiddle. A most captivating jig memorized from his playing I named "Old Man Dillon" in his honor. Like many others of his tunes, it was nameless. Inferior versions of it have since been found, entitled "A Mug of Brown Ale," and I am satisfied this is the original and correct name.

It is a curious coincidence in our experience that all solitary musicians—that is those who play for their own enjoyment mainly—seldom vary from song or marching time in the execution of dance music.

A fine old traditional tune, "Drive the Cows Home," although classed as a double jig, was evidently a clan march. William McLean, from whose piping I picked it up, played it in marching time on the Highland pipes.

To Bob Spence, a fellow boarder, in 1870, I am indebted for our setting of "Happy to Meet and Sorry to Part," a grand and spirited double jig not found in any previous Irish collection, although printed in one American volume of miscellaneous dance music. Spence was a devoted student, and while he patiently sawed away on his fiddle, a receptive memory enabled me to learn his tune and retain it.

Another excellent jig is "The Joy of My Life," unnamed and unpublished as far as we know. It was a favorite with Delaney, Early and McFadden, and some others.

A German bandmaster in Troy, New York, was so pleased with its rhythm that it fills a favored place in his repertoire. To impress a German leader favorably is high honor indeed for an Irish jig.

When I heard that affable Highlander, Joe Cant, play *Bodach an Drantain*, its Irish origin appeared indisputable, and, being a "new one," it was retrieved as the "Grumbling Rustic," its translated name. Incidental corroboration of its identity and my judgment came to light by finding an elaborate version of it with four variations in that extremely rare volume, McGoun's *Repository of Scots and Irish Airs*, published about the year 1800. It was named "Gillan na Drover" and classed as Irish. The first and second words were plainly corrupted from the Gaelic *"Giolla na"*—servant or attendant of. What Irish word "drover" stands for is still a mystery. In our desperation for an intelligible title, this march in O'Neill's *Irish Music for the Piano or Violin* is called "Gillan the Drover."

The "Tailor's Wedding," which I heard played on the Highland pipes by my cherished friend, Joe Cant, had a suspiciously Irish swing to it. And so it proved to be, although printed in Scotch music books. It was known to McFadden and Early as "Skiver the Quilt," and by that name we found it printed in both ancient and modern collection. Yet it does not appear in Petrie's *Complete Collection of Irish Music.*

An almost forgotten melody is the *"Cailin Deas Donn,"* or "The Pretty Brown-haired Girl." The Irish song to this air I remember only in a fragmentary way, and it is doubtful if the Folklorists have preserved a copy. Overlooked when preparing our first volume, it has been since printed in the *Dance Music of Ireland.* O'Farrell included it in his *Pocket Companion for the Irish or Union Pipes* (1810) as "Calleen Das Dawn."

Two versions of "The Tenpenny Bit" were procured from James Kennedy and Abram S. Beamish, representing Leitrim and Cork respectively. Its existence in counties so far apart proclaims its antiquity, although no trace of it has been found in Petrie's *Complete Collection of Irish Music,* by that or any other name.

A willing and valued contributor to our musical stores was Timothy Dillon, a much respected member of the Chicago police force, from which he has since been retired on pension. A violinist of the old traditional style of playing, he possessed many fine jigs and reels with which we were entirely unfamiliar, among them being "The Boy from the Mountain," "The Woodcock," "The Belles of Liscarroll," "The Chorus Jig," "Church Hill," and "The Yellow Wattle," double jigs; *"Bothar o Huaid,"* or "The Northern Road," single jig; "Dillon's Fancy," "The Long Strand," and "The Lady Behind the Boat," reels. His style was airy and florid and quite distinct if not original in its sweeping slurs. An almost identical setting of "The Chorus Jig" is printed in Dr. Joyce's recent work, before mentioned, as an unpublished tune. The tune of that name published by Bunting in his third collection is in two-four time and was obtained by him in 1797 from "McDonnell the Piper," its author and date of composition being unknown. This tune is identical with "The Rocks of Cashel," printed in other collections. An early and simple version of it under the latter name is to be found in McGoun's *Repository of Scots and Irish Airs,* printed about 1800, and in Aird's *Selection of Scotch, English, Irish, and Foreign Airs,* volume 4, published about 1791. In *A Philosophical Survey of the South of Ireland,* published in 1778, the author, Dr. Campbell, says, "We frog-blooded English dance as if the practice was not congenial to us; but here they moved as if dancing had been the business of their lives. The 'Rocks of Cashel' was a tune which seemed to inspire particular animation."

One of the old timers is "The Three Little Drummers," which I remember from boyhood. Dr. Petrie's collections include three settings of it, one of them being printed without a name. Our version has three strains; the third, learned in Chicago, is identical with the second strain of Dr. Petrie's unnamed setting. Highland pipers seldom play any other Irish jig for dancers but this, and it is to be found in most of their books or bagpipe music.

Recently I learned that "The Little House Under the Hill," an old jig of no special merit, was composed by the famous "Piper" Jackson, who flourished about 1750. A version of it closely resembling the simple melody I learned when a boy is named "Link About" in Aird's *Selection of Scotch, English, Irish and Foreign Airs,* published from 1782 to 1797. Strangely enough, the tune named "The Little House Under the Hill," in an earlier volume of the same work, is a reel of unknown origin. The jig is also to be found in *The Hibernian Muse* as an air from *The Poor Soldier*. It was evidently in more repute a century ago than it is today, for an elaborate setting of it in eleven strains, under its proper name, was printed in O'Farrell's *Pocket Companion for the Irish or Union Pipes*, published in 1804.

Many years ago the writer picked up an unpublished jig from Daniel Rogers, a native of East Clare, who consoled himself for many privations and disappointments in life by merrily whistling the many rare tunes which a musical ear, had stored in his memory. He had learned it, he told me, from a County Clare fiddler named Tom Hinchy, in New York. As usual, there was no name to it, so we called it "Hinchy's Delight." No trace of it has been found in Petrie's *Complete Collection of Irish Music*, and the only one of our local musicians who had even a variant of it was Edward Cronin.

Among the many Irish melodies interspersed throughout Mooney's *History of Ireland* was one entitled "Ella Rosenberg." It was a new one to all of us, and so enthusiastic was one of our club over its tonal beauties that it came to be known as "Father Fielding's Favorite." His Reverence induced the good sisters in his parish to teach it to their most promising music pupils, while he cheerfully accompanied them on the flute.

But we are not always loyal to our first love, and "Ella Rosenberg" was not the only one to feel the pangs of neglect and inconstancy. Her admirer, the musical clergyman, heard a piper named Burns play a different version of it in Waterford, while his Reverence was on one of his annual pilgrimages to Ireland. Since his return to Chicago he has been endeavoring, with poor success, to substitute the new for the old version which first captivated his fancy.

A spirited jig named the "Humors of Castle Lyons," noted down from the writer's dictation, is probably not a very ancient composition. It was not known, evidently, to any collectors of Irish Folk Music before Dr. Hudson obtained a setting of it from a noted piper named Sullivan, in the County of Cork, whose rivalry with Reillaghan is the subject of a story in a later chapter. The tune has found its way into American collections of harmonized melodies.

No one but an Irishman would think of naming an air or a tune "The Man Who Died and Rose Again." Where Patrick Touhey, the famous piper, obtained this rare unpublished jig, we are unable to say.

Few tunes learned in boyhood days left such an indelible impression on my mind as "The Blooming Meadows," which I heard Mr. Timothy Downing, a gentleman farmer at Tralibane, play in his own home. Although instructed by him on the flute, I did not venture to be too inquisitive in regard to tunes not a part of my studies, and therefore did not learn its name at that time. The melody has been previously printed under various names, but no setting has the artistic second finish to the last strain except ours. Although Dr. Joyce printed a setting of "The Blooming Meadows" in his *Ancient Irish Music* in 1873, a slightly different version of it, named "Trip It Along," appears in his latest work, *Old Irish Folk Music and Songs*.

Other names by which this splendid double jig is known are "Down With the Tithes," "The Humors of Milltown," and "The Hag and Her Praskeen." The latter was the Connacht name by which it was known to David Quinn, the celebrated piper. It has also been called "Cover the Buckle," but I have since ascertained definitely that the name refers to a special dance and not a special tune.

Most Irish jigs in six-eight time are "Double Jigs," commonly termed "Doubles" in Leimster and some other parts of Ireland. Such jigs are also popularly known, at least in Munster, by the appellation of *Moinin* or *Moneen* jigs, a term derived from the Irish word *moin*—a bog, grassy sod, or green turf—because at the fairs, races, hurling matches, and other holiday assemblages, it was always danced on the choicest green spot or *moinin* that could be selected in the neighborhood. A separate classification of "Single Jigs," and the first ever made in a printed volume, was initiated in O'Neill's *Dance Music of Ireland*.

The following description of that variety is taken from *The Petrie Collection of the Ancient Music of Ireland*, published in 1855. Like the common or "Double Jig," the "Single Jig" is a tune in six-eight time, and having eight bars or measures in each of its two parts. But it differs from the former in this, that the bars do not generally present, as in the "Double Jig," a succession of triplets, but rather of alternate long and short, or crochet and quaver notes. "Battering," as applied to this variety of jig, is called "single battering." The floor is struck only twice—once by the foot on which the body leans, and once by the foot thrown forward.

In considering Hop Jigs or Slip Jigs, as they are called, according to locality, a quotation from Wilson's *Companion to the Ballroom* may not be out of place. The author, who styles himself "Dancing Master from the King's Theatre Opera House, London," was not handicapped by any shrinking modesty which would restrain him from criticising others in his profession, says in his preface: "In the progress of this work a number of tunes have been collected together in nine-eight, as they require in their application to the figures, either in country dances or reels, what are technically termed Irish Steps. Few tunes of this measure are to be found in collections of Country Dances; and the

An Irish Jig.

reason is, those who are but indifferent dancers are not acquainted with proper steps.

"Some are apt to imagine that an Irish tune must be uniformly danced with Irish steps. This, however, is a mistake. It is to the tune, and not the nationality of the tune to which the steps in question are applied, and tunes in nine-eight always require Irish steps, whatever may be their origin; while Irish tunes of six-eight or common time are danced like others. This variety of Irish time has little or no recognition in modern music, and some persons appeared incredulous when arrangement in nine-eight time was mentioned."

"The Rocky Road to Dublin," probably the most widely known of Hop or Slip Jigs, is not one of the oldest. The earliest printed versions which we have found are in *The Citizen* magazine, published in Dublin, in 1841. The musical editor, Dr. Hudson, says it is a "modern Irish dance." It is said the name is taken from a road so called in the neighborhood of Clommel. It is the air which is sung by the nurses for their children in a great portion of the southern parts of Munster, and they frequently put forward as one of their recommendations that "They can sing and dance the baby to 'The Rocky Road'." Under the above name a version of it was printed without comment in Petrie's *Complete Collection of Irish Music,* and a variant also appears as "Black Rock," a Mayo jig. As "Black Burke" it was found in a publication the name of which is forgotten. Our setting of this famous tune, obtained from John McFadden, consists of three instead of the ordinary version of two strains.

An uncommonly fine tune of this class, in three strains, obtained from John Ennis, is "Will You Come Down to Limerick?" Simpler versions are known to old-time musicians of Munster and Connacht, and in Chicago. Ennis had no monopoly of it, for it was well known to Delaney, Early, and McFadden. As an old-time Slip Jig it seems to have been called "The Munster Gimlet," a singularly inapt title; but when it came into vogue by its song name, we are unable to say.

It would be too tedious to discuss in detail the many excellent and hitherto unpublished Hop Jigs gathered and printed through patient and persistent efforts maintained from year to year, so we will conclude the discussion of Jigs by a brief allusion to "The Kid on the Mountain."

This unpublished tune in six strains was introduced among our experts by the "only" Patsy Touhey, the genial, obliging and unaffected wizard of the Irish pipes. A version of this tune, with the puzzling title, "Bugga Fee Hoosa," I find is included among the numbers in Dr. Joyce's *Old Irish Folk Music and Songs*.

To hear Touhey play this jig as he got it from his ancestors was "worth a day in the garden" to any one interested in the Dance Music of Ireland.

"Oft have I heard of music such as thine,
Immortal strains that made my soul rejoice,
Of wedded melody from reed and pipe, the voice,
And woke to inner harmonies divine."

CHAPTER VI

STORIES OF TUNES WITH A HISTORY
DANCE MUSIC (CONTINUED)

> "The pipes with clear and humming sound,
> The lovers' whispering sadly drowned;
> So the couples took their ground—
>   Their hearts already dancing.
> Merrily with toe and heel,
> Airily in jig and reel,
> Fast in and out they whirl and wheel—
>   All capering and prancing."

It was while listening to Barney Delaney's wonderful music one Sunday evening many years ago at John Doyle's hospitable home that I first heard that slashing reel called "The Milliner's Daughter." "Ah, that's me darlin'!" exclaimed our host, with delight. "None of them can bate that." Neither could they. Played on the Irish pipes and fiddle together, by capable performers, the melody and rhythm of Johnny Doyle's favorite reel, no words of mine can adequately describe.

Mr. Doyle was a gentleman and a genius and an ardent lover of the music of his native land. After years of service as locomotive engineer he became an engineer in the Chicago fire department. A skilled mechanic, it was his pleasure during leisure hours to make bellows for the pipers on an improved plan of his own invention. Never before nor since were such serviceable equipments manufactured. A music lover, but not a musician, he had a fiddle and a set of Irish pipes in his house all ready for any performer who chanced to call. And seldom was he without callers, for every one felt that the kindly welcome and hospitality of Mr. and Mrs. Doyle were genuine, and not mere formalities, until his death at a patriarchal age put an end to the festivities.

Bunting's strange dogma, that "A strain of music once impressed on the popular ear never varies," finds no support in our experience. In fact, the exact contrary is almost invariably true. Farquhar Graham, in his introduction to Wood's *Songs of Scotland,* exposes the fallacy which Bunting maintained. "I shall only, therefore, state here that as a result of my own experience as a collector of our melodies, that I rarely, if ever, obtained two settings of an unpublished air that were strictly the same," writes Dr. Petrie in dissenting from Bunting's views, "though in some instances I have gotten as many as fifty notations of the one melody."

This diversity is well exemplified in the case of "The New Demesne," a reel new to us, which James Kennedy played with great spirit and smoothness. "The College Grove" reel, with two additional strains obtained from John Ennis, a Kildare man, was plainly a variant of Kennedy's tune, which the latter learned from his father in County Leitrim. A careful comparison established a relationship between the reels above named and "The Green Jacket," which Edward Cronin learned in his youth in Tipperary. Recently the writer made the acquaintance of "Miss Corbett's Reel" in Aird's *Selection of Scotch, English, Irish and Foreign Airs,* published in the latter part of the eighteenth century. Its close resemblance to Kennedy's tune proves conclusively that it was the original progenitor of all the versions of that popular reel. In corroboration of this view, Sergeant Early informs me that piper Quinn always referred to the tune as "Miss Corbett's Reel."

An unpublished reel of ancient Connacht lineage is "*Bean a tigh ar lar,*" or, as it is called in English, "The Woman of the House." It was a great favorite with "Jimmy" O'Brien, the Mayo piper, who died in this city over thirty years ago; and it was no stranger to Early and McFadden, who, if they did not know it before, learned it from David Quinn in Chicago. Delaney and Touhey also played it.

This traditional tune, like a great many others, is not to be found in Petrie's so-called *Complete Collection of Irish Music;* but Dr. Joyce introduces it in his recent work as an unpublished tune under the title of "Cows Are a-Milking."

For the best effect, it should not be played in faster than marching time, and as it is rich in phrasing and peculiar in an arrangement requiring sixteen bars in each strain, it presents exceptional advantages for the display of talent and technique at the hands of a skilful musician.

While a great majority of the dance tunes printed in old collections, such as Playford's *Dancing Master,* Aird's *Selections,* etc., etc., and *The Hibernian Muse,* are out of date and forgotten, "The Mason's Apron" still retains its popularity. Settings of it little varied by time or locality have been printed as "The Mason's Cap," "The Masson Laddie," and "Miss Hope's Favorite," and for a tune preserved in type as far back as 1785, at least, it bids fair to hold its own with the best of them in the future. As "Lady Carbury," Dr. Joyce includes it as an unpublished reel in his latest work, *Old Irish Folk Music and Songs.*

Were any one to ask which was the most popular reel, the answer would not be a subject for speculation, for the verdict would be unanimous in favor of "Miss McLeod's

Reel." While the name under any form of orthography would indicate a Scottish origin, we have not found it in any of the old published collections. Upon examination, its evolution or adaptation from "The Campbells Are Coming," or rather the still older Irish air, *"An Seanduine,"* or "The Old Man," is clearly apparent.

O'Daly in *Poets and Poetry of Munster,* Grattan Flood in *A History of Irish Music,* Fitzgerald in *Stories of Famous Songs,* and others, agree on the Irish origin of the music of "The Campbells Are Coming."

Beranger, a French traveler, mentions "Miss McLeod's Reel" among six favorite tunes played by the Irish pipers for his entertainment at Galway in 1779, and that is the earliest mention of the name which we have found in print.

The rapid decadence of Folk Music in Ireland since the regrettable suppression of the "Patrons" and farmhouse dances does not appear to have unfavorably affected "Miss McLeod's Reel," for it is universally hummed, lilted, whistled and played throughout the island; and in some parts of the country no other reel is heard. In fact, it was the only reel played for the dancing classes at the Munster *Feis* in 1906, when competing for prizes.

That it has not been burdened, according to custom, with numerous other names, is quite remarkable for a tune which has been in circulation in Ireland for at least one hundred and thirty years.

"The Enterprise and Boxer," or "The Enterprising Boxer," is the only other title for this tune which we have discovered in our researches.

That well-known reel, "Peter Street," can hardly be regarded as a tune with a history. In the matter of general distribution it is well up towards the top of the list, for it may be found in most American piano publications which include reels and hornpipes among their numbers.

Its ringing tones assail the ear from self-player pianos, and as "Miller's Frolic" it appeared in Howe's collections, printed in Boston when our parents were young. "Peter Street" is by no means a characteristic Irish reel, and for that reason its paternity has always been to me a matter of uncertainty, although a florid setting of it with variations was received from Mr. John Tubridy, a school teacher at Tulla, County Clare, and a prize winner on the violin at a Leinster *Feis*. It does not appear in Dr. Petrie's *Complete Collection of Irish Music*. Neither does it find a place in Dr. Joyce's collection of *Old Irish Folk Music and Songs*.

Its discovery at last as "Sweet Peter Street" in Clinton's *Gems of Ireland*, published in 1841, furnished the first particle of authentic evidence which came to hand establishing its Irish origin.

One of McFadden's finest traditional tunes was the "Shaskan," or "Shaskeen Reel," included among the hornpipes in O'Neill's *Music of Ireland*, but properly classed as a reel in the *Dance Music of Ireland*. It turns out to be one of the rare old Connacht tunes which remained unpublished and but little known except through our belated efforts.

As a Christmas present which was sure to be appreciated, I forwarded in 1907 to Rev. Dr. Henebry, at Waterford, Ireland, a box of Edison phonograph records which Sergeant Early generously permitted me to select from his treasures. Among them was "The Shaskeen Reel," played by Patrick Touhey. The clergyman's comment is best expressed in his own words:

"The five by Touhey are the superior limit of Irish pipering. One of his, especially 'The Shaskeen Reel,' is so supreme that I am utterly without words to express my opinion of it. It has the life of a reel and the terrible pathos of a *caoine*. It represents to me human man climbing empyrean heights and, when he had almost succeeded, then tumbling, tumbling down to hell, and expressing his sense of eternal failure on the way. The Homeric ballads and the new Brooklyn Bridge are great, but Patsy Touhey's rendering of 'The Shaskeen Reel' is a far bigger human achievement. Why, there is no Irish musician alive now at all in his class! If things were as they ought to be, he should be installed as professor of music in a national university in Dublin. And that is what I think of Patsy Touhey and his pipering."

When Edward Cronin, a new star of uncommon brilliance, first appeared on our musical horizon, great interest was manifested in the long-forgotten treasures which his sweeping bow introduced.

That which first claimed attention was a hornpipe of smooth and easy rhythm, a stranger to us all. Not a single air or tune having resemblance or relation to it has yet been discovered. Although learned in his native Tipperary, Mr. Cronin never heard it named, but to make amends for the deficiency he christened it "Chief O'Neill's Favorite."

On account of its peculiarly Irish tonality, some people refer to it as "The Brogue Hornpipe." Regardless of the name, it is a prime favorite with dancers, and its permanent popularity is assured.

"The Cloone Hornpipe" and "Old Man Quinn," obtained from Sergeant Early and John McFadden, originally came from the celebrated piper whose name is memorialized in one of them.

David Quinn possessed a wonderful repertory of Irish Folk Music which, descending to his pupil and friend, and by them communicated to Sergeant O'Neill, has been pre-

PATRICK J. TOUHEY,
Irish Piper and Comedian.

served in our publications for future generations. Mr. Quinn's tunes, few of which had been noted by former collectors, were given wide circulation in this city by the musical twain above named, and to their knowledge of his music can be traced directly or indirectly not a few of the best numbers in our volumes.

An excellent hornpipe of no great antiquity, which has won the favor of many, is "Dunphy's Hornpipe." Nameless, like too many others, it was called after the man from whose playing it was reduced to notation by our scribe. This unpublished tune had some circulation in County Kilkenny, for Father Fielding, also, we found had heard his mother lilting it.

When we heard of "The Rights of Man" hornpipe, it was supposed that it was a new composition which had attained rapid popularity in Ireland, because neither the name nor the tune had any place in our memories. It was not long, however, before John McFadden acquired a setting of it, which he played in his own inimitable way. It was distinctly Irish in tone and structure, as it ought to be, for Sergeant O'Neill recalled a version of it as played by his father in Belfast many years ago. Obtained too late for insertion in the *Music of Ireland,* it was printed in the *Dance Music of Ireland,* issued in 1907.

Dr. Joyce prints a version of it as an unpublished tune in his new work, *Old Irish Folk Music and Songs,* and a duplicate of it, No. 294, is simply called "Hornpipe." A florid setting of this favorite as played by Mrs. Kenny, a noted violinist of Dublin, was brought to Chicago by Bernie O'Donovan, the "Carberry piper," but in that style it gains no advantage for the dancer.

Ordinarily such a common tune as "The Devil's Dream" would not be expected to call for special mention. How or when it came to be so named cannot now be stated. A version of it found in many Scotch publications is called "The Devil Among the Tailors," and in Alday's *Pocket Volume of Airs, Duets, Songs, Marches, etc.*, published in Dublin, *circa* 1800, it is printed without a name, being simply referred to as "A Favorite Hornpipe." An unexpected coincidence in the setting is that, like John McFadden's, it has three strains, all other printed versions having but two.

The earliest printed set of it entitled "The Devil's Dream" so far encountered is in Wilson's *Companion to the Ballroom,* published at London in the year 1816.

"The Liverpool Hornpipe" has not entirely escaped misunderstandings, for in Aird's *Selection of Scotch, English, Irish and Foreign Airs* a peculiar version of it is also named "Blanchard's Hornpipe."

The most popular and best known hornpipe in my boyhood days did not even have a name. It was the great favorite with all the crack dancers who gave exhibitions of their Terpsichorean abilities on certain occasions by dancing on the kitchen table or on a door unhinged for the purpose and laid on the floor.

Dancing experts invariably were equipped with "dancing-shoes"—light and elastic—to drum out the fancy steps, with telling effect to the ear, as well as enable the dancer to exhibit to the eye his skill in this line of entertainment.

The most renowned dancer of his time in our neighborhood was Jerry Daly, my brother-in-law, now a nonagenarian resident of Chicago; and it was for him the tune was named "Jerry Daly's Hornpipe." Even at that advanced age he still delights in showing the boys how it ought to be done.

An inferior variant of this tune as a reel is to be found

in Levey's *Dance Music of Ireland,* under the name "The Poor Old Woman." As a song air entitled "The Poor Woman" it is printed in Dr. Joyce's late work, before mentioned, but the appropriateness of either name is open to question, for there is nothing in the phrasing, structure, or tonality of the tune in the slightest degree suggestive of the *"Sean Bhean Bhocht,"* or "The Poor Old Woman," sung by every peasant, young and old, throughout Munster, at least in the last century.

Another unpublished, unnamed and unknown tune, except to the writer, was "Kit O'Mahony's Hornpipe," so called after my mother, from whose lips it was learned in childhood. Many musicians of a later generation, among them relatives who had grown to manhood at the old home, assured me they had never heard it. Not even a variant of this tune had been found in print until the publication of Dr. Joyce's *Old Irish Folk Music and Songs,* where a version appears entitled "Miss Redmond's Hornpipe." A note explains that it was sent to the editor many years before by Grattan Flood. How a tune of such extreme rarity came to be known only at two places so far apart as Enniscorthy, County Wexford, on the east coast, and Bantry, County Cork, on the west coast of Ireland, is not easily accounted for.

Still another hornpipe on the same order, and also learned from my mother, is named in O'Neill's *Music of Ireland* "The Banks of the Ilen." This tune, better known than the preceding, was printed in Levey's *Dance Music of Ireland* as "Six Mile Bridge," and quite recently in Dr. Joyce's work, before mentioned, as "The Queen's County Lasses"; but it is missing from Dr. Petrie's *Complete Collection of Irish Music.*

When quite young I heard an indifferent fiddler named

Crowley, at Drimoleague, in West Cork, play a fine tune which he called "O'Dwyer's Hornpipe," the tones and triplets of which haunted me more or less distinctly through life. The third strain seems to have come to me by intuition, for it is not one of the three which Crowley played. This hornpipe is an old traditional tune in Munster, but wellnigh forgotten in this generation. Somewhere, years ago, a poor and limited version of it was seen in a piano pamphlet, disguised as "De Wier's Hornpipe." Like scores more of the numbers in O'Neill's *Music of Ireland* and *The Dance Music of Ireland*, this hornpipe also appears in Dr. Joyce's *Old Irish Folk Music and Songs*, under the name "Prime's Hornpipe."

A fine old traditional hornpipe in five strains, entitled "The Groves" and said to be one of "Piper" Jackson's compositions, was preserved in the Petrie collections; but the setting printed in O'Neill's *Music of Ireland*, was not derived from that source. The tune came to us through Sergeant Early, from Patrick Touhey, the famous Irish piper. A few bars of it found lodgment in my memory since John Hicks played it at St. Bridget's Bazaar in this city thirty years ago. We were overjoyed on recovering this rare tune, because we had despaired of being so fortunate. A much different version of it, known as "The Drunken Sailor," but not identical with Dr. Petrie's setting, is one of the numbers in O'Neill's *Irish Music for the Piano and Violin*, First Series.

"Youghal Harbor" as an air is frequently mentioned by writers on Irish music, but our search for the notation of it was unrewarded until it was eventually found in Mooney's *History of Ireland*. As the arrangement seemed better suited for a hornpipe, it was so classed. Since then the Bunting and Petrie collections have been searched for it in vain, but it was found in Lynch's *Melodies of Ireland,* published in 1845.

The air named "Youghal Harbor, or, I'm Sadly Thinking," in Haverty's *Three Hundred Irish Airs,* 1858, is a different tune altogether. Dr. Joyce prints at least two vocal versions of it in his recent work, frequently alluded to, and he speaks of Forde having seven versions of "Youghal Harbour" among his manuscripts.

There was a fiddler of great renown in County Longford, named Sault, of whom our music-loving friend, Mr. Gillan, speaks in glowing terms. One of his compositions, donated by the latter, which we named "Sault's Own Hornpipe," is decidedly unique and surprising at first glance to the performer. It is in common time and the second bar consists of four eighths with rests—from G above the staff to G below. As an instance of originality in dance music, this tune has scarcely an equal.

A tidy clog brought to Chicago many years ago by Bernard Delaney, our celebrated Irish piper, became a great favorite, especially among the dancers. It circulated for a time without a definite name, but was later identified by James O'Neill, our scribe, as a tune which he had heard called "The Londonderry Clog" in Ulster. By that name it is known and printed in our collections. The tune consisted of but two strains originally. Turlough McSwiney, the "Donegal Piper," while playing in Lady Aberdeen's Irish Village at the Chicago World's Fair in 1893, improvised a third strain which Miss Nellie Gillan improved. Some few months later the writer was surprised to hear Delaney play "The Londonderry Clog" with an additional or fourth strain, in fine style. In this form it became still more popular, and there seemed to be enough of it to suit the most exacting. The end had not yet been reached, for among some neglected papers we came across an unnamed tune which was unmistakably related to "The Londonderry Clog," and to that thrifty favorite our two unclaimed strains were added, making altogether an excellent hornpipe or clog of six strains, unsurpassed by any composition of that class ever printed.

Although this dance tune, only slightly varied, appears to have been known in districts so widely apart as Donegal, Londonderry, Down, Tipperary and Kings counties, it is not to be found in any printed collection of Irish music before our time. It is just barely possible that it originated later than the early part of the nineteenth century, when that patriotic Irishman and enthusiastic collector, George Petrie, was in his prime.

After Ed Cronin had been aroused from the lethargy into which his isolation in Lake View had plunged him, he began to indulge in original composition and adaptation, with unexampled assiduity. Of course, all who woo the Muses can hardly hope to produce an unbroken line of masterpieces. As specimens of latent talent born of his brain after the day's weary and monotonous toil in a machine shop, we invite attention to "The Bantry Hornpipe" and "Caroline O'Neill's Hornpipe," with four strains in each.

Songs innumerable have been written to the air of "The Cuckoo's Nest" in the three kingdoms. Ordinarily it consists of two strains, and is to be found in various settings and under divers titles in many old printed collections. Bunting's version in three strains, he states, was taken from an old music book dated 1723. He adds that the air is "very ancient, author and date unknown."

"Come Ashore, Jolly Tar, and Your Trousers On," is the peculiar title under which it is printed in Aird's *Selec-*

tion of Scotch, English, Irish and Foreign Airs, published in 1782-97. It has four strains and is evidently the version from which the Highland pipers derived the transposed style of it which they play.

In Wilson's *Companion to the Ballroom*, published in 1816, the simple setting therein printed is named "Jackey Tar," but a footnote informs us that this tune, with a little alteration, constitutes what is now called "The Cuckoo's Nest," from which it was taken. "The Mountain Dew," a ballad by Samuel Lover, is sung to this air.

Long before the writer ever expected to tread on the soil of County Clare, "Paddy" Mack's fame as a fiddler had been well sung in Chicago. He was blind, of course, as almost all others were who lived by their musical skill in Ireland. It was our good fortune while traveling in the year 1906 to meet and be entertained by two of his pupils—Michael Touhey and John Allen—at their homes, as well as at Clashmore House, the residence of Mr. James Conway, our hospitable host. Both were charming fiddlers whose free and easy style of bowing gave their tunes that delightful spirit and swing peculiar to the best traditional Irish musicians.

Old Mr. Touhey, familiarly called "Darby Simon," who had known Mrs. O'Neill in her girlhood, summoned his son Michael from the hayfield to play for us. Flattered by Mrs. O'Neill's recollection of his skill and agility as a dancer, the old man, verging on to eighty years of age, but still active and erect, stepped onto the "flag of the fire" and "battered" one of "Paddy" Mack's hornpipes thereon in a manner few of the present generation could equal, and he didn't seem at all distressed by the exercise.

Here was a scene worthy of the brush of Hogarth and the pen of Carleton. The interior of a peasant's cottage, with cupboard and dresser and settle ranged against whitewashed walls, affords a study not unworthy of the artist's talent. The large open fireplace, with comfortable seats on either side, served as a frame for the picture of the octogenarian father dancing a hornpipe to the fiddling of his own son. What a subject for a word-painter! — and where else but in Ireland could such a sight be seen?

An enjoyable evening spent at Ayle House as the guests of John Walsh, Esq., J. P., left many pleasant memories. We were entertained with much excellent music by members of the family, and it was an unexpected delight to find in the vicinity of Feakle so little evidence of the musical decadence which is noticeably affecting the spirits of the people in other parts of Ireland.

"Paddy" Mack is long since dead, but his memory lives and his pupils are worthy of his reputation.

Among the many fine tunes played by Touhey and Allen night after night in Mr. Conway's house were two reels and one hornpipe that were entirely new to me. Much as I tried to memorize them as of old, the effort was not altogether successful, and I was indebted to Mr. Tubridy, a school teacher from Tulla, for sending me the notation later on. He was himself a prize winner at a Dublin *Feis*, and contributed an uncommon reel not included in our first volume, O'Neill's *Music of Ireland*. None of the four tunes thus obtained were known by name, so the hornpipe, to commemorate the old blind musician, was named "Paddy Mack," and the reels "The Maid of Feakle," "Johnny Allen's Reel," and "The Humors of Scariff," contributed by Touhey, Allen and Tubridy, respectively.

Those four dance tunes secured in a locality within twenty miles of the city of Limerick show how incomplete has been the work of the unselfish souls who had devoted both time and money to the collection of Irish Folk Music.

Previously unknown to the members of our "Irish Music Club," those tunes are now in circulation, and one of them particularly, "Johnny Allen's Reel," is a prime favorite, on account of the fascinating tenderness of its melody. It is most effective when played in marching time, a style quite suitable for the elaborate steps of the Munster dancers.

One of the earliest recollections in my memory is "The Downfall of Paris," as the name of a *Rinnce Fada,* or Long Dance. Little hopes had we of ever getting a version of the melody. But the unexpected happens, sometimes. To our unutterable joy, Edward Cronin not only played that elusive tune, but many others, ancient and obsolete, with which we were entirely unfamiliar. This old-time favorite consists of four strains.

Of the fifty-odd collections, containing more or less Irish music, in the writer's library, Wilson's *Companion to the Ballroom* alone had a setting of this Long Dance, and that volume was only recently acquired.

The author states that it was originally composed for a quick-march in opposition to "Ca Ira," the French national air. It has since become a favorite dance, particularly with good dancers, as it requires a very long figure not easily performed by tyros in the art.

Only one strain of twelve bars of "The Ace and Deuce of Pipering" was known to Mr. Cronin, but the second strain was obtained from another source.

A different version of this rare old Long Dance in three strains was subsequently contributed by Sergeant Michael Hartnett, whose quiet and retiring disposition betrayed no indications of the wealth of Folk Music his memory preserved. A good setting of this tune was printed in Dr.

Joyce's *Ancient Irish Music,* and identical with that in Dr. Petrie's *Complete Collection.*

Another of Ed Cronin's historic Long Dances, and one of which he alone had any knowledge, is "Planxty Davis," or "The Battle of Killicrankie." Hardiman, author of *Irish Minstrelsy,* and Grattan Flood, author of *A History of Irish Music,* tell us that the melody was composed by Thomas O'Connellan, the great Irish harpist, on the occasion of the battle of Killicrankie, in 1689. "Its Irish origin," writes Grattan Flood, "is sufficiently clear from the fact that in a Northumbrian manuscript of the year 1694 this tune appears as "The Irish Gillicranky." As in the case of many other tunes encountered in our researches, the modern versions have been much embellished and improved, at least for modern taste.

In this opinion we are sustained by no less an authority than Alfred Moffat, the learned author of *The Minstrelsy of Scotland* and *The Minstrelsy of Ireland.*

When Dr. Joyce penned the explanatory note to "The Orangeman," the third number in his *Old Irish Folk Music and Songs,* he was not aware that this tune had been already printed years before in O'Neill's *Music of Ireland,* as "The Orange Rogue," which Mr. Cronin learned in his youth at Limerick Junction, Tipperary. "I woke up from sleep one night whistling this fine air in a dream," he says, "an air I had forgotten for years. Greatly delighted, I started up—a light, a pencil, and a bit of paper, and there was the first bar securely captured. I have never seen this air written elsewhere, except in one County Limerick manuscript." Our version, first classed as a jig, has been transferred to the Long Dances, where it properly belongs, in *The Dance Music of Ireland.*

Other Long Dances and Set Dances, previously unknown

to us, and contributed by the same custodian of old Irish dance tunes, are "The Barony Jig," "The Blackthorn Stick," "John O'Dwyer of the Glens," and *"Bfuil an fear mor astig?"* or "Is the Big Man Within?" The latter, in its Irish name, sometimes abbreviated to *"Fear Mor,"* is peculiar in having the first strain in *nine-eight* time and the second in *six-eight* time. The four tunes above named were printed in O'Neill's *Dance Music of Ireland* for the first time. Under the name, "How Are You Now, My Maid?" Dr. Joyce prints a version of the last of them in *Old Irish Folk Music and Songs,* just fresh from the press.

A remarkably fine Long Dance is the "Three Captains," contributed by Sergeant James O'Neill. That name, as well as "Three Sea Captains," is occasionally seen in print, but the airs to which they are attached seem scarcely worth preserving. None of our local musicians knew this splendid tune, and nothing even resembling it is to be found in any collection of Irish music but ours, although a version of it, named "Mr. William Clark's Favourite," is printed in McGoun's *Repository of Scots and Irish Airs.*

While endeavoring to enlarge our store of unpublished and forgotten Irish airs, little did we suspect that our unassuming friend, Sergeant Michael Hartnett, next door neighbor to our scribe, was the custodian of so many musical gems utterly unknown to others in our circle. Although we obtained from his dictation that fine flowing composition, "Bonaparte's Retreat," we would not be justified in classing it as his exclusively, for it turned out that it was one of Ed Cronin's best Long Dances also. This tune was probably of Munster origin, for it was not known even by name to any of our people born outside of that southern province. Many natives of Munster also, among them the writer, were equally ignorant of its existence.

The other Long Dances, "The Lodge Road" and "The

Jockey at the Fair," previously unpublished, were contributed by our scribe, Sergeant James O'Neill.

Just in time for classification among the Long Dances in our second volume, *The Dance Music of Ireland*, we obtained another stranger, named "Hurry the Jug," from Bernie O'Donovan, "the Carberry Piper," a young musician of fine promise, lately arrived from Ireland. In giving this rare dance tune publicity, we have preceded Dr. Joyce by two years. Two versions of it are printed in his latest work, already mentioned—one under its proper name, as a Set Dance, and the other as a Jig, named "I Rambled Once." The means by which O'Donovan contrived to learn it himself, throws a flood of light on the secretiveness, or rather selfishness, of certain musicians on both sides of the Atlantic, who treat rare tunes as personal property, to be guarded with as much care as trade secrets.

There was and still is in the city of Cork a whistling cobbler named Creedan. His cheerfulness was no greater than his covetousness in saving his tunes from circulation. Should any of his patrons display any interest in the tunes which he often whistled unconsciously, from force of habit, by listening or inquiring the name of any of them, the flow of melody ended then and there.

Our friend O'Donovan was presumed to be "very hard on shoes," on account of his frequent visits with damaged footgear; but, being fully aware of the cobbler's idiosyncrasy, he was careful to be apparently absorbed in reading, with the paper hiding his face. From this it can be seen that Creedan's bill was in exact proportion to his customer's ability to memorize the tunes.

It was under such circumstances that O'Donovan picked up "Hurry the Jug" and other airs. His experience would be merely an incident likely to excite our merriment, were

Bernie O'Donovan

not Creedan the type of a class, members of which, I regret to say, are found right here in Chicago.

> "Oh! while the soul of music yet was flowing,
> The listener paused, for too intensely strung
> The passionate chords, that, with a spirit glowing,
> Kindled and trembl'd as the minstrel sung."

CHAPTER VII

DIVERSITY OF TITLES—TUNES WITH MORE THAN ONE NAME

"Strange power hath memory to fill the ear,
With music wafted from the distant past;
From scenes and times that would not, could not last;
When cherished strains, melodious deep and clear,
Burst from the lips of friends and kindred dear."

THE bewildering variety of settings or versions of traditional Irish tunes is fully equaled by the confusing diversity of names by which many of them are known.

To the collector of fugitive melodies within a limited territory in Ireland, the few difficulties of this nature encountered are inconsequential. When the field of inquiry is extended, the perplexities arising from the multiplicity of titles in different localities increase, until they reach the maximum in America, where natives of probably every parish in Ireland are to be met.

Were melodies known by but one name, the classification of variants and the avoidance of duplicates would be quite a simple matter.

No doubt this diversity and duplication of titles, increasing in the flight of years, existed from the earliest times of which we have any authentic records.

In looking over any printed or manuscript collection of Irish music, our hopes of finding something new under names to us unfamiliar, are not infrequently doomed to disappointment, for the title only too often disguised the identity of a well-known tune.

Every number must be played over and carefully considered, for many tunes have been previously published under different names, and, besides, many others prove to be merely variants of tunes already in our collections.

The writer, a native of Cork, the county in which Forde compiled much of his manuscript collection, and contiguous to County Limerick, where Dr. P. W. Joyce obtained most of the music which he has published, recognizes a large portion of it, especially the dance tunes, as the same, slightly varied and differently named, which he had learned in his boyhood days, and subsequently published in O'Neill's *Music of Ireland* and in *The Dance Music of Ireland.*

The reader can form some idea of the tremendous amount of research necessary in order to acquire even a fair knowledge of the subject, from the following instances:

A ballad called "The Fair at Dungarvan" was a great favorite in Munster, at least in the middle of the last century. The air, which I remembered since boyhood, was noted down and printed under that name, no other being known for it at the time. It developed, however, that it was an air of great antiquity, much varied by time and taste, but never beyond easy identification. As "Rose Connolly," Bunting printed it in 1840 in his third collection, *The Ancient Music of Ireland,* and notes that it was obtained in Coleraine in 1811, "author and date unknown." It is to be found under that name also in Surenne's *Songs of Ireland,* published in 1854. Probably its most ancient title was "The Lament for *Cill Caisi,*" or "Kilcash," a setting of which is to be found in Dr. Petrie's *Complete Collection of Irish Music.* Among the songs which I find are sung to this air are: "Alas, My Bright Lady," "Nelly, My Love, and Me," "There is a Beech-tree Grove," and "Were You Ever in Sweet Tipperary?"

One of the earliest recollections of youth is my father's

singing of a very affecting song, the last line of every verse being *Mo Muirnin na Gruaige Baine*. This fine old air is mentioned in Hardiman's *Irish Minstrelsy*, published in 1831, as another of these wandering melodies well known among the peasantry of the southern and western parts of Ireland.

The original Irish stanzas of the song are preserved in volume 1, of that now rare work, but no trace of the melody has been found in any of the old printed collections of Irish music.

Neither the above name nor its English equivalent, "My Fair-haired Darling," appears in the index to Dr. Petrie's *Complete Collection of Irish Music*, 1892-7; but No. 202, a nameless air obtained from Teige McMahon, of County Clare, and an air named "One Evening in June; or, Youth and Bloom," contributed by Paddy Coneely, the Galway piper, particularly the latter, are variants of the melody which I learned from my father and printed in O'Neill's *Music of Ireland* and O'Neill's *Irish Music for the Piano or Violin*.

"Dobbin's Flowery Vale," in Dr. Joyce's *Ancient Irish Music*, closely resembles our setting of the air. He speaks of it as one of the best known tunes all over Munster. Conceding that it was, who can explain why such a delightful melody has been overlooked so long, especially after Hardiman brought it into such prominence? Other songs sung to this air are "The Maid of Templenoe" and "The Charmer with the Fair Locks."

That popular melody best known as "The Rose Tree" has many other titles. It is probable but not certain that its original name was *"Moirin ni Chuileannain,"* or "Little Mary Cullenan," from a song written to the air by the Munster poet, John O'Tuomy, who died in 1775.

O'Keeffe introduced it in *The Poor Soldier* in 1783, with

PADDY CONEELY,
Dr. Petrie's Famous Galway Piper. 1840.

verses beginning "A Rose Tree in Full Bearing," hence the name by which Moore inserted it in his *Irish Melodies* as the air to his verses beginning, "I'd Mourn the Hopes that Leave Me." It was also called "The Rosetree of Paddy's Land," and in Oswald's *Caledonian Pocket Companion,* printed in 1760, a version of it was called "The Gimlet." As "The Irish Lilt," Thompson included it in his Country Dances for 1764. In Aird's *Selection of Scotch, English, Irish and Foreign Airs,* volume 1, published in 1782, a setting of the air is called "The Dainty Besom Maker," and in Gow's *Second Collection,* published in 1788, it is included under the name "Old Lee Rigg, or Rose Tree." Mullhollan introduces it among his *Irish Tunes* in 1804 as "Killeavy," and it is printed under that name also in Thompson's *Original Irish Airs,* 1814-16.

Other names by which the air is known are "Maureen from Gibberland," "Forgive the Muse that Slumbered," and "Fare You Well, Killeavy." A version of it in the *Forde Collection,* entitled "Captain MacGreal of Connemara," is to be found as an unpublished air in Dr. Joyce's *Old Irish Folk Music and Songs,* issued in 1909.

"The Green Woods of Truigha" is a melody of great antiquity, as is proved by its structure and by the fact of its being known by so many names in different parts of the country. Besides the above name, which it bears in Ulster, it is known in Leimster as "Ned of the Hill" (*Eamonn an Cnuic*); in Connacht as "Colonel O'Gara," and in Munster as "*Mor no Beag*" ("Big or Little"), with a variety of other aliases.

That delightfully poetic name, "Oh, Arranmore, Loved Arranmore," in Moore's *Melodies,* has come to be better known than "Kildroughalt Fair," the air to which it is set and which was included in Holden's *Periodical Irish Melodies,* printed from 1806 to 1808. It is also included under the latter name in Lynch's *Melodies of Ireland,* published in 1845. Variants of this air were "Lough Sheeling," "Old Truicha," and "Thy Fair Bosom."

Another setting of "Kildroughalt Fair" is "Bridget O'Neill," one of the numbers in Bunting's second collection, published in 1809. An older version of this air is printed under the name "My Lodging Is Uncertain," in O'Farrell's *Pocket Companion for the Irish or Union Pipes,* published in 1804.

One of Gerald Griffin's poems, "The Wanderer's Return," commencing, "I've come unto my home again," is set to the music of "Kildroughalt Fair" in Moffat's *Minstrelsy of Ireland.*

A very popular old Irish marching tune was *"Domhnall na Greine,"* first printed in O'Farrell's *Pocket Companion for the Irish or Union Pipes,* in which the name appeared as *"Donald na Greana,"* and twice elsewhere in the same collection, whether unconsciously or not, as "O, My Dear Judy" and "The Boney Hilander."

The old Irish title means in English "Daniel of the Sun" or "Sunny Dan." The origin of the name is thus explained by John O'Daly, editor of *The Poets and Poetry of Munster.* Domhnall was a fellow who loitered his time idly basking in the sun, as his cognomen would indicate, and consequently he became a fitting subject for the poets to display their wit upon. O'Daly, who gives many specimens of this wit in Irish and English, prints one epic of thirteen verses in the original Irish, with a rhyming English translation describing Dhonal's mock heroic accomplishments.

In Moore's *Melodies,* "Thady you Gander" instead of *"Domhnall na Greine"* is given as the air to which the verses beginning "Oh, 'tis sweet to think," are sung; yet curiously enough no mention is made of the air by that name in any other publication except where Moore's song is copied. We are indebted to Alfred Moffat for the information that said air is included in Holden's *Old Established Irish Tunes,* produced in 1806, as "She Is the Girl That Can Do It." That the tune was old and established is evidenced by the fact that it is known by so many names, such as "Bully for You," "I Gave to My Nelly," "Girls of the West," "The Leg of a Duck," "From the Court to the Cottage," "You May Talk as You Please," and "Bucky Highlander," the latter being the Scotch name burlesqued by some Irish wag in verses often heard by the writer, commencing "Potatoes and butter would make a good supper for Bucky Highlander."

Few tunes have enjoyed such wide circulation and universal popularity as *"An Rogaire Dubh,"* or "The Black Rogue," a Munster jig formed on the air, "Brigid of the Fair Hair," according to Dr. Petrie's notation. A comparison of both tunes proves that they had a common origin at least.

It appears that the jig version of it penetrated in some way to Dumfries, in that part of Scotland visible from County Down, Ireland, on a clear day, and soon came to be known as "Johnny MacGill," the name of the fiddler who gave it publicity, claiming it as his own composition. In course of time it came to be known as "Come Under My Plaidie," the name of a popular song written by Hector Macneill to the catchy music. Under the latter name it is regarded as a Scotch tune and printed as such in several collections.

Its true origin is conceded, however, by R. A. Smith, who included the air "Johnny MacGill" as one of the numbers in *The Irish Minstrel,* published at Edinburgh in the year 1825.

Tom Moore also set his song, "Life Is All Checkered

with Pleasures and Woes," to the air of "The Bunch of Green Rushes," the name by which the melody is known in Forde's *Encyclopedia of Melody*, published in London early in the last century, and in several other collections.

Few if any tunes had more names, or songs sung to them, than this, among them being the following: "Michael Malloy," "Tom Linton," "The Little Bunch of Rushes," "God Bless the Grey Mountain," "The Bark Is on the Swelling Shore," "Nature and Melody," "The Humors of Donnybrook Fair," "Inishowen," "The Irish Lady," "The Irish Lass," "O, Pleasant Was the Moon," " 'Tis a Bit of a Thing," and "What Sounds Can Compare?"

In the present generation few realize that the waning favorite, "Kate Kearney," once so popular as a waltz tune, was an ancient Irish melody long before Lady Morgan wrote the song of that name.

Edward Bunting printed it as "The Beardless Boy" in his *General Collection of the Ancient Irish Music*, 1796, and under the same name it is to be found in Crosby's *Irish Musical Repository*, 1808.

In his second volume—*A General Collection of the Ancient Music of Ireland*, 1809—Bunting again includes a practically identical setting of this air as "The Dissipated Youth," the same title under which Haverty published it fifty years later in his *Three Hundred Irish Airs*.

The melody is called "Kate Martin" in Murphy's *Irish Airs and Jigs*, printed in 1809.

As a waltz tune, "Kate Kearney" had but one drawback—it lacked a serviceable second part or strain. This, however, was supplied by some orchestra leader, but it was essentially German in composition, and devoid of any trace of Irish feeling. O'Farrell, a celebrated Irish piper, who published in London six small volumes of music suitable for his instrument—1797 to 1810—attempted two variations on "Kate Kearney" with indifferent success.

The old air known by the corrupt Irish title "Savourneen Deelish" has come to be called by a variety of other names, such as "The Molecatcher's Daughter," "Miss Molly, My Love, I'll Go," "The Exile of Erin," "I Saw from the Beach," "There Came to the Beach" and " 'Tis Gone, and Forever." Moore's song by the latter name was first printed in the sixth number of the *Melodies* in 1815.

In Shields' opera, *The Poor Soldier*, 1783, "Farewell ye Groves" was sung to this air, which was also called "Erin go Draugh" in O'Farrell's *Irish Music for the Union Pipes*. As "Savournah Deelish" it was known in Arnold's opera, *The Surrender of Calais*, 1791. By that name also, according to Alfred Moffat, it was printed in Adam's *Musical Repository*, 1799, Nathaniel Gow's *Collection*, 1800, Holden's *Collection*, 1806, and Murphy's *Collection* in 1809, and even now in Moore's *Melodies*.

An air in Dr. Petrie's *Complete Collection of Irish Music*, of recent date, called *Ta na la*—in English, "It Is Day"—I find is a version of that spirited tune commonly called "Tow Row Row," and also "Paddy, Will You Now?"

Under these names the tune has been printed in several collections. Variants of the strain as lullabies have been noted by Dr. Joyce. The chorus to the old song ran as follows:

"Tow, row, row! Paddy, will you now?
Take me now, while I'm in humor;
And that's just—now!"

Who has not heard of "The Rakes of Mallow" and the life they led, with their "Beauing, belleing, dancing, drinking," according to the song?

The air was first printed in Burk Thumoth's *Twelve*

English and Twelve Irish Airs about 1745. As "The Rakes of London" it was included among Johnson's *Two Hundred Country Dances,* published in 1751. In the *Compleat Tutor for the Guitar,* issued a few years later, the same publisher prints it as "The Rakes of Marlow." Aird numbers the tune among his *Selection of Scotch, English, Irish and Foreign Airs*—Glasgow, 1782—under the name, "The Rakes of Mall." Alfred Moffat tells us that Arnold made good use of the air in his opera, *Auld Robin Gray,* 1794.

Mallow, a thriving town in Cork, famous for its Spa, was much frequented by young gentlemen in the last century, who took the waters for their health.

One of the most popular Long Dance or Set Dance tunes, especially in Munster, is "The Humors of Bandon." Our setting, as played by James O'Neill and Ed. Cronin, has sixteen bars in the second strain. Although not printed in any old Irish collection of music, it is an ancient tune, for a nice version of it named "The Humors of Listivain" was printed in Aird's *Selection of Scotch, English, Irish and Foreign Airs,* Vol. 3, published in 1788, with ten bars in each strain. Neither title appears in the Petrie collections, but an indifferent version of the tune in regular measure, called "The Merry Old Woman," and another version without a name and having only six bars in the second strain, are to be found in the first part of Petrie's *Complete Collection of Irish Music*. A jig named "The Humors of Bandon" in Levey's *Dance Music of Ireland,* London, 1858, differs but little, except in the key, from Petrie's "Merry Old Woman."

A friendly critic not long ago among other alleged discoveries informed us that a jig entitled "The Kinnegad Slashers" in O'Neill's *Music of Ireland,* was "The Land of Sweet Erin," and he was right. Yet so were we, for as "The Kinnegad Slashers" it was printed in O'Farrell's *Pocket Companion for the Irish or Union Pipes,* Vol. 3, published in 1804, and in Powers' *Musical Cabinet,* issued six years later.

Additional names by which this popular tune is known are "O! an Irishman's Heart," "O! Merry am I," "Powers of Whiskey," and "Paddy Digging for Gold." None of those names appears in the index to the Petrie Collections. The Scotch have annexed the tune also, among whom it is known as "The Bannocks o' Barley Meal."

That excellent Irish jig best known as "The Frost is All Over," has a variety of other appellations, such as "The Praties are Dug," "The Mist of Clonmel," "On a Monday Morning" and "What Would You Do if You Married a Soldier?"

One setting of this tune as "The Frost Is All Over" obtained in the County Armagh and two other versions by different titles are printed in Dr. Petrie's *Complete Collection of Irish Music.*

The fame of "Father O'Flynn," Alfred Perceval Graves' inimitable song, is world wide, and there is reason to believe that the spirited air, "The Top of Cork Road," to which it is sung, contributed something to its popularity.

It was not by any means a rare tune in West Cork in my boyhood days, and the version of it remembered was printed in our publications. We are not aware that it is included in Dr. Petrie's *Complete Collection of Irish Music,* but it was printed without comment in Dr. Joyce's *Ancient Irish Music* in 1873.

The tune found its way into three English Collections of Country Dances, and one Country Dance Card between the years 1770 and 1781 as "The Yorkshire Lasses." Alfred Moffat tells us that its first publication distinctly connected with Ireland was in Holden's *Masonic Songs,* Dublin, 1798.

The second strain of "The Irish Lilt" in Vol. 1 of Aird's *Selection of Scotch, English, Irish and Foreign Airs,* printed in 1782, and the second strain of "The Top of Cork Road" bear a very close resemblance. It's being known as "The Irish Lilt" at such an early date disposes of any English claim to the tune.

Other names by which the air is known are "Trample Our Enemies," "To Drink With the Devil" and "The Rollicking Irishman."

Who has not heard of "Tatter Jack Walsh," and who has not wondered as to the meaning of that peculiar title? Patient investigation disclosed the fact that the correct name in English is "Father Jack Walsh." The title in connection with the tune, it appears, was originally written down *"An t-athair* Jack Walsh," the first and second words being idiomatic Irish for Rev'd Father. In transcribing that name, some one, probably ignorant of the Irish language, corrupted *"t-athair"* into "Tatter," hence the meaningless error which has been perpetuated to this day.

A ballad called "Kitty of Ballinamore," has been sung to this air, and as a double jig it has also been printed under the name "To Cashel I'm Going."

It is generally believed that "Billy O'Rourke is the Bouchal" was the original name of that popular tune to which is sung a modern favorite, "The Fair of Windgap" or *Aonach Bearna Gaoithe* (geeha). Such, however, is not the case, for we find the same tune in the *Encyclopedia of Melody* as "The Day I Married Susan," while in *The Hibernian Muse,* published in 1787, it is printed under the name "Mrs. Casey," from the opera of *Fontainebleau.*

It is one of the numbers in Lynch's *Melodies of Ireland,*

printed in 1845, under a slightly altered name—"Billy O'Rorke Is the Boughal"—and in Surenne's *Songs of Ireland*, by the same name, a little improved in spelling.

In *Stories of Tunes with a History*, I alluded to "Jimmy O'Brien's Jig," so named for the piper from whose playing the writer memorized it. In *The Bee, A Collection of Irish Airs*, published early in the last century, and in Clinton's *Gems of Ireland*, printed in 1841, a version of it is entitled "Copey's Jig" and ascribed to "Piper" Jackson.

Probably the oldest version of it is found in Aird's *Selection of Scotch, English, Irish and Foreign Airs*, published in the latter part of the eighteenth century, where it is named "Cassey's Jig."

Who has not heard of "Lannigan's Ball," a serio-comic song of great popularity fifty years ago. This sprightly air or jig tune is to be found in Aird's *Selection*, etc., before mentioned under the name "Dribbles of Brandy." In the same volume the Hop Jig, known to us as "Drops of Brandy," is called "The Cudgell."

From Thomas Broderick, a Galway man, my school director at Edina, Missouri, the writer picked up a reel called "My Love Is Fair and Handsome." To some it is known as "Paddy McFadden," under which title it is printed in an American publication. The discovery of a version of it in Aird's *Selection*, etc., before quoted, as "John Roy Stewart," was quite unexpected, as the easy flowing style of its rhythm would not indicate an origin dating back to the eighteenth century.

The old melody known as "The Rakes of Kildare" can boast of a respectable antiquity. A version of it printed in Aird's *Selection of Scotch, English, Irish and Foreign Airs*, published 1782 to 1797, is simply called "A Jig." Compared with "Get Up Early," in Bunting's *Ancient Music of Ireland*, issued in 1840, they betray a common origin. Bunting obtained his tune, which is in reality a march, from a Mayo musician in 1802, and he notes that the author and date of composition were unknown. Tom Moore's "Swift from the Covert" is sung to a version of "The Rakes of Kildare," and an American piano pamphlet contained a variant of it which was named "The Barndoor Jig."

"The Priest in His Boots," or, as a translation from the Irish title would indicate, "The Priest and His Boots," is one of the old-time Country Dances or Set Dances. A good version of it printed in the appendix to Moffat's *Minstrelsy of Ireland* was copied from C. & L. Thompson's *Complete Collection of 120 Favorite Hornpipes*, 1765-77. We find the tune also printed in Aird's *Selection, etc.*, 1786, as "The Parson in His Boots."

In Crosby's *Irish Musical Repository*, "The Priest in His Boots" is given as the air of a song entitled "Paddy's Trip from Dublin," a few pages further on it is again named as the air to, "Murphy Delaney." Both may have had a common origin, which time and taste have varied, yet "Murphy Delaney" as now known appears to have been derived from "A Jig to the Irish Cry," one of Burk Thumoth's *Twelve Irish Airs*, published in 1742.

"The Irish Washerwoman" shares with "Miss McLeod's Reel" the reputation of being the most universally known dance tune wherever the English language is spoken. Its being named "Jackson's Delight" in Forde's *Encyclopedia of Melody* clearly betrays its origin as one of Jackson's jigs. In the same publication it also appears as "The Irishwoman," which we hoped was its true name originally. Our confidence in that view has been rudely shaken, however, by finding what we believed to be the corrupted name —"The Irish Washerwoman"—in Aird's *Selection, etc., etc.*, 1782; McGoun's *Repository of Scots and Irish Airs*, published *circa* 1800, and in Wilson's *Companion to the Ballroom,* issued in 1816, and other old printed collections. In reviewing O'Neill's *Irish Music for the Piano and Violin* in the Journal of the *Irish Folk Song Society* of London, Mrs. C. Milligan Fox, the honorable secretary, alludes to it as "The Washerwoman."

Edward Cronin alone of our Chicago musicians remembered any strains like the reel called "Lough Allen" in the Petrie collection of *The Ancient Music of Ireland,* published in 1855. That circumstance entitles it to special mention, for the tune is printed in one form or another no less than six times, without names and by various names, in Petrie's *Complete Collection of Irish Music,* recently published.

Concerning "Lough Allen," in the volume published under Dr. Petrie's personal supervision in 1855, he tells us that "It has been a very popular dance tune in County Leitrim, where it most probably had its origin." An almost identical setting, No. 258, in the so-called "Complete Collection," is without a name, and so is No. 154, a variant of it. No. 396, another version in the same volume, is entitled "The Mill Stream, a County of Cork Reel."

Other versions or variants of this widely distributed reel are No. 888, called "Box About the Fireplace, A Munster Reel," and No. 896, which is simply called "A Munster Reel." When we come to consider No. 911, which bears the name "Lough Allen," we find a reel in four sharps, which, if not a different tune, has scarcely any resemblance to the "Lough Allen" first named or its variants. Such confusion in a collection of Irish music—the work of one talented individual—is truly bewildering.

A reel once popular throughout the southwest of Ireland, at least, was known in West Cork in my boyhood days as "Rolling on the Ryegrass."

Periodically, Mary Ward and her two daughters, who had been driven to mendicancy as a result of the famine, made our farmhouse their headquarters for a week or so at a time. They were always very welcome, for the old woman had all the news of the country to relate. In fact, it was through her and her like that news was disseminated in the absence of newspapers in those times. Besides, she could sing a good song, and lilt a good tune in spite of her blindness and poverty. That explains the source of the writer's acquaintance with "Rolling on the Ryegrass" and many another tune either lost or forgotten in this generation. Other names by which this favorite tune was known are "Old Molly Ahern," "The Piper's Lass," "The Rathkeale Hunt," "Maureen Playboy" (Father Fielding gave me that as the Kilkenny name), and "The Shannon Breeze." The latter name is also applied to another reel printed in our collections under the name "Winter Apples."

As an instance of the fascination which certain tunes have for individuals, and even families, "Rolling on the Ryegrass" well serves our purpose. An American-born family of gigantic men and women named Sullivan manage an immense farm a dozen miles beyond the limits of the city of Chicago. They are all musical, and several of them can dance a jig or reel as cleverly as if they were born in Ireland. Of course, there is no scarcity of tunes in such a family, but no tune ever played warms the cockles of their hearts or gets their feet in motion quicker than the strains of "Rolling on the Ryegrass." Both parents came from the Glens on the north shores of Bantry Bay, and it is a curious fact that their preferences, musical and mental, have suffered no diminution in transmission to their offspring, born and brought up in a cosmopolitan American community.

Were the writer to attempt to enter into the details of all his contributions of unpublished tunes to our collections, the reader would be justified in thinking that personality was being given entirely too much prominence; yet what is more natural than that personal reminiscences would constitute the greater part of a story of this nature?

One of the earliest recollections of my childhood days was a sprightly song called "Get Up, Old Woman, and Shake Yourself," which my mother and sisters sang frequently. This air or jig tune was promptly dictated to our scribe. Another jig, named "Go to the Devil and Shake Yourself," occasionally obtruded, and although by many confused as the same tune, they were in reality entirely different. Having inadvertently omitted the latter tune from O'Neill's *Music of Ireland,* we were bound to insert it in *The Dance Music of Ireland,* and we did, with a vengeance. The music seemed strangely familiar, though, and for good reason, too, because "Go to the Devil and Shake Yourself" proved to be identical with "When You Are Sick Is It Tea You Want?" and also "The Penniless Traveler," both jigs already printed under those names in our collections.

Few tunes can boast of such ancient popularity as "Go to the Devil and Shake Yourself." In a volume comprising nine collections of Country Dances, published in London in 1798, this jig appears six times, while a different tune is printed under that name once. It is exceptional in having no variants, because it has been preserved in print for over a century, instead of being dependent on the uncertainty of tradition for perpetuation. But yet another complication arises, for under the above title my tune, "Get Up, Old Woman, and Shake Yourself," is to be found in Alday's *Pocket Volume of Airs, Duets, Songs and Marches,* Dublin, 1800, and in Haverty's *Three Hundred Irish Airs,* published in New York in 1858.

Another mystifying conflict of titles is found in the case of "Fisher's Hornpipe," one of the numbers in Wilson's *Companion to the Ballroom.* In a footnote the author says that the tune is also called "The Egg Hornpipe." The tune appears in Alday's *Pocket Volume,* etc., etc., under the title "Lord Howe's Hornpipe." In the second volume of the same work the tune is again presented as "Blanchard's Hornpipe." To add to the confusion, Forde in the *Encyclopedia of Melody* prints it as "The College Hornpipe," while Dr. Joyce in his recent work calls it "The Blacksmith's Hornpipe."

Still people will wonder when they find a familiar tune with a strange name.

Examples of this character, exemplifying the almost endless diversity of names by which so many Irish airs, marches, dance tunes, etc., have been known and are still known, could be prolonged indefinitely, and our only reason for mentioning them in this connection at all is to convey to the reader some idea of the endless embarrassments to be met with in collecting and classifying Irish Folk Music.

In the conflict of titles, the multiplicity of names, and the diversity of settings, the avoidance of duplicates becomes a task of no little difficulty.

> "Music, all powerful o'er the human mind,
> Can still each mental storm, each tumult calm;
> Soothe anxious care on sleepless couch reclined,
> And e'en anger's furious rage disarm.''

CHAPTER VIII

DUPLICATION OF TITLES—DIFFERENT TUNES WITH SAME NAME

"Songs of our land, ye are with us forever;
　The power and the splendor of thrones pass away,
But yours is the might of some deep-rolling river,
　Still flowing in freshness thro' things that decay.
Ye treasure the voices of long-vanished ages;
　Like our time-honored towers, in beauty ye stand;
Ye bring us the bright thoughts of poets and sages,
　And keep them among us, Old Songs of our land."

THAT historical events influence not a little contemporaneous music, as well as poetry and song, is well illustrated in a volume comprising nine collections of Country Dances in the writer's library, published in London in 1798, the year in which the French fleet sailed into Bantry Bay. In Lavenu's Collections there is a tune, in six-eight time, named "Bantry Bay." Another tune of the same name, in common time, is to be found in Preston's Collection of Country Dances. A jig, called the "Bantry Bay Boys," appears in Thompson's Collection; while E. Riley prints "The Bantry Boys," also in jig time, in his collection.

Notwithstanding the similarity of titles, those tunes are independent compositions.

To add to the confusion, one of my own best traditional hornpipes is known as "Bantry Bay." Unsuspicious of any existing duplication of titles, our versatile friend, Ed Cronin, christened one of his compositions "The Bantry Hornpipe."

Thus six dance tunes, originating from six different sources, by a remarkable coincidence are so similarly named as to suggest some relationship, at least in their composition. Yet none whatever exists.

In like manner, Bonaparte's meteoric career so affected the impressionable Irish mind that his name is memorialized in at least five traditional tunes. "Bonaparte Crossing the Rhine," or the Alps, as some would have it, a spirited march, is the best known of them. "Madam Bonaparte's Hornpipe," which, by the way, is a Long Dance, was much in vogue in years gone by. Superior to all others commemorating the great military captain, is "Bonaparte's Retreat," a march or Long Dance overlooked by all collectors of Irish music before our time. The name was dimly remembered, and but little hopes of recovering the tune was entertained until, to our great delight, the silent and modest Sergeant Michael Hartnett, who incidentally dropped into Sergeant O'Neill's residence next door, one day informed us that he knew the tune since his boyhood.

Before he left the house that elusive treasure and several other rare strains long forgotten, but retained in his tenacious memory, were among our collections. An almost identical setting of "Bonaparte's Retreat" was also known to Edward Cronin, another Munsterman, whose acquaintance we had not formed until some years later.

A variant of this rare tune, which John Carey called "The Answer to It," we called "Bonaparte's Defeat," to preserve the name and sentiment. Being regular in structure, it was classed with the hornpipes.

Still another memorial of the brilliant Corsican is known as "In Comes Great Bonaparte," printed in *Ancient Irish Music*, by Dr. P. W. Joyce, who states that he learned the tune from his father.

From the fact that such an excellent tune as "Bonaparte's Retreat" was unknown to our best musicians outside of Munster, where it was popular in more than one county, we are inclined to believe that all Bonaparte tunes had their origin in that province. None of the tunes above named are to be found in Dr. Petrie's *Complete Collection of Irish Music*. Neither is there any other tune commemorative of the Bonaparte name in that work.

The instances in which tunes having neither resemblance nor relationship are known by identical names are comparatively limited. Whether such duplication of titles was the result of coincidence, carelessness, or design, is uncertain, but whichever may have been the cause, it can well be imagined how it leads to confusion and embarrassment.

When one finds the name of an air or dance tune printed or written over a composition entirely different from the one expected or known to us by that name, the thought of there being two melodies of the same name seldom or never occurs to the inquirer, and the supposed mistake is sure to be attributed to the editor's ignorance.

In Crosby's *Irish Musical Repository*, published in 1808, there is an air called "Within This Village Dwells a Maid." Yet this identical title appears over an entirely different composition in Thomson's *Select Collection of Original Irish Airs*, volume 1, printed in 1814. The source from which the air had been derived, the editor did not mention—contrary to his usual custom. Bunting includes in his third collection—*The Ancient Music of Ireland*, published in 1840—a melody entitled "In This Village There Lives a Fair Maid," which was obtained at Ballina, County Mayo, in the year 1792, the author and date of composition being unknown.

This air, like Crosby's, is in three-four time, but in a different key. Their descent from a common origin is plainly evident, however, regardless of the discrepancy in key and title.

"*Cuisle mo Chroidhe*" (Cushlamachree), or "Pulse of My Heart," is one of the oldest traditional Irish melodies. Although first printed in 1815 as the air to "Come Over the Sea," in the sixth number of Moore's *Melodies,* it has been printed in many other publications since that date. From Alfred Moffat's *Minstrelsy of Ireland* we copy a fragment of the old song associated with this air:

> "*Cuisle mo chroidhe,*
> Did you but see
> How the rogue he did serve me?
> He broke my pitcher, he spilt my water,
> He kissed my wife, and he married my daughter—
> *O! cuisle mo chroidhe*"—etc.

There is another Irish air of the same name, in three-four time, which bears not the slightest resemblance to that which we have just discussed; but where we obtained the setting of it as printed in O'Neill's *Music of Ireland,* I cannot now recall.

Besides the two melodies mentioned, there is a third, "*Cuisle geal mo chroidhe,*" or "Bright Pulse of My Heart," contributed by Sergeant James O'Neill. This is a melody of singular beauty, which had never been printed before its appearance in our collection.

"The Dandy O," so frequently mentioned in printed collections of Irish music and Irish minstrelsy as the air to which certain songs were sung, invited no special attention until a spirited marching tune, in common time, under that name was encountered in the second volume of O'Farrell's *Pocket Companion for the Irish or Union Pipes,* volume 4, published in 1810. This tune differed from all other versions of the air of that name so far encountered.

Investigation disclosed a surprising amount of inaccuracy and confusion in connection with this air. It developed that there were two melodies called "The Dandy O," one of which Tom Moore utilized as the air for his song, "The Young May Moon," in six-eight time, and the other, much varied, for "O! Weep for the Hour," or "Eveleen's Bower," in common time, noting the latter "air unknown."

In Surenne's *Songs of Ireland*, "The Pretty Girl of Derby O" is given as the air for "Eveleen's Bower." Lynch in his *Melodies of Ireland* varies the name as "The Maid of Derby"; while in Smith's *Irish Minstrel*, published in Edinburgh in 1825, "The Dandy O," to which the Scotch poet, James Hogg, wrote "Go Home to Your Rest," and "The Maid of Derby," are separately printed and in different arrangement. "This Is the Ranting Season O" and "I'll Follow My Own Figary O" are modern names for this air.

That reliable authority, Alfred Moffat, in his *Minstrelsy of Ireland*, tells us that the air designated "The Dandy O" was introduced by Shield as an "Irish tune" in his comic opera, *Robin Hood*, in 1784, and it was printed as "Pat and Kate" by George Thomson in 1805. In Pringles *Reels and Jigs*, Edinburgh, 1801, it is called "The Irish Wedding."

"The Dandy O," as a title, is an abbreviation of one of the lines in the second verse of *Robin Hood*, which reads, "And I'm her a-dandy O." This air is entirely different from "The Dandy O" in Brysson's *Curious Selection of Fifty Irish Airs*, 1791, and in O'Farrell's *Pocket Companion, etc.*, before alluded to.

A very early setting of "The Dandy O" to which Moore set "Eveleen's Bower" escaped the attention of the vigilant Alfred Moffat. It is printed in Aird's *Selection of Scotch, English, Irish and Foreign Airs*, volume 3, *circa* 1786, and is entitled "Peggy of Darby; or, The Dandy's Irish." This title combines the suggestion of both names above quoted from Smith's *Irish Minstrel.*

No less than three airs are in print under the appellation *"An Cnoicin Fraoich,"* or "The Little Heathy Hill." There are some traces of resemblance, but practically they are different tunes. The earliest printed is the air in O'Daly's *Poets and Poetry of Munster,* published in 1851. The next and best is the melody obtained from piper James Buckley and printed by Dr. Joyce in his *Ancient Irish Music,* brought out in 1873. This is the version sung by the peasantry in my native barony in West Cork. The third air is to be found in Petrie's *Complete Collection of Irish Music,* 1902-5.

An unusual departure was made in directing "The Rough Little Heathy Hill," an entirely distinct air, to be played "lively," a tempo which is manifestly unsuited to this plaintive strain. The writer when a schoolboy remembers hearing this air sung daily for a week to a direful ballad picturing the eternal woes of the unrepenant at a church mission which was drawing to a close.

The version of "The Foggy Dew" in Bunting's third collection, *The Ancient Music of Ireland,* published in 1840, scarcely bears any trace of resemblance to the folk song of that name as sung in South Munster. Dr. Joyce states, without any qualification, that the airs are entirely different. The version which I learned in my native place and another closely resembling that published by Bunting, are printed in O'Neill's *Music of Ireland.* Bunting notes that "The Foggy Dew" was procured from J. M. Kneight, Belfast, in 1839, and that it was "very ancient; author and date unknown."

If those settings or versions have been derived from a common source, they furnish striking evidence conflicting with Bunting theory that a strain of music never changes.

In Moore's *Melodies* and other works copied from that volume without discrimination or question, "Love's Young Dream" is set to the traditional air called in English "The Poor Old Woman," but better known by its Irish name, *"An Sean Bhean Bhocht"* (shan van vocht). The writer was accustomed to hear a distinctly different air of that name in common circulation in his boyhood days in West Cork. To find such a distinguished authority as Dr. Joyce on our side of the question is reassuring, for he includes a version of "The Shan Van Vocht" in his late work, *Old Irish Folk Music and Songs*, which varies but little from our setting in O'Neill's *Music of Ireland*.

Moore undoubtedly obtained the melody from Bunting, for a setting of it in B flat is to be found in his second volume, published in 1809, with the correct title in Irish, but an abbreviated one, "The Old Woman," in English.

An air called *"An Bhean Bhoct;* or, The Poor Woman," in Dr. Joyce's book, is easily identified as "Jerry Daly's Hornpipe," but neither of them betrays any traces of the traditional air above mentioned.

A favorite term of endearment in Ireland was *"Gradh Geal Mo Chroidhe"* (Gra gal machree), or "Bright Love of My Heart," for there are no less than six airs published under that name. Three of them are to be found in the Petrie collection, but they are variants of an original air. The two airs so named in O'Neill's *Music of Ireland* differ from them and from one another and from the sixth and latest air among the Forde manuscripts included in Dr. Joyce's recent work, previously mentioned.

Still more intensely expressive of acute affection is the phrase or title *"A Cuisle Geal Mo Chroidhe,"* or "Bright Pulse of My Heart." Two airs, one in the Petrie collections and the other in Dr. Joyce's recent volume, *Old Irish*

Folk Music and Songs, are published under the Irish title. It appears that Dr. Petrie originally obtained this setting from Dr. Joyce, so that the latter is really responsible for both versions.

"The Pearl of the White Breast," or "The Snowy-breasted Pearl," translated from the same original Irish name, is a title by which more than one melody is known. The air of the latter name printed in Bunting's first volume, published in 1796, bears no resemblance to the air of the same name in Moffat's *Minstrelsy of Ireland.* Moffat obtained the melody from Prof. Eugene O'Curry, a native of West Clare, who learned it from his father.

It was the O'Curry melody which Dr. Petrie printed in *The Petrie Collection of the Ancient Music of Ireland,* published in 1855, when he was president of the *Society for the Preservation and Publication of the Melodies of Ireland.*

"The Pearl of the White Breast" is a melody strongly marked as belonging to the class of airs known among the Irish as sentimental or love tunes. Its cadences are all expressive of an imploring and impassioned tenderness, according to Dr. Petrie, but wanting in those expressions of hopeless sadness or wailing sorrow with which the *Caoines* or elegaic airs are so deeply stamped.

In his latest work Dr. Joyce introduces an air, being the third with the above title, but it is entirely distinct from the Bunting and O'Curry melodies.

Two settings of the air—in common and three-four time —resembling, but not identical with Bunting's,—are to be found in O'Neill's *Music of Ireland.*

Whatever may have been its origin, the name, "*An Gearran Buidhe,*" or "The Yellow Garron," is traditionally well commemorated in at least five different melodies printed under that title. One appears in Bunting's

General Collection of the Acient Music of Ireland, published in 1809. There are four airs of the name in Petrie's *Complete Collection of Irish Music,* and while traces of a remote relationship may be detected in certain phrases, they may be regarded as consisting of two distinct airs at least. A version in six-eight time was copied from a manuscript dated 1780.

In his latest volume, before alluded to, Dr. Joyce introduces three distinct tunes similarly named, and remarks that they do not resemble either the Bunting or Petrie melodies. The air entitled "The Young Garron," in O'Neill's *Music of Ireland,* contributed by Sergeant O'Neill, varies but slightly from Bunting's version, except in being in a different key.

Comparing the loveliness and charms of woman to the beauty of the rose has had great vogue at all times with bards and poets. In Bunting's third collection, produced in 1840, we find "The Black Rosebud" and "The Little Black Rosebud" in the index, although both melodies are named "The Black Rosebud" in the body of the work and noted as being "very ancient; author and date unknown." They are not distinct airs, however, but different versions of the same original air.

Dr. Petrie says that in the entire range of Irish melodies there is perhaps scarcely one of more widely spread popularity amongst the Irish peasantry than the air called *"Rois Geal Dubh,"* and sometimes *"Roisin Dubh"*—the first signifying "Fair or White-skinned, Black-haired Rose," and the second "Black-haired Little Rose."

Two settings of the air mentioned appear in O'Daly's *Poets and Poetry of Munster,* and under both titles also. Dr. Petrie, who criticises them as wanting in Irish vocal character, on account of having probably been obtained from some piper or fiddler, gives a version of his own in

The Ancient Music of Ireland, published by him in 1855. Songs without number have been sung to those airs.

The name *Rois Geal Dubh* (Rose gal dhuv) literally translated is "Bright Black Rose," and under that name it has been printed more than once.

There is still another melody in the rose family, entitled "The Blood-red Rose," contributed by Sergeant O'Neill and printed in O'Neill's *Music of Ireland.*

Among the nine versions of "Rose" airs we find published by Bunting, O'Daly, Petrie and O'Neill, there appear to be but three distinct melodies, all others being but variants.

"The Dawning of the Day" was also a favorite name for several Irish airs. One of them, obtained from Patrolman William Walsh, a versatile musician and a native of Galway, proved to be a Welsh air of that name. Having read somewhere that O'Carolan was the composer of "The Dawning of the Day," the fine setting which we printed was classed with his compositions in O'Neill's *Music of Ireland,* but we have since learned that it is one of O'Connallon's productions. A third air under that title in Dr. Joyce's *Old Irish Folk Music and Songs* is distinct from those just mentioned and from "The Dawning of the Day" printed in his *Ancient Irish Music,* which was published in 1873. That setting differs in the key only from the version obtained by Dr. Petrie in 1854 from Kate Keane and printed in his so-called *Complete Collection of Irish Music.*

An old version of O'Connallon's composition, entitled "The Dawning of the Day. Irish," is to be found in Aird's *Selection of Scotch, English, Irish and Foreign Airs,* volume 3, *circa* 1788. It varies considerably from the modern setting.

"*Mairin ni Chuillionain,*" or "Little Mary Cullinan," is

one of those allegorical names by which Ireland was known in Irish Song. It is the same air as "The Rosetree," to which Tom Moore adapted his verses commencing "I'd mourn the hopes that leave me." In another article, the many and various names by which that melody has been known are dealt with; but what concerns us in this connection is that Dr. Joyce in his new work prints another and distinctly different air under practically the same title, viz., "*A Mhaire ni Chuillionain.*" He gives no account of its origin or the source from which it was obtained, but refers to the melody, in O'Daly's *Poets and Poetry of Munster,* as a different air.

Up to a century ago the term "jigg" was not infrequently applied to any lively music; but one would hardly expect to find obsolete classifications persist so late as the year 1840, when Bunting published his third and last collection, *The Ancient Music of Ireland.* "A Highland Reel" in the *Caledonian Muse,* published about 1785, is in six-eight time.

One of Bunting's numbers is "The Chorus Jig," in two-four time, which he notes he obtained from McDonnell, the piper, in 1797. This tune is identical with "The Rocks of Cashel," printed as early as 1782, previously mentioned. An entirely different composition, in six-eight time, called also "The Chorus Jig," we obtained from Timothy Dillon, a native of County Kerry, and included in *The Dance Music of Ireland.* A variant of Dillon's tune, under the same name, I find is printed in Dr. Joyce's late work, *Old Irish Folk Music and Songs.* Mr. Dillon was a fine violinist of the old traditional school, whose memory was stored with many rare strains.

There was still another "Chorus Jig," in two-four time, found in an American piano publication; but a much better version of that tune in four strains was contributed by James Kennedy, of County Leitrim, and printed as "The Chorus Reel" (which it was, in reality) in O'Neill's *Music of Ireland*.

Few jigs are more widely known than "The Frost Is All Over." Dr. Petrie noted down a setting of it under that name from County Antrim, in the far north. In South Munster it was commonly called "The 'Praties' Are Dug and the Frost Is All Over." Yet our friend Dr. Joyce in his latest work prints a hornpipe entitled "The Frost Is All Over," without comment or explanation.

In our collections, a reel called "The Scolding Wife" varies but little from the tune of that name in the Petrie collections. I find, however, a reel similarly named in Dr. Joyce's *Old Irish Folk Music and Songs*, which bears not the slightest resemblance to the other alluded to.

A traditional Irish jig of marked individuality, entitled "The Lark in the Morning," was first printed in O'Neill's *Music of Ireland*.

It was contributed by James Carbray, of Quebec, who learned it from a Kerry fiddler named Courtney. It was a special dance in olden times; but how a tune of such beauty and character could have been lost or forgotten, passes comprehension. In his latest volume Dr. Joyce also prints "The Lark in the Morning" from the Forde manuscripts, which is an entirely different and much inferior tune. "The Lark in the Blue Summer Sky," in the same work, is also a distinct air.

The melody called "Carolan's Cap," in Bunting's Second *Collection of The Ancient Music of Ireland*, published in 1809, is entirely distinct from the air of that name which appears in the Joyce collection found among the Pigot manuscripts.

"The Shanavest and Caravath," a simple tune which appears in Dr. Joyce's *Old Irish Folk Music and Songs*, claims no relationship to the much superior tune of that name printed in his *Ancient Irish Music,* published in 1873. Dr. Petrie includes the latter setting in his collections and two other versions of this spirited march or hornpipe, one being named "John Doe," while the third is printed anonymously.

A rather smooth-flowing jig named "Green Sleeves" was discovered in our researches, and being apparently evolved from a Clan march, was printed in O'Neill's *Music of Ireland.* The "swing" of it as well as the name pointed strongly to an Irish origin. It appears that we were in error, however, for the air is as old in England as the time of Queen Elizabeth. It was printed in *Playford's Dancing Master,* published in 1686. Even Shakspeare mentions it twice in the *Merry Wives of Windsor.*

Another jig with that identical title was in circulation in County Limerick over half a century ago, for Dr. Joyce includes it in his *Old Irish Folk Music and Songs.* He says that the tune was noted down by him from the playing of James Buckley, a celebrated Irish piper. Dr. Joyce's "Green Sleeves" was printed in O'Neill's *Music of Ireland* in 1903 under the name "Hartigan's Fancy," as played by John Carey, a Limerick fiddler long a resident of Chicago.

One of the numbers in Bunting's *Ancient Music of Ireland* is named "The Hare in the Corn," which he obtained from a piper in 1800, the author and date being unknown.

All of Bunting's airs are supposed to have been previously unpublished, but in looking over Aird's *Selection of Scotch, English, Irish and Foreign Airs,* volume 5, published about 1795, we find the identical tune, classed properly as a jig, and under the same name. It seems to have been quite a favorite, for it appears in Clinton's *Gems of Ireland* as "The Hare in the Corner," and in various publications in later years as "The Absent-minded Man," "The Royal Irish Jig," and "The House on the Corner."

The lilting lines sent me by Ernest McGaffey, our genial Poet of Nature, will doubtless reawaken tender memories in the minds of many readers.

THE HARE IN THE CORN.

Beyond, in the distance,
  Goes by the gray moon,
And from the far sea-wall
  Comes up a gay tune.
The music drifts nigh me,
  And, sure as you're born,
'Tis a piper lad playing
  "The Hare in the Corn."

How it quickens my pulses,
  That lilting old tune,
And brings back the time
  When, a merry "gossoon,"
I tripped it with Peggy
  From night until morn,
And the piper's best tune was
  "The Hare in the Corn."

Ah, Peggy, sweet Peggy,
  The stars on the sea
Shone never so bright
  As your blue eyes on me.
Small need of a ribbon
  Your locks to adorn,
As we jigged it so lightly—
  "The Hare in the Corn."

'Twas backward and sideways,
  And then an advance
Like a feather you floated
  Along in the dance.

> We'd never a fiddle,
>   No flute, nor a horn,
> Just the piper lad playing
>   "The Hare in the Corn."
>
> Faith! then was the day
>   I'd walk many a mile
> For the touch of your hand
>   And the light of your smile.
> Sure a Queen or a Princess
>   You'd put them to scorn,
> As I faced you when dancing
>   "The Hare in the Corn."
>
> But alas for us both,
>   For you faded from sight,
> And the ghost of my youth
>   Walks beside me tonight;
> And the faint echoes o'er me
>   Sound sad and forlorn,
> 'Tis a piper lad playing
>   "The Hare in the Corn."
>
> ERNEST McGAFFEY.

In his descriptive text Bunting tells us that "The Hare in the Corn" was an ancient tune for the pipes, in which there is an imitation of a hunt, including the sound of the huntsmen's horns, the crying of the dogs, and finally the distress and death of the hare. This performance can only be given on the Irish pipes, the chanter of which, when pressed with its lower end against the performer's knee, can be made to produce a smothered sobbing tone, very closely resembling the dying cry of the hare, but difficult to imitate or describe in musical notation.

Another jig, also called "The Hare in the Corn," with three strains, possessing more evidence of ancient Irish character than the first mentioned, was found in an American compilation of Dance Music. It is decidedly more favored by our present-day pipers than Bunting's tune, and has been incorporated in our collections for that reason.

We have also two distinct reels entitled "The Four Courts," one being obtained from John Ennis, of Kildare, and the other from Edward Cronin, of Tipperary.

"The Mountain Lark" had been given to us as the name of two reels which have nothing in common but the time. One was contributed by James Kennedy, a native of Leitrim, and the other printed under that name in a modern compilation. The latter tune was in general circulation among our Chicago musicians and known as "The Steam Packet." This title seems to be chronologically improbable, as the composition bears internal evidence of a far greater antiquity than the invention of steam navigation.

An unpublished reel of uncommon excellence, called "Touch Me if You Dare," was obtained from Miss Ellen Kennedy, a native of Ballinamore, County Leitrim. It had almost escaped her memory since she had heard her father play it, and we counted ourselves fortunate in securing such a fine tune, especially as it was unknown to all our musicians.

Sergeant O'Neill also remembered he had a reel of that name, from the County Down, but it turned out that it bore no resemblance to Miss Kennedy's tune. In the Ulster idiom it was sometimes called "You Rogue, You Dar'n't Meddle Me!" and under that name it was printed in our first work, *The Music of Ireland,* so as to preserve the quaint title also.

Few names are better known than "The Sailor's Hornpipe," yet when called for by dancers, "Rickett's Hornpipe" and "The College Hornpipe" or "Jack's the Lad" are the tunes almost invariably played.

The only tune printed under the title "Sailor's Hornpipe" which we have been able to discover was in Forde's *Encyclopedia of Melody,* published by Cocks & Co., of London, *circa* 1845. It had never been heard by our Chicago musicians before its discovery in that work. Still they are dancing Sailors' Hornpipes on the stage, at picnics and other entertainments, with unabated fervor—not to the real "Sailor's Hornpipe," but mainly to the tunes above mentioned.

That well-known Long Dance, "The Job of Journey-Work," is to be found in the Petrie collections and in Dr. Joyce's *Ancient Irish Music,* as well as in O'Neill's *Music of Ireland.* The tune of that name in Aird's *Selection of Scotch, English, Irish and Foreign Airs,* volume 3, published in 1788, is a different tune. It is a Long Dance also, varying from ours in another respect, that is, in having but twelve bars in the second strain, instead of fourteen.

The category of duplications of titles is not by any means exhausted, but as the instances given are no doubt sufficient to illustrate a neglected subject, we will conclude with one of uncommon interest.

"The Twisting of the Rope" printed in Bunting's first collection of *Ancient Irish Music,* published in 1796, was chosen by Moore as the air to which he wrote "How Dear to Me the Hour!" for the second number of the *Melodies,* in 1807. The original Irish song was printed in Hardiman's *Irish Minstrelsy* in 1831, but the English translation is not given.

An entirely different air of this name, copied from the Pigot manuscripts, has been lately published by Dr. Joyce in his *Old Irish Folk Music and Songs.* Pigot notes that he obtained this unpublished melody from Paddy Walsh, a Mayo piper, in 1850.

True love never did run smoothly, and a good instance

in illustration of this proverbial saying is furnished by the incident which is said to have been the theme of the song called "The Twisting of the Rope."

A Connacht harper, having quartered himself, according to tradition, in the home of a wealthy farmer, ingratiated himself with one of the young women of the family. This did not escape the notice of the mother, who promptly conceived a scheme for getting rid of the presumptuous bard. She procured some hay and playfully requested him to twist the rope, or "sugaun," for her, and seated herself so that as the rope lengthened the harper would in backing away from her eventually pass through and beyond the outer doorway of the house.

At the opportune moment this crafty matron slammed the door in his face and then threw his harp out of the window after him.

Of course, a comedy of that nature was recorded in song, the name of which, suggested by the occurrence, is likely to outlive the best classics in the language.

> "The master hand upon the harp string laid,
> By way of prelude such a sweet tune played
> As made the heart with happy tears o'erflow,
> Then sad and wild did that strange music grow."

CHAPTER IX

TUNES OF DISPUTED ORIGIN CLAIMED AS SCOTCH OR ENGLISH

"Songs of our land—to the land of the stranger
   Ye followed the heartbroken exile afar;
Ye went with the wand'rer through distance and danger,
   And gladdened his desolate path, like a star;
The breath of his mountains, in summer long vanished,
   And visions that passed like a wave from the strand,
And hope for his country—the joy of the banished
   Were borne to him oft in the songs of our land."

THE author of *Stories of Famous Songs* justly reproaches the Irish for their neglect to preserve their heritage, in his chapter on "Irish Songs Ancient and Modern." "Had Irish chroniclers been as industrious as have been the Scottish," he says, "English people would not have remained so long in ignorance of the magnificent store of legendry, political, pathetic, and humorous, ballads and lyrics, which is so near at hand, but which has never been properly investigated and explored." Those remarks are equally pertinent as regards Ireland's musical remains, much of which have been forgotten or purloined during the seventeenth and eighteenth centuries.

"It is but to repeat an accepted fact that Ireland in her earliest ages, when the inhabitants of Britain were semi-savage, was the centre of a cultivation of surprising extent and refined quality," continues the same author. "Her harpers and bards who in later years developed into wandering minstrels and itinerant musicians, were honored for their art, for their precepts, and their practice."

As early as 1807 Thomas Moore in his correspondence with Sir John Stevenson deplores the result of this indifference as far as it relates to Folk Music. "We have too long neglected the only talent for which our English neighbors ever deigned to allow us any credit. Our national music has never been properly collected, and while the composers of the continent have enriched their operas and sonatas with melodies borrowed from Ireland, very often without even the honesty of acknowledgment, we have left these treasures in a great degree unclaimed and fugitive. Thus our airs, like too many of our countrymen, for want of protection at home, have passed into the service of foreigners."

Eibhlin a Ruin, or EILEEN A ROON

Of all Irish airs which "have passed into the service of the foreigners," *"Eibhlin a Ruin,* or Eileen Aroon," claims first attention, as no air has been the subject of so much discussion in this respect.

The origin of this "Queen of folk airs," as Moffat calls it, has been the subject of controversy for generations. As "Robin Adair" it is well known in Scotland, but the Scotch claim to the air has been disproved, even by one of their own countrymen—the learned Alfred Moffat, author of *The Minstrelsy of Scotland,* and *The Minstrelsy of Ireland.*

In *Grove's Dictionary of Music and Musicians* we read that Gerald O'Daly, the harper, is reputed to have composed the music of "Aileen-a-Roon," but this opinion is not universally accepted. A sheet song was printed in London about 1740 by Walsh with the title, *Aileen aroon, an Irish ballad sung by Mrs. Clive at ye Theatre Royal.* What is more natural than that Kitty Clive, an Irish singer, should sing the songs of her native land? Moffat says that the earliest printed copy of "Aileen-a-Roon" which he has been able to find is in Coffee's *Beggar's Wedding,* 1729, first performed in Dublin, and later in London under the title *Phebe.* After this its popularity increased, so that it was incorporated in many Scotch collections, such as Oswald's *Caledonian Pocket Companion,* Bk. 5, c, 1750. M. Lean's *Collections,* 1772, *Edinburgh Musical Miscellany,* 1793, and half a dozen others. A song entitled "You're Welcome to Paxton, Robin Adair," was published in 1765 at Edinburgh in a song-book called *The Lark.*

Its being sung, printed, and designated "an Irish ballad" long before its appearance in a Scotch collection, refutes their claim to this air, although many Scotch songs were sung to it in the eighteenth century.

So important has the history of "Eileen" or "Aileen Aroon" been considered, that S. J. Adair Fitz Gerald devotes a whole chapter to its discussion in *Stories of Famous Songs.* According to several authorities "Eileen Aroon" dates back previous to the sixteenth century, when living money was still in use, for in the second stanza the hero says he would spend a *cow* to entertain his lady love. While endeavoring to verify this statement the writer, after some disappointment, discovered that there are two songs in Irish named "Eileen a Roon" to be found in Hardiman's *Irish Minstrelsy,* fifty-four pages apart, in Volume 1.

The author's notes, printed elsewhere, and even the text of Fitz Gerald's story, have reference only to the second song, which in the index is called "Old Eileen a Roon."

Bunting says there are as many different sets of words to this melody as there are counties in one of our provinces.

The air was a great favorite with the Irish harpers and wandering minstrels, and as was to be expected Bunting found no difficulty in noting it down in 1792 from the playing of the famous harper, Denis O'Hempsey or Hempson, then almost a centenarian. Born in 1695, Hempson died in 1807, at the extraordinary age of 112 years. When eighteen years of age he undertook a tour of Scotland, which lasted three years, and of course much of his music, including "Eileen Aroon," was picked up and circulated by the Highland minstrels. During Hempson's second visit to Scotland, in 1745, he was taken into the young Pretender's presence by Col. Kelly, of Roscommon, and Sir Thomas Sheridan, where he played a number of airs, among them "Eileen Aroon."

It turns out also that Robin Adair, whom the Scotch have honored with songs, was a real personage and an Irishman at that. There were two of the name, however, and the author of *Stories of Famous Songs* believes that the real romantic Robin was a grandson of Patrick Adair, Ballymena, County Antrim, and not the Robin Adair, ancestor of Viscount Molesworth, of Holly Park, County Wicklow.

The first Irish number in Burk Thumoth's *Twelve Scotch and Twelve Irish Airs*, printed in London about 1742, is "Ailen Aroon" with variations. The setting is quite elaborate, consisting of twelve staffs of eighty-four bars, and harmonized.

"Aileen Aroon," with variations in thirteen staffs, was printed in Paul Alday's *A Pocket Volume of Airs, Duets, Songs, Marches, etc.*, published in Dublin, *circa* 1800, and in simpler form in works too numerous to mention.

The romantic story of the incidents which gave rise to this composition is best told in the words of Hardiman, author of *Irish Minstrelsy*, published in 1831.

"Carol O'Daly, brother to Donough *Mor* O'Daly, a man of much consequence in Connacht, was one of the most accomplished gentlemen of his time, and particularly excelled in poetry and music. He paid his addresses to

DENIS O'HEMPSEY, or HEMPSON.
Born 1695, Died 1807.

Ellen, daughter of a chieftain named Kavanagh, a lovely and amiable young lady, who returned his affections, but her friends disapproved of the connection. O'Daly was obliged to leave the country for some time, and they availed themselves of the opportunity which his absence afforded of impressing on the mind of Ellen a belief of his falsehood and of his having gone to be married to another. After some time they prevailed on her to marry a rival of O'Daly. The day was fixed for the nuptials, but O'Daly returned the evening before. Under the first impression of his feelings he sought a wild and sequestered spot on the sea shore, and inspired by love composed the song of "Eileen a Roon," which remains to this time an exquisite memorial of his skill and sensibility. Disguised as a harper he gained access among the crowd that thronged to the wedding. It happened that he was called upon by Ellen herself to play. It was then, touching his harp with all the pathetic sensibility which the interesting occasion inspired, he infused his own feelings into the song he had composed, and breathed into his softened strain the very soul of pensive melody; appealing to her in Irish, "*A tiocfaidh tu no fanfaidh tu (will you come or will you stay) Eibhlin a Ruin*"?

It was from the last verse of this famous song that the characteristic motto of Irish hospitality, *Cead mile failte* (a hundred thousand welcomes), was derived. The ardent wooer thus gave expression to his rapturous feelings when the object of his passion yielding to his pleadings replied:

> Oh, yes! oh, yes! with thee
> I will wander far and free,
> And thy only love shall be
>   Eileen Aroon.
>
> A hundred thousand welcomes,
>   Eileen a Roon.

> A hundred thousand welcomes,
>   Eileen a Roon.
> Oh, welcome ever more
> With welcome yet in store
> Till love and life are o'er,
>   Eileen a Roon.

To reward his fidelity and affection, the fair one contrived to elope with him that very night, and in keeping with the true spirit of romance in all such cases, it is presumed they lived happily ever after.

A rivalry even more intense than the contentions concerning the claim to "Eileen Aroon," exists regarding the origin of

MAGGY LAIDIR OR MOGGY LAUDER.

While the Scotch in the face of indisputable evidence reluctantly conceded the Irish claim to the first named air, they treat with disdain all Irish pretentions to ownership of the latter, although evidence favorable to the Irish contention is strongly presented by Dr. Grattan Flood in *A History of Irish Music* and Adair Fitz Gerald in *Stories of Famous Songs.*

Hardiman, author of *Irish Minstrelsy,* in his notes to the song "Maggy Laidir," composed in Irish by John O'Neachtan in the seventeenth century, tells us that "the air as well as the words of the song, though long naturalized in North Britain, is Irish. When our Scotch kinsmen were detected appropriating the ancient saints of Ireland (would that they rid us of some modern ones) they took a fancy to its music. Not satisfied with borrowing the art, they despoiled us of some of our sweetest airs, and amongst others that of Maggy Laidir. This name signifies in the original Strong or Powerful Maggy and by it was meant Ireland, also designated by our bards under the names

Sheela ni Guira, Graine Uaile, Roisin Dubh, Caitilin ni Uallachain, Moirin ni Chuillionain and *An Londubh* or The Blackbird. By an easy change the adjective *laidir* was converted into Lauder, the patronymic of the Scotch family, and the air was employed to celebrate a famous woman of questionable reputation."

In the preface to his *Select Melodies of Scotland*, Thomson, the friend of Robert Burns, says: "Some airs are claimed by both countries (Scotland and Ireland), but by means of the harpers or pipers who used to wander through the two, particular airs might become so common to both as to make it questionable which of the countries gave them birth." After quoting the writer's extract and much more from Hardiman, Farquhar Graham, editor of Wood's *Songs of Scotland*, vigorously defends the Scotch claim. "We are quite at a loss," he says, "to understand Mr. Hardiman's assertion that the air as well as the words of 'Maggy Laidir,' though long naturalized in North Britain, is Irish. He offers no proof of the Irish origin of the air, which, known in Scotland as 'Maggie Lauder,' bears no resemblance in style or construction to the airs of Ireland in the seventeenth century. Bunting does not give the air in any of his collections, but alludes to it as an Irish air in his third collection, and gives Hardiman as his authority."

David Laing, an eminent antiquary editor of Johnson's *Scots Musical Museum*, is of the opinion that the old Scottish song of "Maggie Lauder" was written by Francis Semple about the year 1642.

On this point Alfred Moffat, author of *The Minstrelsy of Scotland*, is not convinced, because the statement was made on the not very reliable authority of Semple's grandchildren. "Although probably belonging to a much older date," he remarks, "this fine song first appears in *Herd's Collection of Scottish Songs*, Volume 2, 1776. We have not been able to find the air in any collection of Scottish music prior to Adam Craig's *A Collection of the Choicest Scots Tunes*, issued in 1730."

Stenhouse, another Scotch writer, informs us that Gay introduced the air of "Maggie Lauder" in his musical opera of *Achilles*, printed in 1733. The same air had previously been used for a song called *Sally's New Answer—set to the tune of Mogey Lauther*—as well as for a song in the *Quaker's Opera*, written by Thos. Walker and acted in 1728. The air was sung in the *Beggar's Wedding* in the following year as "Moggy Lauther."

While admitting that John O'Neachtan wrote the original Irish song "Maggie Laidir" about the year 1676, Grattan Flood contends that Hardiman could furnish no proof of the Irish origin of the air, merely relying on tradition for his authority. "Fortunately I have succeeded in tracing the tune as far back as the year 1696, when it was sung by the Anglo-Irish actor, Thomas Doggett, in his comedy of *A Country Wake*," says Grattan Flood, "and again by him in the variant of the same play under the title of *Hob, or the Country Wake*, at Drury Lane, in 1711."

Adair Fitz Gerald in his *Stories of Famous Songs* states that though claimed by the Scotch, "Maggy Laidir" is of pure Irish creation and dates from the seventeenth century. Aside from quoting Hardiman and Moffat in support of his opinion, he throws scarcely any additional light on the subject. In the chapter on Scottish music "Maggie Lauder" is disposed of with the remark "only a certain not very edifying version is Scottish—the original is Irish."

Grattan Flood's success in tracing the air back to the year 1696 gives the Irish claim an advantage of thirty-four years, the earliest Scottish publication of the tune being in 1730, as already stated.

A fine setting of "Maggie Lauder," with four variations,

is printed in McGoun's *Repository of Scots and Irish Airs*, published in or about the year 1800—an interesting but rare work.

An Seanduine—THE CAMPBELLS ARE COMING

Anyone hearing the two settings of *An Seanduine* in O'Daly's *Poets and Poetry of Munster* can readily recognize their resemblance to "The Campbells are Coming," the Scotch version of that fine old melody. In O'Neill's *Music of Ireland* another and a simpler setting learned from my mother is printed. It is less involved than O'Daly's, but bears a closer relationship to the Scotch version than the others. The memory of the old Irish verses sung to this popular air in the glens of West Cork has not yet been entirely obliterated.

But let us get down to the evidence of its Irish origin. O'Daly, more concerned with Gaelic poetry than airs, merely mentions that the air is a great favorite in Scotland, where it is known under the name "The Campbells Are Coming."

In *A History of Irish Music*, Grattan Flood informs us that *An Seanduine*, or "The Old Man," was published in 1745. It was promptly annexed by the Scotch and set to the song of "The Campbells Are Coming," first printed in Oswald's *Caledonian Pocket Companion* in 1750. Moffat places the date of its publication by Oswald two or three years earlier. It was also printed in Bremner's *Scots Reels or Country Dances*, Bk. XI, 1761.

In Rutherford's *Two Hundred Country Dances*, c. 1748-56, its title is "Hob or Nob," and by that name the tune was known in England.

"The Campbells Are Coming" is to be found also in Aird's *Selection of Scotch, English, Irish and Foreign Airs*, volume 1, published in 1782.

In *Stories of Famous Songs* the author classes "The Campbells Are Coming" among the Irish Airs and mentions the incident as told by O'Daly, which originated the Irish song called *An Seanduine,* or "The Old Man."

Andrew McGrath, an intellectual but erratic Munster bard, in the course of his wanderings chanced to meet with a disconsolate young married woman on the roadside, weeping bitterly. A short interview disclosed the cause of her grief. She told of having been influenced by her parish priest to marry an old man on account of his wealth and possessions. Whether it was on account of his age or natural coldness, their married life was anything but harmonious or satisfactory. MacGrath, whose heart was sensitive and sympathetic, was moved by this narrative of unrequited love to compose a song, which resulted in his undoing, although it brought his name undying fame. The popularity of the song was instantaneous, but the sentiment was such, that the bard incurred the implacable enmity of all old men between whom and their wives there was much disparity in years.

The poet McGrath found it advisable to make himself scarce in that part of the country thereafter. The song and the music, like some of our modern "hits," circulated far and wide and traveled via the minstrels into Scotland, caught the popular fancy at once and still retains it undiminished to this day. Following are two of MacGrath's verses translated into English:

"Out on the highway I met with a bold man,
 A rogue of a priest, who wed me to an old man;
 It's little he cared, so he fingered the gold man,
 If I found the old vagabond's comfort but cold man."

"O, you old dotard, with you I won't tarry,
 Bad luck to the schemer that forced me to marry;

May I soon see the day when your master, Old Harry,
To his mansion below will the pair of you carry.''

Following is the first stanza of another version:

''A priest made me marry, for better or worse,
An old wretch who had naught but his money and years.
Ah! 'twas little he cared, but to fill his own purse,
And I now look for help to the neighbors with tears.''

THE WHITE COCKADE

The Scottish claim to this tune has been so insistent that we naturally look for it in the *Minstrelsy of Scotland,* by Alfred Moffat. Contrary to our expectations, however, that excellent authority has seen fit to include it in the *Minstrelsy of Ireland* instead. He tells us that "The White Cockade," a Scotch tune, or "O an ye were died guidman," probably crept into Ireland about the year 1745, and criticises what he terms "the barbarized piper's version of it" in John O'Daly's *Poets and Poetry of Munster.*

"As far back as 1687," he says, "we find Playford printing an early version of "The White Cockade" as a Scots tune in *Apollo's Banquet.* He calls it "The Duke of Buccleugh's Tune." In Walsh's *Compleat Country Dancing Master,* 1718, the air is printed as "Fidler's Morris." Oswald introduces the air as "1 wish you were dead, good man," in his *Caledonian Pocket Companion,* about the year 1748.

"The White Cockade," commonly believed to mean a military ornament, literally signifies a bouquet or plume of white ribbons, with which the young women of Munster adorned their hair and headdress on wedding and other festive occasions. O'Daly says the custom prevailed early in the seventeenth century, as a verse will show, translated from an Irish poet of that period named *Muiris Mac Daibhi*

Duibh Mac Gearailt (Maurice, son of black David Fitz Gerald:

> "O, brown-haired maiden of the plume so white,
> I am sick and dying for thy love's sweet aid;
> Come, then, with me and be my delight,
> For I dearly love you and your White Cockade."

This direct reference to the White Cockade, or, in Irish, *Chnotadh Ban,* in literature of the early seventeenth century, is a strong link in the chain of evidence favorable to the Irish claim.

In his short sketch of "The White Cockade" Grattan Flood tells us it was "a popular air of the period 1615-30, and was one of the two airs played by the war pipers of the Irish Brigade at Fontenoy on May 11, 1745. The Scotch subsequently appropriated it, but it was not printed as a Scotch tune until 1778."

The year in which the Irish Brigade distinguished themselves at Fontenoy happens to be the year in which Moffat tells us "The White Cockade" probably crept into Ireland. As the other march played by the war pipers at that battle was "St. Patrick's Day in the Morning," it is too much of a strain on our credulity to believe that a tune coming into Ireland so recently from Scotland would be familiarized and played by the pipers on such a sanguinary occasion.

The author of *Stories of Famous Songs* quotes O'Daly in regard to the origin of the name of this noted tune, but mentions a song beginning, "King Charles, he is King James' Son," which was sung to the air in 1745, and therein the "White Cockade" is turned to military account.

"The Ranting Highlandman," a Scotch version of "The White Cockade," is the first number in volume 1 of Aird's *Selection of Scotch, English, Irish and Foreign Airs,* brought out in 1782.

WILLIAM WALSH.

Many Scotch and Irish songs have been set to this popular strain. The chorus to one which the writer remembers commenced, "Will you list, will you list, will you list, young man?"

O'Farrell gives an excellent setting of "The White Cockade," with variations, in the *Pocket Companion for the Irish or Union Pipers,* volume III, printed in 1804-10. The author was reputed to be a fine performer on the Irish instrument and from the style of his settings in his published works in comparison with others of that period we are convinced he was a musician of taste and talent.

THE HIGH CAULED CAP

Although familiar with this tune from childhood, when a song commencing "What shall I do for starch and blue for my high cauled cap?" was in general circulation, the first printed setting of it found under that title was in O'Daly's *Poets and Poetry of Munster,* published in 1849.

About the middle of the eighteenth century a singularly unsightly and unbecoming article of female headdress called the "High Cauled Cap," came into fashion. It became a subject of unsparing satire from the Munster poets, but, notwithstanding their bitterest shafts, the offensive headgear maintained its defiant elevation for forty years. Its decline began in the early years of the nineteenth century, but it was not abandoned by certain conservative old dames for many years after. As O'Daly remarks, "Even poetry and satire it will thus be seen are not omnipotent."

Many songs of which only fragments are now remembered were composed to this air. William Walsh, an Irishman and a member of the Chicago Police Force, played this tune in fine style on the Highland pipes at the Caledonian

Society's picnic in this city in 1908. His execution was warmly applauded, but the patriotic Highland women would not for a moment entertain the idea of its being an Irish air because a version of it was known to them and their parents as "The Highland Laddie."

Moffat in his *Minstrelsy of Scotland* disposes of it with few words. The Ettrick Shepherd in his *Jacobite Relics* includes the air to verses first published in *Remains of Nithsdale and Galloway Song*, 1870. The air for the song "Where ha'e you been a' the day?" in Moffat's work is said to be the oldest of six different airs designated "The Highland Laddie." A tune of that name in Aird's *Selection of Scotch, English, Irish and Foreign Airs*, late in the eighteenth century, bears no resemblance to the air in question, and still another of that name but distinct from all is to be found in *Wilson's Companion to the Ball Room*, published in 1816.

The Calliope, or The Musical Miscellany, 1788; *The Caledonian Muse,* 1785; *The Edinburgh Musical Miscellany,* 1793; and *The Miniature Museum,* parts 1, 2, 3, 1815, make no reference to the airs or songs alluded to, but Farquhar Graham, editor of Wood's *Songs of Scotland,* traces the Scotch air back to an English origin in the time of Cromwell, when it was known as "Cockle Shells" and printed under that name in Playford's *Dancing Master,* first edition, 1657. Thus too much research disposes of our vain conceits.

Strangely enough, neither the "High Cauled Cap" nor "The Highland Laddie" is mentioned by Grattan Flood in *A History of Irish Music,* 1905, nor by Adair Fitz Gerald in *Stories of Famous Songs,* 1906.

What seems so difficult to understand is how a so-called Scottish air ignored by so many Scotch collectors could be so well known all over Ireland, even among the glens, far from the ordinary routes of travel in the extreme southwest, where so much native music existed unknown beyond a limited district until recently.

"The High Cauled Cap" is one of the special tunes mentioned by O'Keefe and O'Brien in their timely and much needed work, *A Handbook of Irish Dance*. Its existence in Munster early in the eighteenth century, before the introduction of the whimsical fashion from which it took its name, denotes an antiquity that entitles it to a secure place in the list of Old Irish Airs.

THE GIRL I LEFT BEHIND ME

Who would ever imagine that the iconoclasts were questioning the Irish origin of "The Girl I Left Behind Me"—our old friend of bygone days, the *"Spailpin Fanach?"* Such is the case, however, for it is included as an English air in Chappell's *Old English Popular Music*, published in 1893.

This air the author tells us is contained in a manuscript of date about 1770, and several manuscript collections of military music of the latter half of the eighteenth century. As a march it is entitled "The Girl I Left Behind Me, or Brighton Camp."

Mr. Chappell then goes on to tell of encampments along the south coast of England in the years 1691-93, but admits he finds no trace of the words or music in the many publications of the first half of the eighteenth century. There were later encampments, he says, when British admirals were watching the French fleet, 1758-59, and with the complacent confidence of a man who had made a great discovery he adds, "the song of 'The Girl I Left Behind Me' may be dated with great probability in 1758." (*Quod erat demonstrandum.*)

In discussing Chappell's reasons for claiming the melody as English, Alfred Moffat in his *Minstrelsy of Ireland* says: "All this may be true enough, but it by no means proves that the air was not originally imported from Ireland. It has a decidedly Irish flavor about it."

The author of *Stories of Famous Songs* effectually disposes of the English claim, founded on flimsy evidence as the following quotation will show: " 'The Girl I Left Behind Me' is of indisputable Hibernian origin, though the exact date of its composition is not known, but Arthur O'Neill, the celebrated harper, informed Bunting that it had been taught him while he was little more than a child (he was born in 1730) by Owen Keenan, his first master, who had it from a previous harper. Chappell gives the date of the music 'eighteenth century words about 1759,' but the air was certainly known to the harpers a century earlier than that. It is very easy to prove that the words of the song as given by Chappell could not possibly have been written in 1759, for the simple reason that in the second verse the fifth line runs, 'But now I'm bound to Brighton Camp.' Now, Brighton was always called by its original name, Brightelmstone, until quite 1787, and was not generally known as Brighton until twenty years later.

In one of the regiments then quartered in the south of England there was an Irish bandmaster who had the not uncommon peculiarity of being able to fall in love in ten minutes with any attractive girl he should chance to meet. It never hurt him much, however, for he fell out again as readily as he fell in, and so acquired a new sweetheart in every town the regiment passed through. Whenever the troops were leaving the place where he had a sweetheart he ordered the band to play 'The Girl I Left Behind Me,' which even then was an old melody.

Other bandmasters, at the request of the officers and soldiers, began to use the melody as a parting tune, and by the end of the century it was accounted disrespectful to the ladies for a regiment to march away without playing 'The Girl I Left Behind Me.'

This air was well known to the Irish minstrels long before the date assigned to it by Chappell and it was popular even as a street song in Dublin early in the eighteenth century."

ALLY CROKER, OR THE SHAMROCK

This air, as well as "Believe Me, If All Those Endearing Young Charms," has been omitted from Sir Charles Villiers Stanford's edition of Moore's *Melodies* because, on the authority of Chappell, he does not believe it is an Irish air. That Chappell is not an infallible authority has been proven more than once, and his judgment that "The Shamrock" is an English air because it first appeared in *Love in a Riddle* in the year 1729, cannot be accepted as final.

The original air to which Moore composed "The Shamrock" was called "Ally Croker." We are informed by Crofton Croker, a very reliable authority, that the song and music of "Ally Croker" were composed about the year 1725 by Lawrence Grogan, of Johnstown castle, County Wexford, a gentleman piper whose name has been immortalized in the opening lines of "The County Limerick Buckhunt," written in the year 1730 by Pierce Creagh, a County Clare poet:

> "By your leave, Larry Grogan,
> Enough has been spoken;
> 'Tis time to give over your sonnet—your sonnet."

There is nothing improbable in the Irish origin of an air printed in *Love in a Riddle,* in 1729, in view of the statement of Crofton Croker that the music was the composition of an Irish musician of prominence five years earlier. English operas of that period abound in Irish airs, not infrequently picked up from itinerant ballad singers, and thus recorded and preserved.

EVELEEN'S BOWER

This fine strain, probably one of the many unidentified compositions of the renowned bard O'Carolan is another of the airs expelled from *Moore's Irish Melodies Restored,* by Sir Villiers Stanford on the authority of Mr. Chappell, who claims it as English.

To enumerate the many collections of music published within a century in which it is specifically designated as Irish, may not be considered as convincing evidence, yet this fact must not be lightly disregarded.

In Moore's *Melodies* and in many other works "The Dandy O" is given as the original air, but Alfred Moffat in his *Minstrelsy of Ireland* leaves nothing to conjecture. Few are aware that there are two distinct airs of that name; one to which "The Young May Moon" is sung and the other the original air of "Eveleen's Bower." The latter "Dandy O" was printed in Brysson's *Curious Selection of Fifty Irish Airs,* 1791, and in O'Farrell's *Pocket Companion for the Irish or Union Pipes,* volume 4, 1810.

According to the same author the air, "Denis, Don't Be Threatening," printed in 1796, is the progenitor of "The Dandy O." A version of it was used by Shield in the *"Poor Soldier,"* 1783, set to verses beginning "Out of my sight or I'll box your ears."

THE LIMERICK LAMENTATION, OR LOCHABER

The wandering propensities of the Irish and Scotch Minstrels were proverbial, but we think it will be conceded that the former were more decidedly addicted to that habit than their kinsmen.

There can be no question that "The Limerick Lamentation" and "Lochaber No More" had a common origin. The point to be determined is, which is entitled to the claim of seniority. In *Poems of Ireland* Samuel Lover devotes nearly four pages to the discussion of this subject.

In the British Museum there is to be seen a volume entitled *New Poems, Songs, Prologues and Epilogues never before printed, by Thomas Duffet, and set by the most eminent musicians about the Town. London, 1676*. This volume has among its contents a song commencing "Since Coelia is my foe," the lines of which are headed thus, "Song to the Irish Tune" instead of having the name of the composer recorded as in other pieces.

A singular interest attaches to this old song, Lover says, as it establishes beyond a doubt that the beautiful air which the Scotch claim under the title of "Lochaber" is Irish. Allan Ramsay, who wrote a song in the *Tea Table Miscellany* entitled "Farewell to Lochaber, Farewell to My Jean," set to this melody, was not born until 1696—twenty years after the publication of Duffet's "Song to the Irish Tune." Furthermore, the *"Tea Table Miscellany,"* in which *"Farewell to Lochaber"* was printed, appeared in 1724.

Farquhar Graham in *Wood's Songs of Scotland* directs attention to a trifling resemblance which it bears to a much older air of but one strain called "Lord Ronald." While conceding the similarity he says "Lochaber" is a much more modern air than "King James' March to Ireland." Now, James the Second landed at Kinsale in 1689, and "The Irish Tune" was already a favorite in London thirteen years before that event.

The earliest printed copy of the air bearing the title

"Limerick's Lamentation," which is only a modification of "The Irish Tune," Moffat informs us, appeared in Daniel Wright's *Aria di Camera, being a Choice Collection of Scotch, Irish and Welsh Airs, circa* 1730. This Lamentation was sometimes called "Sarsfield's Lamentation." There is, however, a lament of that name entirely distinct from it.

The original air or "The Irish Tune," Adair Fitz Gerald, in *Stories of Famous Songs*, positively assures his readers, was the composition of Myles O'Reilly, the famous harper of the County Cavan, and passed into Scotland through Thomas O'Connellan, the renowned Sligo harper, who spent much of his time in that country.

O! NANNY, WILT THOU GANG WITH ME?

More than once have we read and heard that the above named air was Irish, but as the statements were unsupported by any definite evidence, the question of its origin was left to the future.

Of course, the idiom stamps the name indelibly as Scotch, but from the circumstance of its having been sung as "O! Nanny, Will You Go With Me?" in the Vauxhall Gardens, London, in 1773, it has also been claimed as English.

To Adair Fitz Gerald, in *Stories of Famous Songs*, we are indebted for the information that all three claims are justifiable. When Mrs. Nanny Percy was relieved of her duties as nurse to the infant Prince Edward, son of George the Third, in 1773, and returned home to her disconsolate husband, he greeted her with the verses, "O, Nanny, Will You Go With Me?" The affecting ballad gained such immediate favor that in the *Gentleman's Magazine* of 1780 is was mentioned as "the most beautiful song in the English language."

It appears that the verses were originally written in English, without any Scottish expressions at all. Although it was subsequently incorporated in *Popular Songs and Melodies of Scotland,* the editor conceded its English origin. But where does the Irish claim come in? The answer is simple enough. The music of the song was composed by C. F. Carter, "The Milesian," an Irishman born in Dublin in 1735. He studied for a time under his father, Timothy Carter, an organist in one of the principal churches of that city.

The composer of the music of "O, Nanny," etc., died in London in 1804, having been musical director in the Royalty Theatre some few years previously.

THE PRINCESS ROYAL

This fine air was composed about 1725 by O'Carolan in honor of the daughter of MacDermott Roe, his great friend, the representative of the old Princes of Coolavin, County Sligo. It is now more commonly known as "The Arethusa," and is regarded by many as an English air because Shield inserted a song of that name in his opera, although he never claimed it as his composition. It first appeared under that name in the first edition of *The Lock and Key.* The tune was printed about 1730 in Walsh's *Compleat Country Dancing Master,* as "The Princess Royal the new way," and also in Wright's *Country Dances,* 1735. In 1787 McGlashon included it in his *Scots Measures.*

The early English music publishers seized greedily upon any fine Scotch or Irish airs they could find, and their Country Dance collections especially teem with such tunes, according to Alfred Moffat.

The first to claim the air as one of O'Carolan's compositions seems to have been O'Farrell, in his *Pocket Companion for the Irish or Union Pipes,* in 1804. Bunting obtained a fine version of it from Arthur O'Neill in 1800. The latter explained that the Princess Royal honored was Miss MacDermott Roe, and not a scion of English royalty.

A poor and incorrect setting of this air is included in Messrs. Parry and Rowland's *Cambrian Minstrelsie,* with the following remark: "Though the title of the air is English, there can be no question of its Welsh origin." "Assertions of this description scarcely deserve notice," adds Moffat; "they are easily made and are certainly not worth refuting."

"BELIEVE ME IF ALL THOSE ENDEARING YOUNG CHARMS" or "MY LODGING IS ON THE COLD GROUND"

The air of that popular favorite whose name heads this inquiry, has come to be regarded by not a few musical authorities as being originally English instead of Irish. Very naturally, any such claim contrary to the time-honored belief will by Irishman, at least, be considered ridiculous.

It has been excluded by Sir Villiers Stanford from his edition of Moore's *Melodies (Restored)*. Neither does Alfred Moffat include it in his interesting work, *The Minstrelsy of Ireland,* 1895. We do not find that the melody was among the airs played by the great harpers, and it is not to be found in any Irish collection of music prior to 1787, when as "The Irish Mad Song" it was printed in *The Hibernian Muse,* published in London by S. A. & P. Thompson.

Without indicating its origin, a quaint variant of "My Lodging Is on the Cold Ground" is printed in Aird's

Selection of Scotch, English, Irish and Foreign Airs, volume 1, published in 1782.

In three English publications printed in 1665, 1666 and 1669, respectively, mentioned by William Chappell in his *Old English Popular Music,* London, 1893, a song is printed, the first line of which reads, "My lodging, it is on the cold ground, and, oh! very hard is my fare." Several parodies followed, but the original air composed for this song by Mathew Lock was discarded before the end of the seventeenth century and that now universally known took its place.

A song to the tune "My Lodging Is on the Cold Ground" was printed in a ballad opera in London in 1737. A copy of the music as then printed can be found on page 140 of Chappell's work, before mentioned, Vol. 2. The author concludes his discussion of this air as follows: "The words and music are printed in 'Vocal Music,' or 'The Songster's Companion,' 8vo, 1775, and it has been a stock song in print from that time."

If an error has been made in classifying "My Lodging Is on the Cold Ground" as an Irish air, the Irish can disclaim responsibility, for, besides the publications above named, the tune was printed and classed as Irish by R. A. Smith in *The Irish Minstrel,* published in Edinburgh, and by William Forde in *The Encyclopedia of Melody,* published in London.

Like many other Irish airs, it may have found its way into England in the early part of the eighteenth century and on account of its superior merit been substituted, as it really was, for Lock's original air.

If originally an English composition, to paraphrase Moffat in discussing "Black-eyed Susan," it must be admitted that more than a century's residence in the Emerald Isle has by no means proved a drawback to it;

on the contrary, the Irish form appears to be infinitely finer than the original English version, and for that reason, if for no other, it may be considered an Irish melody.

A discussion of this nature might be prolonged indefinitely, as the list of tunes whose origin has been called in question is far from being exhausted; but as the disquisition relating to the tunes already mentioned is sufficient to direct attention to a subject that has received but slight consideration from writers heretofore, and is but little understood by most readers, my purpose is accomplished as far as this branch of the subject is concerned.

> "Music's the language of the blest above;
> No voice but music can express
> The joys that happy souls possess,
> Nor in just raptures tell the wondrous power of love.
> 'Tis nature's dialect designed
> To charm and to instruct the mind."

CHAPTER X

CURIOUS AND INCOMPREHENSIBLE TITLES

"O native music! beyond comparing
 The sweetest far on the ear that falls,
Thy gentle numbers the heart remembers,
Thy strains enchain us in tender thralls.
  Thy tones endearing,
  Or sad or cheering,
The absent soothe on a foreign strand;
  Ah, who can tell
  What a holy spell
Is the song of our native land?"

THE confusion arising from unintelligible titles, as well as the duplication and diversity of names, by which dance tunes as well as old Irish airs are known, entails no end of trouble to the collector of Folk Music. Popular songs and ballads have been, in days gone by, wedded indiscriminately to any ancient air found suitable to the verses, and in course of time the name of the old air was liable to be forgotten and supplemented by that of the later songs adapted to it.

How so many Irish tunes, found worthy of preservation, and in many cases chosen by poets and song-writers as airs for their compositions, happen to be without names, is something not easily accounted for. Such notations as "Name unknown," "Name unascertained," "Unknown air," etc., so noticeable in certain Irish musical publications, betray a heedlessness which is truly lamentable.

Ten of the sixty melodies in Thomson's *Select Collection*

of *Original Irish Airs,* published in 1814-16, were, the editor states, "communicated without a name by a friend," and two others were submitted by names not original.

The first two hundred eighty-eight numbers in Petrie's *Complete Collection of Irish Music* are nameless, and all through to the end of the third series, anonymous tunes are not by any means rare.

Further instances would be superfluous to illustrate the extent to which musical strains have been preserved traditionally, while the titles, original or modern, have been regarded with unconcern and forgotten altogether.

Corrupt and abbreviated so-called Irish titles, often meaningless and unintelligible in their published form, but add to the collector's embarrassment. Although some of them have been deciphered by resourceful Irish scholars, not a few remain, which defy the skill of the linguist and lexicographer to unravel their mysteries. Ridiculous names, purporting to be Irish, still continue to be printed generations after the first untranslatable attempts at phonetic Irish were committeed to paper; and however leniently we may be inclined to look upon the absurd mistakes of strangers, it is not easy to understand how Irish-born men could be so utterly lacking in a knowledge of the Irish language in the eighteenth century.

The Englishman who in naming one of the tunes in *A Handefull of Pleasant Delites,* printed in 1584 as "Calen o custure me," furnished our first published puzzle. It has been rendered into Irish by Grattan Flood as *"Cailin og a stuiro mo."* The tune was included in several English collections in the seventeenth century and entitled "An Irish Air," and also as "Callino Custurame." Some of our best Irish scholars, such as Dr. Petrie and Dr. Stokes, equated it as "Calleen oge asthore," which freely translated means "My Dear Young Girl." In Chappell's *Old English*

Popular Music, the air is headed, "Calino Casturame," or "Colleen oge astore."

But is the puzzle solved? As Dr. Flood points out, the final *me* (Irish of *my*) persists in all the readings—which would hardly be the case were "Colleen oge asthore" the correct interpretation.

The oldest printed collections containing Irish airs in the writer's library are *Twelve Scotch and Twelve Irish Airs with Variations* and *Twelve English and Twelve Irish Airs with Variations,* by Mr. Burk Thumoth, printed in London in 1742 and 1745, respectively. Even the author's name is not free from the prevailing absurdities (the correct name is said to have been Mr. Thomaus Burk).

Of the Irish airs in those volumes, "Yemon O nock" first attracts attention. This name we have no difficulty in identifying as *"Eamonn an Chnuic,"* or "Ned of the Hill." Under the same grotesque title it appears in *The Hibernian Muse,* published in 1787. In *A Pocket Volume of Airs, Duets, Songs, Marches, etc.,* printed by Paul Alday in Dublin about 1800, it improves slightly as "Emon O Knuck." O'Daly, in *Poets and Poetry of Munster,* prints the name *"Eamonn an Chnoic,"* from which orthography Grattan Flood deviates by spelling the final word *"Chnuic."*

As it would prove tiresome to enter into details in all such cases, we must pass on to Burk Thumoth's next absurdity—"Chiling O guiry."

This name, we may as well explain at once, was intended to represent *"Sighile ni Gadhra"* (Sheela ni Gara); in English, Celia, or Cecelia, O'Gara.

What the publishers did to it can be seen from the following: The Thompsons in *The Hibernian Muse* faithfully copied Thumoth. In Goulding's edition of Aird's *Selection of Scotch, English, Irish and Foreign Airs,* volume 1, 1782, it is "Shilling O'Gairey" and "Sheling a

Gairey." Other forms of the name are "Sighile ni Gara," "Sheela ne Gaura," and "Sheela na Guira," as in McCullach's *Collection of Irish Airs for the Flute and Flageolet* and Forde's *Encyclopedia of Melody*. A dance tune in nine-eight time is printed in different editions of Aird's *Selection*, etc., as "Sheela na Jigg" and "Shella na gigg."

A very popular air must have been "Health to King Philip," under its Irish name, *Slainte Righ Pilib*. Burk Thumoth prints it *Slaunt Ri Plulib*, in which ridiculous reading it is copied in *The Hibernian Muse*, 1787, and in Thomson's *Select Collection of Original Irish Airs*, 1814-16.

The word *Ri* is excusable, being phonetic, but *Plulib* would be laughable were it not absurd and meaningless. No one, it seems, who obtained airs from Thumoth's collections, cared to inquire the significance of his titles, and as a result we find the original but erroneous phrases copied and perpetuated to the present day.

"Drimen Duff" is a long departure from *"Dromfionn Dubh,"* but as its meaning, or rather the intention of its author, is apparent, we will let it pass without further comment, except to say that in English it signifies a "white-backed black cow." The name, like that of many other Irish airs, is allegorical. Bunting wrote it in one word, *"Druimindubh"* and translated it "The black-backed cow." In *The Bee* and in Clinton's *Gems of Ireland* and other works it is corrupted into *"Drimindoo."* It was a popular tune during the Jacobite wars by the party favoring the exiled monarch.

Grattan Flood in *A History of Irish Music* tells us that the exquisite air entitled *"An Ceann dubh dilis,"* or "The Black-headed Dearie," was composed about the commencement of the seventeenth century. It was printed in *Playford's Dancing Master* in 1713, and is to be found in

Burk Thumoth's first volume as *"Curri Koun Dilich."* This is quite a departure from the original.

It appears as *"Ceann dubh dileas,* or Black but Lovely," in McGoun's *Repository of Scots and Irish Airs;* "Black but Lovely" in Aird's *Selection, etc., etc.;* "*Can dubh deelish"* in Forde's *Encyclopedia of Melody,"* and *"Cean Dubh Delish"* in Haverty's *Three Hundred Irish Airs.* It is also to be found in *The Hibernian Muse* as copied from Thumoth. The phrase "Black but Lovely" is by no means a translation of the Irish title, which is intensely expressive of affection and endearment.

Bunting included the air in his third collection of *The Ancient Music of Ireland,* under the title *"Cara Ceann Dills,"* which he translated into "Black-headed Dear." He notes that it was printed by this name in a small collection of Irish airs "published by John and William O'Neale, Christ Church Yard, Dublin, 1726."

"Bumpers Esquire Jones," one of O'Carolan's most celebrated compositions, is one of the *"Twelve English Airs"* in Burk Thumoth's second volume. The air is duly credited to O'Carolan in *The Hibernian Muse,* the editor of which in this instance ventured to doubt Thumoth's infallibility. The title, too, is modified into "Bumper 'Squire Jones," the name under which it was printed in a collection of O'Carolan's airs in 1780, and by which name it has ever since appeared in print and been universally acknowledged as an Irish melody.

This air was composed in 1730 by O'Carolan in honor of Thomas Morris Jones, of Moneyglass, County Antrim,[*] whose hospitality he frequently enjoyed. The original verses in Irish are irretrievably lost. Even the industrious

---

[*] Antrim, Leitrim, Sligo, variously given by Walker, Bunting, Hardiman, respectively.—ED.

Hardiman failed to find a trace of them, although they are said to be O'Carolan's most brilliant effusion. The English verses are from the facetious pen of Baron Dawson, and though they are referred to as a paraphrase on the original, there is no certainty that they are in any way related.

When the bard retired to a private room to compose the air of the celebrated song, a local harper named Moore, who had a keen and receptive ear, overheard him from an adjoining apartment. Moore was also a fair violinist, and when O'Carolan announced that he had now produced a melody which he was sure would please the squire, Moore was prepared not only to insist that the air was an old and common one, but actually to play it note for note on the violin. This of course roused O'Carolan's rage, but when his anger had partly subsided, an explanation was made and the event terminated in a round of conviviality.

A different version of this story leaves out Moore altogether and credits Baron Dawson with having memorized the air and composed the song of eight verses and actually singing them, to the astonishment and embarrassment of the bard, at breakfast next morning.

The first Irish number in Burk Thumoth's *Twelve English and Twelve Irish Airs* is entitled "Balin a mone." The original and correct name is evidently *"Baile na mona,"* or "The Land of Turf or Peat."

Alfred Moffat in his *Minstrelsy of Ireland* states that in John O'Keeffe's *Poor Soldier*, 1780, the song called "You Know I'm Your Priest" was sung to the air "Ballinamona Oro." As "Ballina Mona" it was printed in Johnson's *Choice Collection of Two Hundred Favorite Country Dances,* volume IV, 1748.

The air is called "The Wedding of Ballyporeen" in Forde's *Encyclopedia of Melody* and in Haverty's *Three*

Hundred Irish Airs, but in Clinton's *Gems of Ireland* it is called "The Wedding of Ballinomono."

The seventh Irish number in Burk Thumoth's second volume is entitled "The Dangling of the Irish Bearns." Under the same title it is printed in *The Hibernian Muse,* 1787, and quite a few modern publications. What that name means is beyond our comprehension, and although purporting to be in the English language, neither inquiry nor research has brought us any nearer a solution of its hidden significance.

The earliest printed setting of this melody, according to Alfred Moffat, was in Daniel Wright's *Aria di Camora, being a Choice Collection of Scotch, Irish and Welsh Airs for the Violin and German Flute,* c. 1730. In his comments he maintains that the air bears considerable resemblance to O'Carolan's compositions, although not being attributed to the great bard.

There are other names of airs more or less difficult to understand in Burk Thumoth's volumes, such as "The Irish Ragg," "The Fin Galian's Dance," and that crude attempt at giving "O'Rourk's Feast," or "Planxty O'Rourke," in the Irish language, viz., *"Plea Rorkeh na Rourkough."*

An air named "Caroline" in the index to McGoun's *Repository of Scotch and Irish Airs, circa* 1800, is printed "Carlione, a Favorite Irish Tune," over the music in the body of the volume. The name was evidently intended to convey the idea that it was one of O'Carolan's compositions, for upon examination it proves to be "O'Carolan's Receipt, or Planxty Stafford."

Another air, named "Stack in Virgo," in the same work, was a poser for a time. It was finally equated with *"Staca an Margaidh,"* or "The Market Stake." The first letter of *Margaidh* in conversation is aspirated, hence the phonetic *V* in McGoun's title. This air as printed in Bunting's Second Collection of *The Ancient Music of Ireland,* 1809, is called *"Staca an Mharaga."* In copying the name, Moore's publishers use *Stacca.*

A title which has defied solution by even our best Irish scholars is "Gillan na drover," an old Irish march of nine strains, including variations, in McGoun's compilation. That the first word should be *Giolla,* a boy or man servant, can be seen at a glance, but the word "drover," in either form or sound, suggests nothing in Irish which would complete a rational phrase. The tune has been printed in O'Neill's *Irish Music for the Piano and Violin,* under the name "Gillan the Drover," that being the nearest commonsense phrase I could think of.

"Captain Oakhain" in the same work does not much disguise the plaintive melody "Capt. O'Kane," or "The Wounded Hussar."

Ever since we have been able to read, we have wondered what information or meaning was hidden by the cryptogramic announcement printed over certain tunes— "Air—Gage Fane." In one instance, at least, it was "Gang Fane," but that was no more illuminating than the other. The Irish word *fein* is easily translatable into "self," but no ingenious surmises as to the significance of "Gage Fane" would result in an intelligible name or phrase.

At the moment of returning consciousness from sleep one morning, the solution came to me like a flash. "Gage Fane" stood for *"An Gaedhana Fiadhaine,"* or "The Wild Geese"—the name by which the thousands of Irish were called who fled to France and Spain after the Treaty of Limerick.

Bunting says that this fine melody was composed as a farewell to the gallant remnant of the Irish army who upon the capitulation of Limerick, in 1691, preferred an honorable exile to remaining in the country after their cause was lost.

The mystifying "Gage Fane" confronts us in Smith's *Irish Minstrel*, Moore's *Melodies*, Moffat's *Minstrelsy of Ireland* and many less pretentious publications. It was a relief to find that Perceval Graves in *The Irish Song Book*, issued in 1895, finally broke the monotony of error by printing the correct Irish name.

Grattan Flood in *A History of Irish Music* tells us that Smollett Holden in his *Collection of Irish Tunes*, published in 1804-6, was primarily responsible for this ridiculous error, which has been copied for nearly a century without question or correction.

Who could believe it possible, were not the fact indisputable, that countless editions of Moore's *Melodies* in all English speaking countries, would present to its readers with unvarying monotony the same absurd and meaningless titles originally printed through censurable carelessness if not pitiable ignorance?

Notwithstanding the explanations and corrections of Flood and Graves, it is safe to assume that it may be another century before "Gage Fane" and other names almost equally ridiculous will entirely disappear.

Among the melodies mentioned by Bunting which the harpers played at the Belfast assembly in 1792 is one named "Graga-nish." This title had defied our best efforts to discover the hidden meaning disguised by this combination of letters. It is more than likely that it would have remained inexplicable had I not noticed that the air was known by a name in English also, viz., "Love in Secret."

The idiomatic Irish for this phrase is written *"Gradh gan fios,"* literally "Love Without Knowledge." "Gra gon ios" would represent the Irish name phonetically, hence the puzzling "Graga-nish," as understood by Bunting.

"*Cruachan na Feinne*" (The Fenian Mound or Stronghold), given as the title of an old Irish air to be seen in many collections of Irish music and song besides Moore's *Melodies,* is variously introduced in such forms as "Crooghan a Venee," "Crookaun a Venee," "Croghan a Venee," etc.

As in the preceding case, Perceval Graves breaks away from traditional error, and prints the correct Irish title.

"Gamba Ora" is given as the name of the air to which is sung "Ye Friendly Stars That Rule the Night," a song written by the Scotch poet Tannahill and printed in *The Irish Minstrel,* published by R. A. Smith at Edinburgh in 1825. Down to the present day that titular puzzle continues to be printed in various collections of Irish melodies, presumably for our enlightenment. "Gamba Ora" is neither Irish nor English, but it was evidently intended to convey some information in the former language. It had defied our best efforts to discover its hidden meaning, when a chance ray of light in all likelihood revealed its mystery. Its resemblance to *"Ga Mba ora,"* the name of a tune in Dr. Petrie's *Complete Collection of Irish Music,* attracted attention. A comparison of the two tunes disclosed their practical identity, although in different keys. The name in the latter work, although very corrupt, may be freely translated as "I Wish Them Well," or "May They Have Luck."

It is doubtful if any title in Moore's *Melodies* is so grotesque as *"Sios agus sios liom,"* which in English is literally the self abasing expression "Down and Down With Me." The name intended, "Sit Down Beside Me," is written *"Suidhe sios agus suas liom"* in the Irish language.

Even our learned friend Perceval Graves overlooks this

palpable error and so does the editor of Moore's *Melodies,* translated into Irish by Archbishop McHale. Bunting in his third collection of *The Ancient Music of Ireland* errs but slightly in printing it *"Sin sios agus suas liom,"* which form of the name he copied from Daniel Wright's *Aria di Camera,* published about 1730. In Lynch's *Melodies of Ireland,* 1845, it is printed *"Sios agus sios lionem!"* The editor of the *Hibernian Muse* and O'Farrell in the *Pocket Companion for the Irish or Union Pipes,* published in 1804-10, made a clever phonetic guess at the Irish phrase, which appears as follows: *"Sheen Sheesh igus Souse lum,"* but as Moore's *Melodies* is a household volume its errors will continue to be as widely copied as its beauties are appreciated.

Another perplexing puzzle of an old air is "Noran Kitsa," to which Moore wrote "Wreathe the Bowl."

In Bunting's third collection of *The Ancient Music of Ireland* there is an air named in the index *"Onora an Chisde,"* the translation of which he gives as "Nora With the Cake." Yet over the printed melody appears a somewhat different translation, "Nora With the Purse." How cake can be synonymous with purse is not apparent, and the question naturally arises, which is right? It is an odd coincidence that in O'Neill Lane's *English-Irish Dictionary,* translating the word cake into the Irish *Ciste,* an Irish verse is quoted, the second line of which reads *"Ba maith le Nora ciste."* The correct name, therefore, is *Nora an Ciste.*

The earliest printed copy of this tune which Moffat says he could discover was in Thompson's *Country Dances for 1770,* in which it is called "The Wild Irishman." The oldest setting of it available to the writer was found in the first volume of Aird's *Selection of Scotch, English, Irish and Foreign Airs,* 1782, where it is named "Norickystie, or The Wild Irishman." The title in Holden's *Collection of Irish Tunes* is "Noreen Keesta." In McCullagh's *Collection of Irish Airs*, 1821, it appears as "Noran Kista," while in Forde's *Encyclopedia of Melody* it is "Nora Kista." Clinton in his *Gems of Ireland* and in *The Bee* the title is still further corrupted into "Noresenkeesta." We would hardly expect to find so much confusion concerning Irish names of popular airs at a time when Irish scholars were supposed to be more numerous than they are today. Dr. Petrie does not mention this air among his collections at all.

A very ancient Irish melody is "Baltiorum," and oddly enough it is known only by versions of that name. While euphonious, it conveys no meaning to the reader, and it is commonly assumed that notwithstanding its Latin termination it signifies something in the Irish language. And so it does when understood. The first writer who undertakes to explain it is Edward Bunting. *Baal tigh abhoran*, usually called "Baltiorum," is a tune which might perhaps without rashness, he says, be assigned to the Pagan period, inasmuch as it is still customarily sung at the bonfires lighted on St. John's Eve, the anniversary of the *Baal-tinne*, and has so been sung from time immemorial. He does not give the translation in English, although his dissertation is much more comprehensive than the extract above quoted. To the writer it appears to be the song of praise or worship of Baal, the Fire-God.

The Pagan festivals eventually were wisely turned into account as Christian holidays, and in this instance the *Baal-tinne*, or fire lighted to welcome the *Samhain* or summer solstice, was continued as the celebration of St. John's eve. The melody, Conran tells us in his *National Music of Ireland*, 1850, may be still heard from the groups assembled around those bonfires.

In the writer's boyhood days the melody was forgotten and so was the Pagan significance of the celebration.

In O'Farrell's *Pocket Companion*, etc., before mentioned, the name of the tune is printed "Baulthy Oura." In Aird's *Selection of Scotch, English, Irish and Foreign Airs*, it is "Baltioura." Haverty in *300 Irish Airs* calls it "Baltighoran," the same title given by Bunting over the printed music, regardless of his explanations. The air, or rather dance tune, as "Baltiorum" is also one of the numbers in *Bland and Weller's Annual Collection of Twenty-four Country Dances for the Year 1798*.

A fine traditional old air is the *"Paistin Fionn,"* or "The Fair-haired Child," published in Bunting's *General Collection of the Ancient Irish Music*, 1796. Evidently few collectors cared for correctness in the Irish names of their tunes. So careless were they in this respect that names in the index sometimes differed from those over the printed music. O'Farrell in his work before mentioned published the melody under the title *"Pausteen Feaun."* In *Crosby's Irish Musical Repository*, 1808, and in *Alday's Pocket Volume of Airs*, etc., a few years later it is "Pastheen Fuen," while in an old collection from which the title is missing a still further departure confronts us in "Patheen a Fuen." As "Paistheen Fuen" it is alluded to by Alfred Moffat in his *Minstrelsy of Ireland*. Phonetically, "Paustheen Fune" represents it.

Of the many who have mentioned and published the ancient melody "I'm Asleep and Don't Waken Me," Dr. Petrie alone gives the name correctly in Irish as follows: *Ta me i mo codhladh 's na duisigh me*. Ordinarily only the first half of the name is printed, as in *The Hibernian Muse*, in which the title is abbreviated to "I Am Sleeping." This results in the corrupt Irish abbreviation "Thamama Hulla," or "Thamma Hulla," as in Holden's

Old Established Irish Tunes, 1806. Moore has it "Thamama Halla."

Bunting, who gives quite an interesting sketch of this air, states that it was unwarrantably appropriated by the Scotch, among whom Hector MacNeill had written words to it.

Arthur O'Neill, the great harper, from whose intelligent recital Bunting obtained most of his information concerning harpers, tells the following curious anecdote: "When at McDonnell's of Knockrantry, in the County of Roscommon, I met a young nobleman from Germany who had come to Ireland to look after some property, to which he had a claim through his mother. He was one of the most finished and accomplished young gentlemen that I ever met. When on one occasion Hugh O'Neill and I had played our best tunes for him, he wished to call for 'Past One O'clock,' 'Tha me mo chodladh, naar dhoesk a me,' which he had heard played somewhere before; but for the name of which he was at a loss.

"Perceiving me going towards the door, he followed me and said that the name of his boot-maker was Tommy McCullagh, and that the tune he wanted was like saying 'Tommy McCullagh made boots for me,' and in the broad way he pronounced it, it was not unlike the Irish name. I went with him and played it, on which he seemed uncommonly happy."

Versions of this melody had been printed long before Bunting gave it publicity, although he noted it down from Hempson, the great harper, in 1792. The Scotch claim it also as a Highland melody and in this they are fortified by the fact of a version of it being printed under the Gaelic name *Chami ma chattle,* in a little work entitled *Musick for Allan Ramsay's Collection of Scotch Songs,* published in 1725-6. It was also introduced, says Alfred

Moffat, as "Past One O'clock in a Cold, Frosty Morning" in Coffee's *Beggar's Wedding*, 1731, and in the opera *Flora*, 1732, as "At Past Twelve O'clock on a Fine Summer's Morning."

Space will not permit the full history of this ancient air and its many titles except to state that it was called "Past One O'clock" in Burk Thumoth's *Twelve Scotch and Twelve Irish Airs*, 1742.

In Aird's *Selection of Scotch, English, Irish and Foreign Airs*, published in the latter part of the eighteenth century, there is printed an Irish jig with the mystifying name "Ligrum Cus." Without being at all sure, the writer ventures an opinion that the original name was "*Leig dam cos*," or "Let Go My Foot." However, philologists may yet find Aird's title worthy of their consideration.

Another jig in the same work is named "Jackson's Bouner Bougher." The first word identifies it as one of Jackson's compositions, but what the other words signify must still remain a mystery.

It has never been our good fortune to learn the meaning or derivation of the word or phrase "Langolee" as applied to certain airs in Moore's *Melodies* and other works. Both the "Old Langolee" and the "New Langolee" are much older than Moore's time, for they appear as "Lango Lee" in *The Hibernian Muse*, 1787. In Aird's *Selection, etc., etc.*, 1782, we find "Lango Lee a New Way." Yet on examination it proves to be Moore's "Old Langolee," the same version as printed in O'Farrell's *Pocket Companion, etc.*, 1804. In Paul Alday's *Pocket Volume of Airs, Duets, Marches, etc.*, circa 1800, there is printed an elaborate setting of the "New Lango Lee With Variations," requiring twenty staffs of eight bars each. Its earliest appearance in print was in Thompson's *Twenty-four Country Dances for 1775*.

How often are we asked the meaning of the word "Planxty," a term principally applied to O'Carolan's compositions. Reference to the English-Irish or Irish-English dictionaries within our reach is fruitless, for the word is not to be found in any form.

The best information obtainable is that Planxties are lively or spirited compositions in which the strain may be elaborated to unusual lengths according to the fancy of the composer.

The following is abbreviated from Petrie's definition: The Planxty is a harp-tune of a sportive and animated character, not intended for, or often adaptable to, words; and it generally moves in triplets with a six-eight time, but the Planxty differs from the more ancient jig in having less rapidity of motion, thus giving a greater facility for the use of fanciful or playful ornamentation, and also in its not being bound, as the jig necessarily is, to an equality in the number of bars or beats in its parts. The Planxty, though in some instances it represents such an equality, is more usually remarkable for a want of it; the second part being extended to various degrees of length beyond that of the first.

There appears to be no standard of spelling the term, as it is printed indifferently Plansty, Planxty, Plangsty, Plamgstigh, and Blangsty in questionable English, and Pleraca, Pleireaca, Pleid raca, and Plea Rorkeh in Irish; the latter being Burk Thumoth's version of it.

We cannot but admire the originality and phonetic skill of the genius who arranged the music in Crosby's *Irish Musical Repository*, 1808. The six words in the title of that popular melody, *"An cailin deas cruidte na m-bo,"* or "The Pretty Girl Milking Her Cow," have been adroitly condensed into two, which leave no doubt as to their meaning, viz., "Caleendhas Crootheenamoe."

Irish titles have been subjected to many indignities, but this in its simplicity is excusable because it conveys the sound of the name with tolerable accuracy.

Had O'Farrell in his *Pocket Companion for the Irish or Union Pipes* been as considerate as Crosby, we would not now be worrying over the meaning of *"Thomaus a Moumpus,"* the name of a delightful melody in his sixth volume.

Our best efforts to equate or translate the word "Moumpus" have ended in failure. It is probably a nickname for some Thomas whose peculiarities were aptly indicated, according to a very common Irish custom. Either of two Irish words, *Ampal*—hunger, or *Tormas*—grumbling, may have been corrupted, as in many other puzzling instances.

O'Farrell's orthography in English and Irish is so conspicuously bad that it is doubtful if a proofreader exercised any supervision over the work. It would be too tedious to mention them all, but there is one which we cannot afford to overlook. One of his best jigs is entitled *"Beg vanElla gum."* This name, notwithstanding its oddity in having a capital letter in the middle of a word, is easily translatable as "I Will Have Another Wife," or "I Will Be Married Again." It was evidently an attempt at rendering phonetically the Irish phrase, *"Beidh bean eile agam."* The third word, probably mistaken for a woman's name, was printed Ella and honored with a capital accordingly.

What can be more depressing to a lover of his country's music than to encounter such abortive attempts at Irish names of airs as *"Yogh hone O hone"* in *The Hibernian Muse* and "O Hone What's This?" in Alday's *Pocket Volume, etc.,* before mentioned?

The very absurdity of the titles alone is enough to cause melodies so named to be neglected and forgotten.

Until recently the writer had been unable to ascertain from any source, oral or printed, the origin or meaning of "Moneymusk," the name of the most popular and widely known of all Highland Flings.

Its origin remained a mystery which even our Scotch musicians confessed themselves unable to solve. While looking over the dance section of McGoun's *Repository of Scots and Irish Airs,* published about 1800, I came across a tune called "Sir Archibald Grant of Moniemusk's Reel." Here was the key at last. The reel was our mysterious friend "The Moneymusk" all right, and it was plain to be seen the original name had been abbreviated. "Moniemusk" was simply the name of Sir Archibald Grant's residence or estate.

The battle cry of the Irish Brigade, *"Fag an Baile,"* is historic, yet the phrase in connection with the Irish air of that name has seldom been correctly printed as far as we can remember. It signifies literally, "Leave the Town or Place," although the very free translation as commonly understood is "Clear the Way."

Of course the barbarous orthography is perpetuated even in Perceval Graves' *Irish Song Book,* where in the index it appears as *"Feag a Balleach,"* but as the air to the song "To Ladies' Eyes" it is changed to *"Fag an Bealach,"* or "Leave the Gap or Passage."

In some old collections its form is still further varied, such as *"Fague an Bealeach"* and *"Fagua a Ballagh."* In editing *Moore's Melodies* restored Sir Villiers Stanford evidently did not concern himself with restoring the titles when he tolerates "Faugh a Ballagh."

Alfred Moffat mentions in *The Minstrelsy of Ireland* that *"Fague a Ballagh"* was first published in the seventh number of Moore's *Melodies*. In telling us that the phrase was the warcry of the Munster and Connacht clans he changes the spelling to *"Fag an Bealach."* As the latter form is part of his own diction, he leaves us to infer its correctness.

In the sixth number of Moore's *Melodies,* issued in 1815, the poet sets the song "No, Not More Welcome," to an air which he calls *"Luggelaw."* It is recorded that he obtained it from Petrie, but no explanation is offered as to what the ancient title signifies. Upon investigation *"Luggelaw"* seems to be a corruption of *"Lug na leaca"*— in English, "The Hollow Beside the Hill." It was also printed "Luggela."

A very plausible derivation of the name, which is totally at variance with that found in Dr. Joyce's *Irish Local Names Explained,* is given by Mrs. Plumptre in her *Narrative of a Residence in Ireland* in 1814-15. "The first morning of my stay was spent in a visit to *Loch-Hela,* better known by the name of *Luggelaw,* which sprang originally from a corrupt pronounciation of the name. That of *Loch-Hela*—the *Lake of Hela*—is now so little known that it is very commonly called the *Lake of Luggelaw.* I have seen it called so under an engraving of the spot; nay, I have seen it spelled *"Lugula,"* she says.

Petrie, who copied the tune from P. Carew's manuscript, very naturally copied the name also. There is no reason to believe that *"Luggelaw"* or other meaningless titles will ever be changed while Moore's *Melodies* retain their popularity; and it will continue to be quite satisfactory to all who appropriate the air for other publications.

Mystifying renderings of Irish names and phrases are not exclusively confined to old publications, for in Alfred Perceval Graves' *Songs of Erin,* published in 1901, we find a song entitled "The Stolen Heart; air, Smah Dunna hoo."

Notwithstanding its resemblance, the air has no connection with the surname Donohoe, but as a specimen of phonetic Irish it is certainly unique, and quite unlike the correct idiomatic Irish phrase, *"Is maith an duine tu,"* or "You Are a Good Fellow."

In the same index appears "The Stratagem; Air—Zamba Opa." In that form this alleged Irish name would defy a philologist, but with the discussion of "Gamba Ora" fresh in my memory I readily perceived that the puzzling "Zamba Opa" was another exhibit of that perplexing title.

"Sir Muddin dum da man," given as the air of the poet Graves' song, "The Daughter of the Rock," in the same volume, successfully conceals its secret. No satisfactory elucidation of the phrase into either English or Irish has been thus far effected.

"Sir Muddin" very probably was intended to represent vocally *"'Sa maidin,"* or "In the Morning." The other combination seems to have reference to women, but we may as well admit defeat at once as to speculate further on this philological problem.

Many Irish names of songs or airs as given in old publications are incorrectly printed, and what is still more remarkable is the fanatical fidelity with which modern compilers and publishers continue to copy without question the nonsensical so-called Irish names in editions without number supplied to the public down to the present day.

Dr. Petrie and Dr. P. W. Joyce are of course honorable exceptions, and so is the tuneful A. P. Graves, but is it not about time to eliminate those meaningless and misleading corruptions from a work of such universal circulation as Moore's *Irish Melodies* after a century of complacent toleration?

> "Supplied with paper, pen and ink,
> A poet sat him down—to think;
> He bit his nails, and scratched his head,
> But wit and fancy both were dead—
> Or, if with more than usual pain,
> A thought came slowly from his brain,
> It cost him Lord knows how much time
> To shape it into sense or rhyme;
> And what was yet a greater curse,
> Long thinking made his fancy worse."

CHAPTER XI

AMUSING INCIDENTS AND EXPERIENCES

"No glory I covet, no riches I want,
  Ambition is nothing to me;
The one thing I beg of kind heaven to grant
  Is a mind fit for humor and glee.

With passions unruffled, untainted with pride
  And music for life as my share,
The wants of my nature are cheaply supplied,
  And the rest are but folly and care.

How vainly, through infinite trouble and strife,
  The many their labors employ;
Since all that is truly delightful in life,
  Is what all, if they please, can enjoy."

No sentiment betrays itself more commonly among musicians the world over than professional jealousy. In the early stages of this insidious failing, it may be no more harmful than rivalry, yet it is but too often true that not a few permit their feelings to transgress the limits of pardonable competition.

It would be too much to claim that our Irish musicians in Chicago were exempt from this proverbial failing, and even if its existence must be admitted, it was wisely kept under good control, and never passed the bounds of prim decorum, unlike the case related by Mrs. S. C. Hall, in which the musicians of her native place in Wexford were involved.

"In our younger days every district had its own appointed and particular musician. 'Kelly the piper' belonged exclusively to the sweet seashore of Bannow; 'Andy the fiddler' to the sunny hill village of Carrick, and Tim Lacy to the townland of Ballymitty. Tim's instrument was not specified, for he was a universal master; could take a 'turn' at the pipes, a hand at the fiddle, a blow at the flute, or a 'bate' on the big drum, and was, in fact, so desultory in his habits as hardly to excite the jealousy of any one in particular; for Irish fiddlers and pipers are a most captious and irritable race, as combative for precedence as a bevy of courtiers.

"We remember 'Kelly the piper' and 'Andy the fiddler' challenging each other to a musical contest, which was kept up during five successive Sundays after Mass, and only brought to a conclusion by Andy's letting the music out of Kelly's pipes with a reaping hook; while, in return, Kelly immolated Andy's fiddle on the prongs of a pitchfork."

This occurred over seventy years ago, and while the "Irish Music Club" of Chicago was by no means a mutual admiration society, professional rivalry among its members was never publicly demonstrative or offensive.

Mr. John Conners, dean of the pipers, was an affable, jolly man, good-natured and diplomatic.

Although he had a very flattering opinion of his own abilities, his criticism of others was humorous and tolerant. Generous enough to concede the superiority of "Barney" Delaney and possibly one or two others as jig and reel players, he rather pitied their pretensions to compare with him at all in the execution of airs.

He named his tunes for the benefit of his audience as he played them, and it was well that he did, for his versions were not always either common or conventional.

Like all musicians, he dearly loved appreciation and applause. By the initiated this stimulant was administered sparingly, for his appetite in this respect was so well understood that after a tune or so rarely a word of approval was spoken, lest in a spirit of generosity he would continue his performance indefinitely.

On one occasion, while he was playing at Delaney's residence the silence became chilling and oppressive after a little while, so he unbuckled his pipes and laid them on the table. Deeming it entirely safe at this juncture to be at least courteous, my brother-in-law incautiously ventured to remark, "That was pretty good, Mr. Conners." This belated though qualified approval of his music so touched his sensibilities that, with the pleased inquiry, "Did you ever hear this one, Mr. Rogers?" he buckled on the pipes again and continued the entertainment.

At another time, Mrs. O'Neill came along as Mr. Conners was placing his instrument in the buggy awaiting him in front of Delaney's house, where he had been playing for an hour or two. "Oh, I knew it must have been you, Mr. Conners, when I heard the music, as I approached the house," was the "jollying" greeting which fired his brain. But she paid for it, all right enough, although the result was unexpected, under the circumstances.

"Mrs. O'Neill, you always had such a fine ear for music," he responded, with evident delight, "and even if I am in a hurry I'll play a few 'cunes' for yourself." There was no escaping such kindness, so she simply had to endure it as well as the glowering glances of others who had enough of it already.

He was a much married man and buried his third wife before the dark angel summoned himself to glory at the patriarchal age of eighty-two years.

His last wife's wake was numerously attended and by

the natural process of gravitation the "craft," as the music lovers were termed, assembled in the kitchen to condole with the bereaved widower.

Serious as such occasions are to the family, the majority are little affected by grief and this instance was no exception. The conversation had eventually drifted to music, when in a sly way Delaney remarked, "'The Gudgeon of Maurice's Car' is a fine reel, I always liked it." "Yes," answered Ennis, "it is a good reel, but I can hardly ever think of it. How does it go?" Now this was the widower's pet jig and he couldn't stand for such a mistake as that, so he corrected them. "'Tain't a reel at all, 'tis a jig." "Is that so?" inquired McFadden. "Who knows it?" Sergt. Early thought he could start it, and did, but got stalled at the end of the first strain. All of them—the jokers—pretended ignorance or forgetfulness of the second strain. Poor Mr. Conners, taken off his guard by their apparent earnestness, and for the moment oblivious of the draped casket and its lamented occupant in the front parlor, was tricked into humming the fugitive strain for this gang of schemers!

Who could imagine anything more wierd and incongruous?

The good-natured man did not long survive, but he was game to the last; "practiced" on his beloved pipes, and willed them to "Barney" Delaney. "The only one who could do them justice," he said.

His wishes in that respect were carried out by his children, but not his desire to have Delaney play a lament on them while the casket was being borne from the house to the hearse.

There was a "character" named Murphy living alone in a shanty on city land at the approach to Archer Avenue bridge, whose acquaintance I made soon after my transfer to the Deering Street District. He was nearly blind and kept a semblance of a notion store for a living. There was but little demand for his tobacco and candies, but a black bottle or two carefully placed out of sight in a dark cupboard had many patrons. He pretended to "play the pipes," and never was there so dignified and self-conscious a "performer" as he. His so-called music was simply atrocious, but as those who came to woo his black bottle were seldom discriminating he was complacently regarded as a "joke."

And so he was. His seriousness and egotism were irresistible.

Michael Houlihan, a loose-jointed Kilkenny man, lately appointed, in the exuberance of his spirits gave a neat exhibition of jig and reel dancing on the smooth station-house floor one day while on reserve duty.

"Begor, Mike, you ought to go up and dance for Murphy," was the approving remark of an onlooker. Caught by the compliment, the dancer earnestly inquired, "And who is Murphy?"

Several willingly gave the desired information with an additional eulogy on the fame of the great blind piper.

The writer, being the Desk Sergeant on duty, relieved Houlihan from reserve at once, and before long "Big Pat" stole away to see the fun, and on the arrival of the Lieutenant I was enabled to leave also.

The scene at Murphy's when I arrived was ludicrous beyond description. Houlihan, already alive to the joke, good humoredly pranced about the floor, while the piper, "God save the mark," figured a chanter that emitted spasmodic squeals, which by no stretch of the imagination could be identified as tunes. "Big Pat," who enjoyed the rare faculty of voiceless laughter, was apparently in convulsions.

Patrolman Fitzmaurice, who was off duty, sat in a dark corner, but betrayed his presence by explosions of hilarity which he did his best to control. This jerky jocularity of Fitzmaurice was evidently disconcerting to the piper, for after a few interrogative glances towards the former he reverently put away his "little instrument," as he fondly called it, heedless of Houlihan's compliment, "Begor, Mr. Murphy, you can almost make 'em spake."

The joke was too good to end there, so it went much further.

Far out on the "Northwest Side" of the City lived an airy fellow named Tom Bowlan, who was a good Highland piper and an excellent fluter.

The mention of a blind piper never fails to arouse interest, as most Irish harpers, pipers and even fiddlers until recently were blind or afflicted with some other infirmity. Naturally when "Murphy, the blind piper" from County Clare, was spoken of to Bowlan, he was bound to hear him.

It was arranged that on the next Sunday Bowlan was to dine with me and then we would call on the inimitable Murphy.

We will not enter into the details of what happened except to say that Bowlan rather enjoyed the situation when he found he had been "sold," and invited Murphy to play at the wedding of a friend. This our piper was obliged to decline, although grateful for the offer, on account of his blindness and consequent inability to travel in the night time.

When we reached the street my guest turned on me and said things not ordinarily mentioned in polite society. "That fellow hasn't a sin on his sowl," is the terse way he expressed his opinion of the "bard," meaning that he was mentally irresponsible.

Bowlan played the same game on his neighbor McCabe,

a man who being out of work one winter "turned" a set of Highland pipes for himself, filing down beef bones picked up in the vicinity for mounting instead of ivory.

This latest victim put us all in the shade in the game of practical joking, the final dupe being no less a personage than Alderman Michael McNurney of the old Tenth ward. That dignified official was something of an Irish piper himself, and possesed among his treasures the great set of Union pipes on which the famous Flannery was playing when he dropped dead in Brooklyn, New York, many years ago.

The alderman, accompanied by two or three other dignitaries, drove through the City and out along Archer Avenue, where the magnificence of their equipage attracted much attention.

What transpired in Murphy's store, or what kind of a performance was enacted, except the "Spanish Waltz," which was inflicted on every audience, we never learned, but the musical alderman let it go at that, and meekly submitted to much merry bantering among his acquaintances for some time.

As Murphy had never ventured to embark on the stormy sea of matrimony, he could not have been the subject of the following verses by the poet Ritchie:

"Ould Murphy the piper lay on his deathbed,
  To his only son Tim, the last words he said,
  'My eyes they grow dim, and my bosom grows could,
  But ye'll get all I have, Tim, when I slip my hould,
   Ye'll get all I have, boy, when I slip my hould.

"'There's three cows and three pigs, and ten acres of land,
  And this house shall be yours, Tim, as long as 'twill stand;
  All my fortune is three score bright guineas of gould,
  An ye'll get all I have Tim, when I slip my hould,
  Ye'll get all I have, son, when I slip my hould.

"Go fetch me my pipes Tim, till I play my last tune,
For death sure is coming, he'll be here very soon;
Those pipes I have played on, ne'er let them be sould
If you sell all I have Tim, when I slip my hould,
Should you sell all I have Tim, when I slip my hould.

"Then ould Murphy the piper, wid the last breath he drew,
He played on his pipes, like an Irishman true,
He played up the anthem of Green Erin so bould—
Then calmly he lay down, and so slipt his hould!
Then gently he lay down, and slipt his last hould."

Although poor Murphy shuffled off this mortal coil a score of years ago, his memory endures both fresh and green, and it cannot be said that he had lived in vain either, for he served his adopted country faithfully as a soldier during the Civil war, and furnished much pleasant entertainment for his fellow man for many years thereafter.

At a small party given at my residence on a special occasion, the fiddler Dan Horrigan was seated in what proved to be an insecure chair beside the arch between two parlors, so as to be clearly heard in both rooms. To avoid a ponderous couple that came whirling along, the fiddler leaned back and tilted his chair so that it collapsed and let him fall to the floor in a sitting position. Nothing disconcerted, he continued the music without losing a note, or changing his position, to the end of the set. The situation was decidedly comical and no one enjoyed it more than the fiddler himself.

It not infrequently happens that poor performers are the most insistent in displaying their self-conceived talents in public. Of this class was one John McDonald, a detective at police headquarters, who had some rudimentary schooling on the fiddle. One of his pet conceits was that he was quite a musician, but it was not on that account but because of his officious supervision of the dancing platform and his faculty of "calling off" the quadrilles that he was tolerated.

At a picnic held at Willow Springs I observed him preparing to play during a lull in the orchestra. With an impressive swipe he drew the bow, fresh rosined, across the strings, but only a dull rumble was the response. Repeated effort had no better result, while the circling crowd enjoyed his discomforture.

Inspector Shea, it seems had covertly contrived to have Mac's fiddle strings soaped, that being the only practical way to keep him from wasting time that could be used for more agreeable entertainment.

The peculiar hobby of collecting Folk Music followed by a high police official of a great City, seemed so inconsistent with the nature of his duties that it attracted the attention of the press. Occasional mention of our meetings and proceedings awakened an interest in our favorite pursuit, which worked to our advantage, until ultimately we found ourselves the subject of a full page illustrated article in the Sunday issue of the *Chicago Tribune*. This was honor indeed, and it was a welcome recognition of the intrinsic value of our enterprise.

A dramatic sensation originating in comedy, in which the writer was the central figure, took place soon after.

Wearied by a strenuous day at Police headquarters, and needing relief in the outer air, I thought a drive through the outskirts of the City would be advisable. Starting out from the City Hall late in the afternoon, an uneventful tour of the West Division was made, and finding myself a short distance from Sergt. James O'Neill's residence it seemed a favorable opportunity to make a short call. While contentedly scanning the evening papers in the parlor, happy in the freedom of the moment, in through the kitchen rushed a policeman with bulging eyes to announce that the "Chief was assassinated." This was news to me, but I didn't believe it. With a look of terror he precipitately backed out on seeing me, convinced that it was my ghost which appeared to him, and it was with difficulty he told the Sergeant the outlines of the alleged tragedy.

It appears that after my departure from the City Hall evasive answers were given by Secretary Markham to those who inquired for me, instead of saying that I was out on a tour of inspection. Some wag, whose identity was never learned, started the rumor of my assasination and of course the story spread like a prairie fire.

Reporters from all of the daily papers were put on the case, so that when I reached home at eight o'clock they were encountered on the streets, and on the front porch and even in the parlor.

Next morning I found myself favored by the newspapers with an entire front page profusely illustrated. The artists, whose imaginations were given free rein, depicted me with flute and Sergt. O'Neill with violin, in front of a music stand, engaged in playing old Irish airs, while the rest of the police force was trying to discover my mangled remains.

Great interest was manifested by some of our best musicians in learning certain rare tunes which took their fancy, so that scarcely a meeting took place without several new ones being put in circulation. Sunday evenings were generally devoted to this pleasant pastime at our scribe's residence.

One Monday morning I unexpectedly encountered John McFadden in the corridor outside my office door in the City Hall, and wondering what could have happened since we parted the evening before, I asked, "What brings you here so early, John?" "I want to see you privately in your office, Chief," he quietly replied. To my suggestion that we could transact our business just as well where we were as in my office, where so many were waiting, he did not agree, so in we went through three intervening rooms. When the door was closed behind us Mac did not keep me long in suspense. "Chief, I lost the third part of 'Paddy in London' which you gave me last night. I had it all when going to bed, but when I got up this morning, all I could remember were the first and second parts, and I want you to whistle the missing part for me again."

When he left he had it all once more, and he never forgot it either, for it is one of his favorite tunes which is most admired.

Among the coterie which had banded together for the purpose of indulging in the pleasures of Irish melody, there were a few sly jokers, keen of wit and prone to take advantage of the little weaknesses and peculiarities of their associates.

Like some famous prose writers who fondly fancy they excel in poetry, Irish musicians of acknowledged skill in special lines cherish the belief that they are equally proficient in all, and would resent any hint or suggestion from even their dearest friend, that their style or execution left anything to be desired.

Often the anxiety of such persons to demonstrate their fancied abilities only served to emphasize their shortcomings. This the jokers are aware of, so they request, nay, insist, that their prospective victim play one of his favorite tunes. Being vociferously applauded, he is easily led on amid apparently sincere appreciation into playing another class of tunes in which his defects are displayed, while a sly wink and a poke in the ribs here and there indicate their delight at the success of the scheme which lured the unsuspecting musician into exposing his weakest point.

Another type is the amateur or unskilful piper or fiddler whose intense enthusiasm carries him beyond the bounds of discretion in attempting to play in public. Seemingly unconscious of his imperfections, he is easily persuaded by those clever jokers into giving a performance which may be amusing but not entertaining.

By the majority this practice is not approved, although tolerated, for the reason that to discourage or prevent it, would most likely offend those in whose interest it was done, and who could not penetrate the duplicity which induced them to fill a role similar to that of the clown at a circus.

Others again are so captivated by their own playing that it requires no little diplomacy to prevail on them to give somebody else a chance without lacerating their feelings. So impatient and ill at ease are they when another is winning applause that they find some pretext for cutting short his performance and getting the instrument into their own hands.

One of our club members when much younger than he is now lost the valve from the inner end of the blow pipe or mouthpiece of his Highland pipes, but contrived in its absence to prevent the escape of the wind with the tip of his tongue. After a time this expedient became a fixed habit, as he had mastered the art of substituting his tongue for the valve without inconvenience.

When he passed his instrument to some other piper to take a turn at playing, the latter of course furnished much amusement but no music.

This game was played successfully for quite a while, but eventually the joke came to be transferred to the joker. A piper well known to the writer accepted an invitation to attend the funny man's birthday party, but anticipating what was likely to happen he took with him his own set of bellows pipes, all in fine trim, and quietly left them in the hall unobserved.

The honored yet mellow host, after a prolonged spell of

playing on the trick instrument, insisted on his visitor giving them a few tunes. The latter complied, but it was on his own set, instead of the defective instrument which was handed him.

The visitor's performance evoked such favorable comment that the joker felt his reputation slipping away. In the hopes of regaining lost ground he seized and buckled on the bellows pipes, but his lack of familiarity with this method of inflating the bag proved as disastrous to him as the valveless blowpipe did to his victims.

That night's experience cured him of the propensity to enjoy the discomfiture of others, as it brought forcibly to his attention the fact that no one possessed a monopoly of the possibilities of practical joking.

Rivalry and competition generally ending in contests between pipers were quite common in Ireland in the early part of the nineteenth century. No doubt that spirit would be as common and assertive today were there enough Irish pipers in Ireland to create any real competition.

Mention is made by Carleton of a case in which a piper named Sullivan pursued a rival for eighteen months through the whole Province of Munster before he overtook him, and all in order to ascertain, by a trial of skill, whether his antagonist was more entitled to have the epithet "great" prefixed to his name than himself.

It appears that the friends and advisers of Sullivan's rival were in the habit of calling him "the Great Piper Reillaghan," a circumstance which so roused the aspiring soul of his opponent that he declared he would never rest night or day until he stripped him of the epithet "great" and transferred it to his own name.

Sullivan was beaten, however, and that by a manoeuvre of an extraordinary kind. Reillaghan offered to play against him while drunk, Sullivan to remain sober.

The latter, unsuspicious of any plot, and being anxious under any circumstances to be able to boast of a victory over such a renowned antagonist, agreed and much to his surprise was overcome, the truth being that, like O'Carolan on the harp, his opponent was never able to distinguish himself as a performer unless when under the inspiration of whiskey.

Sullivan, not at all aware of the trick that had been played on him, of course took it for granted that as he had been defeated by Reillaghan when drunk, he stood no show against him when sober, and departed during the night, humiliated and crestfallen by this blight to his cherished ambition.

One of our best Chicago Irish pipers, Adam Tobin, is equally fluent on the flute and fiddle, and being of an accommodating disposition, is correspondingly popular. A young lady of his acquaintance had a date with her sweetheart one evening, but the latter being *persona non grata* with her father, how to circumvent the old gentleman's watchfulness and keep him ignorant of her absence, was no simple problem.

The proverbial resourcefulness of her sex did not fail on this occasion, for she hit on a plan which required but Tobin's kindly coöperation to prove successful. Her father was a great lover of Irish pipe music and enjoyed any discussion relating to that or kindred subjects—so she confided her difficulty to the sympathetic Adam and arranged for him to drop in early in the evening, and of course engross her father's attention until she returned from the theatre.

Everything worked out splendidly except that she did not show up at the appointed time. Tobin, however, possessed the loyalty and fortitude of Casabianca and continued playing and arguing until he collapsed from pure exhaustion long after midnight.

But what happened to the fair lady? Nothing much, only that when she got home, she stole quietly in and upstairs to her dormitory unobserved; her mind being so absorbed between the fear of detection and the delights of the evening, that she never thought of the gallant Tobin and his heroic sacrifice.

The musical number on the programme arranged for the night of Dr. Douglas Hyde's address at the Auditorium in 1905 was so disappointing—ludicrous, it might be termed—and out of all proportion to the importance of the occasion, that the idea of allowing the great Apostle of the Gaelic Revival to return to Ireland under false impressions of Irish musical talent in Chicago could not be entertained. As one humiliated Gaelic Leaguer expressed it, "Something should be done to take the bad taste out of his mouth."

The following from the *New World* gives a fair idea of how the genial Doctor came to change his impressions:

A NIGHT IN IRELAND.

"It is doubtful if anything in Dr. Douglas Hyde's experience while in America was so thoroughly enjoyed by him as the "Night in Ireland" arranged by Father Fielding and Chief O'Neill a few days before he left Chicago. Mr. Bernard Delaney's residence on Forest Avenue was chosen as the meeting place, and at the appointed hour the *"Craoibhin"* arrived, accompanied by Father Fielding and Father Fagan of Galway, Ireland. There was no formality observed at that meeting. It was an Irish meeting, pure and simple. The priests were there, as they used to be in olden times in Ireland, encouraging the national music, songs and dances of their country. Pipers and fiddlers of world-wide renown were present, such as Delaney, Early, Tobin and McCormick, Cronin, McFadden, O'Neill and Clancy, men whose names are familiar at the very cross roads in Ireland to-day. The Irish step dancing of Dan Ryan, the Hennessy brothers, and Richard Sullivan were pronounced by Dr. Douglas Hyde to be the best he had ever witnessed. He heard the songs of his native land sung in Irish and English, by Mrs. P. F. Holden and Father Scanlan. Father Green, Father Fagan and Chief O'Neill chatted with him at intervals in Irish. Father Small, who was toastmaster on the occasion, was particularly happy in his remarks on the Irish Irishman, the English Irishman and the American Irishman. Father Fielding played that beautiful descriptive tune called the Modhereen Rua (or Fox Chase), which Dr. Hyde said an Englishman couldn't even whistle if the Almighty promised to endow him with a sense of humor.

In the midst of this unconventional Irish hospitality, the *"Craoibhin Aoibhinn"* sat for hours listening to those men of Erin pouring forth an inexhaustible flood of music, songs and melodies of the motherland. On several occasions he was visibly affected. He was moved to ecstasy at the thrill of his own music heard in a foreign land. No wonder, for a night with those men above named would put a soul under the ribs of death. The *"Craoibhin"* was astonished at the wonderful proficiency of the players and the inexhaustible extent of their repertoire.

There is nothing in art so grand, so thrilling as the irresistible vigor and mighty onrush of some of the reels they played, filled with the hurry of flight, the majesty of battle strife, the languishment of retreat, the sweep of a rallying charge with a laugh at fate, though yet the whole was ever still accompanied by the complaining magic of a minor tone like the whisper of a far away sorrow. Dr. Douglas Hyde enjoyed that "Night in Ireland" and expressed himself as delighted with what he had seen and heard. He thanked all present, particularly Father Fielding, for arranging such a pleasant meeting, and also Chief O'Neill, whom he complimented on his great efforts in keeping alive in a foreign land the jewels of our fathers which were inherited from them beyond the dawn of history and are still entwined with our very heart strings."

A visit to the county of Clare, in 1906, increased materially our store of unpublished tunes, but in order to reach Clashmore House, our destination near Feakle, I was obliged to engage a jaunting car at Killaloe, but made a brief stop at Scariff on the way to see an old acquaintance.

Hospitality being at all times the order of the day in Ireland, I ventured to drink a glass of porter. Had I any suspicion of its acridity, the most fiery beverage would have been taken in preference.

The driver, who had enjoyed his bottle of stout, noticing my distress, explained the causes which led up to it. "You see, sir, the holy fathers gave a mission in Scariff last week, and, begor, they paralyzed the town. No doubt in the world, sir, what you just drank is the first that came out of that kag in a week!"

The vitalizing effect of the Gaelic League agitation in recent years has been felt throughout Ireland from the centre to the sea, and of course Feakle, an old but small town in East Clare, was no exception.

"Paddy" Mack and "Tommy" Hinchy, fiddlers, great in their day, had long since joined the Heavenly choir, and so had the pipers "Mickey" Gill and "Mickey" Burke, better known as "Mehauleen cuis na thinna." An amateur band was organized and in due time acquired enough proficiency to parade on St. Patrick's Day, marching and countermarching on the one main street of the town, cheered on by tumultuous applause.

No one was more conspicuous in the band and prouder of it than Johnny Doyle, who pounded the bass drum, except his father. When the band countermarched, the old man, Michael Doyle, returned to the public house to have another drink in honor of the day and the event, but he never failed to reappear on the street when the rising flood of music announced the band's return.

After a few repetitions of that performance the father seemed to think his son was not putting enough soul into his work, and he determined to remind him of it at the first opportunity.

When the band came within hailing distance on its next approach, the old man, aroused by the inspiration of the beverage he had imbibed and his son's fancied neglect, stepped out in front menacingly and giving vent to his indignation, fairly shouted at the drummer, "Thanam an dhial a vosthard; hit it, why don't you? Is it afraid of it, you are? Bate it in airnest, you caolaun, you!"

The result was electrical, but as the parade came to an end then and there, Johnny didn't have a chance to redeem himself.

Another story in which Michael Doyle was the leading character, although in no way connected with music or song, may be found not less interesting to the general reader on that account.

Mr. Doyle was much given to speculation and frequently indulged in the excitement of cattle jobbing in a small way. He was by no means an aggressive dealer, but walked about unobtrusively at the fairs on the lookout for a bargain in heifers and calves. Emulating the example of the intrepid explorers of old who ventured into distant lands, Doyle decided to attend a cattle fair at Killarney in the county of Kerry, a two days' journey each way, on foot.

When his destination became known all of his friends from the country around were on the tiptoe of expectation, to hear from him on his return all about Killarney—that wonderful place of world-wide renown—that miracle of picturesque grandeur which defied the power of pen to describe.

Now here was Michael Doyle, their neighbor, trafficker and traveler, actually feasting his eyes on the sublime scenery. What a treat it would be to hear his story, and how they would enjoy the description of nature's magnificence by one who saw and could tell them all about it.

"Yerra, how are you, Michael? And you're looking well after your long journey." "I suppose you must be tired." "How did you make out?" Such were the greetings which assailed him on every side. Hardly waiting for replies to those formal questions, his callers continued: "Killarney must be a wonderful place entirely, Michael, by all the accounts we heard of it. I suppose you traveled it all; the lakes and the castles and the abbeys and everything. Tell us what you think of it."

"Well, then," replied the traveler, ruefully, "they can all say what they like about it, but there's wan thing I can tell ye: Killarney is a dom bad place to buy a chape calf!"

The wonderful skill and proficiency of the classes of youthful dancers, who competed for prizes at the Munster *Feis* in the City of Cork, which I attended in the summer of 1906, was a delight and a revelation. It had never been my good fortune to witness anything even approaching the grace, rhythm, precision, and uniformity of their performance on either side of the Atlantic.

They were a credit to their instructors as well as to themselves.

'Tis very true they were not worried by the introduction of any unfamiliar tunes, for "Tatter Jack Walsh," "Miss McLeod," and "The Rights of Man"—jig, reel, and hornpipe respectively, with monotonous repetition, served for all occasions.

Before the dancers came upon the stage, the piper, a handsome fellow, who I understood was the forceful and moving spirit in the music revival, occupied the centre of the stage, and ostentatiously tuned his instrument in full view of the wondering audience. The round, full, organ tones of the regulators, which the man of music industriously fingered, had roused the awed assemblage to the highest pitch of curiosity and expectation, when out from the wings tripped the blushing boys and rosy colleens to take their places.

Of course they nearly filled the stage, so the piper, in an apparent spirit of accommodation, swung around to one side behind the drapery so adroitly that only his legs and knees, with the wonderful Irish pipes resting thereon, were visible to the audience.

With commendable promptness the dancers and the expectant onlookers, many of whom had traveled far to enjoy and encourage the revival of traditional Irish music, were treated to a "tune on the pipes"? No, sad to relate, but on a French celluloid flageolet which the piper deftly extracted from an inside pocket.

The mute but conspicuous Irish or Union pipes placidly reposing on the piper's knees, Mr. Wayland told me, were an old set of the Egan make, that were a full tone below concert pitch. As they could scarcely be heard distinctly above the drumming of the dancers on the platform, he prudently adopted the expedient described.

The Irish were always noted for their drollery and humor, and this incident but serves to show they have not deteriorated in that respect, even when apparently unconscious of their mirth-provoking absurdities.

While visiting Mr. Rowsome, an excellent Irish piper and pipe maker in Dublin a week later, in strolled John Cash, the aged piper from Wicklow County, who had come all the way to play at the Mansion House reception in connection with the annual Leinster *Feis*.

A well-built and corpulent man he was, deliberate in speech and movement, and well past the scriptural limit in years. After fortifying himself with a generous stimulant he "put on the pipes," a set as wheezy and antiquated as their owner, but his weary and uncertain manipulation of them in the effort to play "*Nora Chreena*," with concords on the regulators, showed all too plainly that age and affliction had unstrung the nerves and broken the spirit of the old bard. In his dignity and helplessness, John Cash was a truly pathetic figure.

In the midst of the stream of gay humanity which entered the Mansion House next evening came John Cash, carrying his instrument in the traditional green bag under his arm.

At the ball which succeeded the reception by the Lord Mayor and Douglas Hyde, the orchestra, which consisted of three fiddlers and an amateur Irish piper, and John Cash, were stationed on a platform which commanded a good view of the ball room.

Several numbers were danced without the intervention of the Wicklow piper, although he had always tuned up and appeared anxious to co-operate. The manager, a bright young fellow, it was noticed, always found some pretext for keeping him out of it, although he was permitted to occupy a place among the musicians as a concession to his age and profession.

Impatient and ill at ease, poor Cash repeatedly essayed

to play, but the resourceful manager as often found means to restrain him, the result being that he never got an opportunity to identify himself with the programme while I was present.

The attitude and movements of Mr. Andrews, the young piper, were all that could be desired, but not a note from his instrument could be heard from any position which the writer could reach, including the balcony immediately above him. The combined tones of the three violins had drowned out the weak voice of the chanter.

Among the dancers a few men wore the ancient saffron-colored kilts. One of them, a lithe young fellow, carried a set of war pipes lately come into fashion again, but there was no indication that their use in a musical way was contemplated.

Here were two Union pipers in the orchestra and one war piper among the dancers; yet the only music to be heard was furnished by three fiddlers. This condition of affairs could hardly have been intended as a joke; still, the situation was not altogether wanting in certain elements of Irish humor and pleasantry.

One could not help becoming reminiscent, taking into consideration the importance of the occasion and other circumstances. And this was in the very heart of the one-time "Land of Music and Song"—the country renowned above all others for the excellence of its music and musicians.

When we come to think of it as the Glorious Green Erin which produced the celebrated bards, Rory Dall O'Cahan, O'Conallon and O'Carolan, and such famous harpers as Gerald O'Daly, Cornelius Lyons, Cruise, Miles O'Reilly, John and Henry Scott, Heffernan, Murphy, Hempson, O'Neill, Fanning, Higgins, Quin, Carr, and

Rose Mooney, we are amazed at the musical degeneracy of our day.

Besides the harpers, there were in those times great Union pipers, whose celebrity extended beyond the confines of their native land—such as Jackson, "Parson" Stirling, Talbot, Gaynor, Ferguson, Crump, Coneely, Gandsey, and a host of others.

We may derive some qualified pleasure in contemplating the prominence of Irishmen by birth or blood who have achieved fame in the world of music in more recent times.

Many scaled the heights of distinction, but their compositions are cosmopolitan and not national. Neither do their productions give promise of a revival of those characteristic Irish strains—typical of Gaelic temperament—which most strongly appeal to the sentiments and aspirations of a regenerated Ireland.

> "Hail, Music, goddess of the golden strain!
> Thy voice can spread new blessings o'er the plain;
> Thou the sad heart can cheat of all its cares,
> And waft soft soothings on thy melting airs;
> Bend the rude soul to wish the gentle deed
> At pity's touching tale to bleed;
> Thy magic can the noblest aims inspire,
> And bid pale terror feel the hero's fire.''

CHAPTER XII

SKETCHES OF EARLY COLLECTIONS OF IRISH MUSIC

"The bards may go down to the place of their slumbers,
  The lyre of the charmer be hushed in the grave,
But far in the future the power of their numbers
  Shall kindle the hearts of our faithful and brave.
It will waken an echo in souls deep and lonely,
  Like voices of reeds by the winter-wind fanned.
It will call up a spirit of freedom, when only
  Her breathings are heard in the songs of our land."

ANCIENT Irish history and literature abound with allusions to music, musicians, and musical instruments, long centuries before the printer's art was invoked to diffuse and perpetuate the melodies for which Ireland had been so renowned.

Although the English and the Scotch had preceded us in one field of activity—the collection and publication of their national melodies—it is at least gratifying to our national pride to be able to claim that an Irishman, William Bathe, a native of Dublin, while a student at Oxford, was not only the first to print an English treatise on music, but that he formulated methods of transposition and sight-reading, that may still be studied with profit, according to Grattan Flood. This work, entitled *A Brief Introduction to the Art of Music,* was "Imprinted at London, anno 1584."

Coincident was the publication of *A Handefull of Pleasant Delites by Clement Robinson and others*—Containing *sundrie new sonnets, newly devised to the newest music.* This was the earliest work containing printed music of which there is any record, and we are told by several authorities that it included a few Irish tunes, one of which, "Calen o custure me," has been discussed in the chapter on "Curious and Incomprehensible Titles."

It is now nearly two hundred years since the first printed collection of Irish tunes came from the press. In the year 1726 there was published in Dublin by J. & W. Neale, of Christ Church Yard, a little volume bearing the modest title, *A Book of Irish Tunes,* and another called *A Collection of Irish and Scotch Tunes.*

Several books of Psalms and Psalters appeared before this date, Grattan Flood asserts; but as Folk Music, and not church music, is our subject, the question of priority requires no further consideration.

Neglect on the part of the Irish to collect and publish their songs and music was taken advantage of by our acquisitive kinsmen, the Scotch, much more than by the English, because the music of Ireland and Scotland was fundamentally the same up to within comparatively recent time; and it was owing to this circumstance that the origin or ownership of so many melodies, claimed by different countries, has been the subject of interminable disputes since the beginning of the nineteenth century.

Moore, Hardiman, Bunting, Petrie, Grattan Flood and Adair Fitz Gerald have submitted convincing evidence in support of the Irish contention, and it is no less gratifying to us than honorable to our opponents that such able Scotch writers as Farquhar Graham, editor of Wood's *Songs of Scotland,* and Alfred Moffat, author of *The Minstrelsy of Scotland* and *The Minstrelsy of Ireland,* concede the justice of many of the Irish claims.

One of the earliest manuscript collections of music in

the "Three Kingdoms," and which includes several Irish airs, was compiled by William Ballet, a Dublin actor, about the year 1594. It is known in musical bibliography as *William Ballet's Lute Book*, and is preserved in the library of Trinity College, Dublin. It was the source from which William Chappell obtained many of the tunes in his *Old English Popular Music*.

Two years later *A new Booke of Tabliture containing sundrie easie and familiar instructions, etc., on the Lute, Orpharion, and Bandora* was printed at London for William Barley.

Many works of a similar nature soon followed, including books of "Ayres," but it was not until 1650 that any great collection of music without words was undertaken. In that year John Playford commenced the publication of *The English Dancing Master—or Plaine and easie rules for the dancing of Country Dances, with the tune to each Dance, London. Printed by John Playford at his shop in the Inner Temple, neere the Church doore, 1651*.

Editions of this work containing many Irish tunes continued to be enlarged and issued down to the year 1725.

Another of Playford's many publications was entitled *Musick's Handmaid*, printed in 1678.

Of Scotch manuscript collections, the most important are the *Skene manuscripts*, 1615-20, and the *Straloch manuscripts*, 1627, now preserved in the Advocates' Library, Edinburgh.

That enterprising English publisher, John Playford, becoming interested in Scotch music, compiled and published the first printed collection of Scotch tunes, entitled *A Collection of Original Scotch Tunes (full of the Highland Humours) for the violin—Being the First of this Kind yet Printed. London, 1700*. This was a small oblong book of but sixteen pages, of which only one original copy is known to exist.

The Orpheus Caledonius or a Collection of the best Scotch Songs set to Music was printed in London in 1725. A volume named *Music for Allan Ramsay's Collection of Scotch Songs* followed in 1726, and *Oswald's Caledonian Pocket Companion,* in twelve serial volumes, was issued from 1742 to 1764.

The foregoing statement concerning English and Scotch collections of music is introduced for the purpose of showing that, being much earlier in the field, English and Scotch collectors had a decided advantage of the Irish in this line of activity, the inevitable result being that, having our melodies or tunes in their books, they have a *prima facie* case in their favor; while the Irish claim to ownership, if not supported by documentary or other convincing evidence, fails to be established.

Even such noted tunes as "St. Patrick's Day" and "Garryowen" first appeared in English and Scotch collections. The former was included in Rutherford's *Two Hundred Country Dances,* issued in 1748, and it was introduced in the opera *Love in a Village* in 1762. Under the name "St. Patrick's Day in the Morning" it was printed in Aird's *Selection of Scotch, English, Irish and Foreign Airs,* volume 3, published at Glasgow, c. 1788.

"Garryowen" first came into notice, Moffat tells us, through having been played in a pantomime called *Harlequin Amulet,* produced in 1800. In a few years thereafter it appeared in several Scotch and Irish collections.

Who would question the Irish origin of the air to Moore's song, "The Harp That Once Through Tara's Hall"? Yet it was included in William McGibbon's *Collection of Scots Tunes, Book 2,* published in Edinburgh in 1746, under the name "Will You Go to Flanders?" That was forty-six years before Bunting obtained a setting of the air as "Molly My Treasure" from Fanning, the Mayo harper, in 1792, although he did not print it until 1840. Sheridan introduced the air in *The Duenna*, set to the stanza commencing "Had I a heart for falsehood framed." As "My Heart's Delight," a dance setting of it was printed in Charles and Samuel Thompson's *Country Dances for 1775*. From that year until 1807, when Moore utilized it, "Gramachree" (phonetic Irish for "Love of My Heart") is to be found in many printed collections, sometimes set to "The Banks of Banna" or "As Down on Banna's Banks I Strayed," and sometimes to a ballad called "The Maid in Bedlam."

Two verses of the old song commencing "Will you go to Flanders, my Molly O?" are preserved in David Herd's *Ancient and Modern Scottish Songs,* printed in 1776.

Although the air is generally admitted to be Irish, the Scotch are slow to relinquish their claim, based on the circumstance of its being printed in Scottish collections long before the Irish made any pretensions to its Irish origin.

The question naturally arises, How did those disputed airs come to be known in Scotland? The explanation presents no difficulties when we realize that Irish harpers were in the habit of making touring visits to Scotland for centuries. Mention is made in history of two occasions in the year 1490 when Irish harpers played at the Scottish Court at the King's command.

In the preface to the *Select Melodies of Scotland,* Thomson, the publisher, says: "Some airs are claimed by both countries, but by means of the harpers or pipers who used to wander through the two, particular airs might become so common to both (Ireland and Scotland) as to make it questionable which of the countries gave them birth."

It does not appear that any of the older Irish airs were committed to writing until the close of the seventeenth or the commencement of the eighteenth century, but that they were formerly handed down by one generation of harpers and pipers to another, according to Farquhar Graham.

We have seen that the first printed collections of English music appeared in 1584, of Scotch music in 1700, and of Irish music in 1726. For the future my remarks will be confined to collections of music exclusively or mainly Irish.

In connection with the early printing of Irish music in Dublin, the authors of *A Handbook of Irish Dance* mention John and William Neale, also Neale, Neill and O'Neill. The works published by the former have already been named, so that obviously *A Collection of Country Dances,* issued about the same date, must be credited to the latter. In addition to the volumes before mentioned, John and William Neale published *The Beggar's Wedding* in 1728 and *Polly,* another opera, in 1729.

Various dates ranging from 1727 to 1730 are given as the time when Daniel Wright published *Aria di Camera, being a choice collection of Scotch, Irish and Welsh airs for the Violin and German Flute.*

It may be as well to state here that I am indebted to Grattan Flood's work, *A History of Irish Music,* Dublin, 1905, for the names and dates of several of the works referred to in this article, not being so fortunate as to have copies of all of them in my library, while at the same time announcing that it contains some few others not mentioned in Dr. Flood's lists.

The Vocal Miscellany, a London publication, was reprinted in Dublin in 1738. Its contents must have been singularly barren of Irish tunes, for its name has not been quoted in any subsequent publications, as far as can be remembered.

The writer owns to a certain pride in possessing splendid copies of those extremely rare volumes published by Mr. Burk Thumoth about 1742 and 1745.

The first of these is entitled *Twelve Scotch and Twelve Irish Airs, with Variations, set for the German Flute, Violin or Harpsichord by Mr. Burk Thumoth. London. Printed for & sold by H. Thorowgood at the Violin & Guitar under the North Piazza of the Royal Exchange.*

The twelve Irish airs are designated as follows: "Ailen Aroon," "Yemon O Nock," "Past One O'Clock," "Chiling O Guiry," "Slaunt Ri Plulib," "The Major," "Drimen Duff," "Curri Koun Dilich," "McCreagh's Irish Tune," "Hugar Ma Fean," "The Irish Cry," and "Jigg to the Irish Cry." The meaning of those absurd names has been explained in a previous chapter. The last named may be easily identified as the original of "Murphy Delany," although Alfred Moffat tells us the latter was evolved from "The Priest in His Boots," a tune printed in C. & S. Thompson's *Compleat Collection of 120 Favorite Hornpipes,* 1765-77.

The title to the second volume is *Twelve English and Twelve Irish Airs with Variations,* etc., etc. This little volume also was *Printed in London for J. Simpson at the Bass Viol & Flute in Sweeting's Alley opposite the East Door of the Royal Exchange.*

The Irish airs in "Book the Second" are: "Balin a mone," "The Rakes of Westmeath," "Molly St. George," "My Nanny O," "Da mihi Manum," "Planks of Connaught," "The Dangling of the Irish Bearns," "The Irish Ragg," "Thomas Burk," "Plea Rorkeh na Rourkagh," "The Rakes of Mallow," and "The Fin Galian's Dance."

Bound in with this collection was *The Ladies' Pocket*

Guide or The Compleat Tutor for the Guitar, published by David Rutherfoord in London, 1755.

There was a small collection of O'Carolan's compositions issued in 1747. As many as six new editions of this work appeared from time to time up to the beginning of the nineteenth century.

The edition issued in 1779 bore the descriptive title, *A Favorite Collection of the so much admired Old Irish Tunes. The original and genuine of Carolan, the celebrated Irish Bard.*

Whether McLean's *Selection of Twenty-two Original Airs,* published at Dublin in 1771, were exclusively Irish or partly Scotch, we are unable to say.

A volume of Jackson's *Celebrated Irish Tunes,* published by Edmond Lee at Dublin, 1774, won immediate popularity and was reprinted three times.

Jackson, at that time famous, was a man of considerable property and lived in the vicinity of Ballingarry, County Limerick. Equally celebrated as a musician and composer, he was known all over Ireland as "Piper" Jackson, on account of his remarkable skill as a performer on the Irish or Union pipes, his favorite instrument. This renowned musician and "Parson" Stirling, of County Antrim, also a famous piper, are said to have been the last who composed Irish tunes and airs in the ancient traditional style.

Originally, all Jackson's compositions bore his name in the titles, such as "Jackson's Rambles," "Jackson's Frolics," "Jackson's Morning Brush," etc., etc. In course of time the composer's name was in most cases discontinued for the sake of brevity, and not infrequently entirely new names were substituted.

Probably the most popular of his tunes which still retain his name is the double jig, "Jackson's Morning Brush," first printed in the collection above mentioned.

It was one of the airs in the opera, *The Agreeable Surprise*, 1781, and it appears as one of the numbers in Thompson's *Country Dances for 1779*. It was also included in Aird's *Selection of Scotch, English, Irish and Foreign Airs*, 1782. Under the name "Such Beauties in View" it was printed in a scarce collection of Old Irish Airs called *The Bee*, published in Dublin, *circa* 1820. Edward Bunting, who obtained a setting of "Jackson's Morning Brush" from a piper in 1797, waited until 1840 to include it in his *Ancient Music of Ireland*. Under the caption, *Author and Date,* is printed "Jackson, County Monaghan, 1775." This seeming contradiction is explained by the fact that Jackson owned estates in both counties.

What the *Hibernian Catch Book,* published at Dublin in 1775, consisted of, cannot be stated, as no reference to it has been encountered except in Grattan Flood's list.

In the year 1786 there appeared from the press that monumental work quoted by all subsequent writers on Irish music: *Historical Memoirs of the Irish Bards interspersed with anecdotes of and occasional observation on the Music of Ireland; also an Historical and Descriptive Account of the Musical Instruments of the Ancient Irish, and an Appendix containing several Biographical and other papers, with the Select Irish Melodies.* By Joseph C. Walker, Member of the Royal Irish Academy.

In addition to the author's essays on the Bards, etc., chapters are devoted to "Inquiries Concerning the Ancient Irish Harp," and the "Style of the Ancient Irish Music," by the Revd. Dr. Ledwich, and "An Essay on the Poetical Accents of the Irish," also "An Essay on the Construction and Capability of the Irish Harp," by William Beauford, A. M., both noted antiquarians.

The magnificent volume, *Walker's Irish Bards,* so called,

was the first work in which Irish music and all that pertains to it, including musical instruments, are treated of scientifically by competent authorities.

The *Hibernian Muse,* which included many of O'Carolan's productions, appeared in 1787. Strangely enough, it was published in London, not by Irishmen, but by S. A. and P. Thompson, brothers, of Scotch birth or ancestry.

Many rare or forgotten Irish tunes, as well as Irish airs from the operas, *The School for Scandal; The Poor Soldier; Love in a Camp; Robin Hood; The Duenna; Rosina; Fontainebleau; The Agreeable Surprise,* and *The Castle of Andalusia,* are to be found in this splendid work.

In 1791 Brysson's *Curious Selection of Fifty Irish Airs* made its appearance. A version of one of them, called "The Dandy O," was the air to which "Eveleen's Bower" was set; but it must not be forgotten that there was an entirely different air of that name, now best known as "The Young May Moon," Tom Moore's love-song.

This was followed in 1794 by Cooke's *Selection of Twenty-one Favorite Irish Airs,* but, not having a copy accessible, the contents cannot be discussed.

Gaudry's *Masonic Songs* were published at Dublin in 1795, and Holden's *Masonic Songs* in 1798; but what bearing such compositions may have on Irish Music cannot be estimated at this date.

The most important step in the preservation and perpetuation of Irish Folk Melodies was taken by Edward Bunting in the publication of his first work, *A General Collection of the Ancient Irish Music,* which he brought out in 1796. It consisted in a great measure of those National treasures which he noted down from the playing of the best harpers in Ireland at the great meeting held

Edward Bunting.

THE NEW YORK
PUBLIC LIBRARY

ASTOR, LENOX AND
TILDEN FOUNDATIONS

at Belfast in July, 1792. Sixty-eight melodies were published in this volume. As church organist at Belfast, Bunting had but a limited acquaintance with native music; but English as he was by descent on his father's side, the charms of traditional Irish melody so fascinated him after his experience with the harpers that he made tours through the north and west of Ireland, and even engaged others to aid him in the search for unpublished melodies.

The result of this zeal took form in the publication of his second collection, comprising seventy-seven additional airs. Both collections were arranged for the pianoforte, and several of the numbers in the latter volume, being accompanied with verses, were also arranged for the voice.

Certain of Bunting's theories and opinions are criticised by Farquhar Graham, editor of Wood's *Songs of Scotland*, and even by his friend Dr. Petrie. The assertion that "a strain of music once impressed on the popular ear never varies" is so palpably erroneous that he furnishes the evidence to refute it in the same volume.

"A Soft, Mild Morning," obtained from Hempson, the great harper, in 1796, is but a variant of "I Am Asleep and Don't Waken Me," scored from the same harper's playing, in 1792. "The Bonny Cuckoo," obtained from Mr. Joy at Ballinascreen and printed in his third collection, closely resembles "The Little and Great Mountain" in the first collection. "O Southern Breeze," published in volume 2, is simply an inferior setting of the air named, "Why Should Not Poor Folk," in volume 3. "The Blossom of the Raspberry," in the first collection, is "The Captivating Youth" in a different key printed in the second, and there are several other instances in Bunting's own collections where variants of the same strain are published as distinct airs.

All through the writer's personal experience as a collector of Irish Folk Music, variants without number are constantly obtruding.

Elsewhere Dr. Petrie has been quoted as saying that he rarely if ever obtained two settings of an unpublished air that were strictly the same, though in some instances he had gotten as many as fifty notations of one melody.

Encouraged by the generous Dr. Petrie, who furnished him with many of his best selections, and finally spurred on by the latter's threat to publish a rival collection, Bunting gave to the world in 1840 his third and greatest work, *The Ancient Music of Ireland arranged for the pianoforte, to which is prefixed a Dissertation on the Irish Harp and Harpers. including an account of the Old Melodies of Ireland*.

The contents of this beautiful and instructive work, comprising, besides historical and descriptive text, one hundred fifty-one numbers, with the sixty-eight and seventy-seven numbers in the first and second volumes respectively, amounting to two hundred ninety-six in all, constitute a magnificent and enduring monument to the skill, industry and patriotism of Edward Bunting.

With the exception of the great and unselfish George Petrie, the contemporary of Bunting, and Dr. P. W. Joyce, whose labors in behalf of Irish Folk Music death alone can terminate, song writers and publishers have been content to avail themselves of the mine of melody conveniently at hand as a result of the labors and researches of others.

Bunting's work, the fruit of nearly half a century's diligence, made Moore's *Irish Melodies* possible, for it was from that source the majority of the airs were selected, although Dr. Petrie and Smollett Holden also generously contributed melodies from their collections. "There can be no doubt that to the zeal and industry of Mr. Bunting his country is indebted for the preservation of her ancient National airs," Moore acknowledges in the preface to his *Melodies.* "They were the mine from which the workings of my labors as a poet have derived their lustre and value."

Collections and publications galore of Irish airs and songs have been rained on the public since then, but the monotony of their contents displays the aversion of their authors and editors to any tunes or airs except those which may be safely pirated or appropriated from the works under discussion.

Bunting complained bitterly of the misuse made of the airs in his first collection by Sir John Stevenson and Tom Moore, who altered them to suit their songs, and bewails the fruits of his labor, caught up as soon as they appeared, to be sent forth again in dress so unlike their native garb.

But to return to the subject. O'Farrell, a famous performer on the Irish bagpipes, who played in the pantomime of *Oscar and Malvina* at London in 1791, compiled and published in 1797-1800 a work in two small volumes, entitled *O'Farrell's Collection of National Irish Music for the Union Pipes, etc., with a Treatise for the most Perfect Instruction ever yet published for the Pipes.* This notable work was supplemented by four more volumes produced in the years 1804-10 and named *O'Farrell's Pocket Companion for the Irish or Union Pipes.* All six are small oblong books neatly printed but cheaply bound.

The settings with variations of many of the tunes indicate that the author was a musician of taste and talent and fertile fancy. A pioneer in publishing music suitable for the once popular Irish pipes, he was also distinguished as being the author of the only competent instructions ever printed for that instrument, although two others—Fitzmaurice, of Edinburgh, in 1805, and O'Flannagan, of Dublin, in 1833—published collections of tunes for the Irish or Union pipes also.

About this time a Belfast enthusiast named Mulhollan published a book of *Irish and Scots Tunes*. Next year, 1805, Miss Owenson favored her country with *Twelve Hibernian Melodies*.

Smollett Holden, a collector of some distinction, came out about the same time, 1804-6, with two volumes entitled *Old Established Irish Tunes,* which were followed closely by Hime's *Selection of the Most Admired Original Irish Airs,* never before printed, 1805-8. Utterly at variance with its promising title, this volume is only remarkable for not containing a single air which had not been already printed, according to Alfred Moffat.

Holden's later publication, *Periodical Irish Melodies,* printed in 1808, is a work of more than ordinary importance, being quoted frequently by Alfred Moffat in his *Minstrelsy of Ireland*.

Crosby's *Irish Musical Repository,* published in London in 1808, preserves quite a few Irish tunes not to be found in other works. "Denis Delaney," an excellent jig in three strains, for instance, being one of them.

Scarcely a year has passed since 1771 without the appearance of some work containing more or less Irish music, although we are discussing only those devoted to Irish melodies almost exclusively.

After Crosby's publication came *A Collection of Irish Airs and Jiggs with Variations, by John Murphy, performer on the Union Pipes at Eglinton Castle,* in 1809; Mulhollan's *Ancient Irish Airs* and *Powers' Musical Cabinet,* in 1810, and Hime's *Collection of Country Dances,* from 1804 to 1814, and then Tom Moore came upon the stage and overshadowed all others.

The publication of Moore's *Irish Melodies* may be regarded as the beginning of a new era in Irish Music and Song.

"Music's the cordial of a troubled breast,
The softest remedy that grief can find;
The greatest spell that charms our care to rest,
And calms the ruffled passion of the mind."

CHAPTER XIII

SKETCHES OF COLLECTIONS OF IRISH MUSIC, COMMENCING WITH MOORE'S MELODIES; ALSO MISCELLANEOUS COLLECTIONS CONTAINING IRISH MUSIC

> Music, oh how faint, how weak,
>   Language fades before thy spell!
> Why should feeling ever speak
>   When thou can breathe her soul so well?
> Friendship's balmy words may feign,
>   Love's are ev'n more false than they;
> Oh! 'tis only music's strain
>   Can sweetly soothe and not betray.

THE first numbers of Moore's *Melodies* were published in the year 1808, and the last in 1834. No work of a similar character in any country achieved such widespread popularity. Unnumbered editions, from cheap to sumptuous, have been and still continue to be printed, and so great has been its repute that the work has been translated into six continental languages.

The *Melodies* of Moore, according to Mooney, the Irish historian, worked miracles in the National sentiment. Their melody and passion awoke the soul of Ireland from the torpor of slavery.

O'Connell felt the sentiment growing up around him which Moore's poetry created, and never failed to point his speeches against tyranny, with the stings supplied, in endless profusion, by the accomplished bard.

The music of Ireland from this date began to revive

rapidly. It was introduced into the theater in overtures and musical interludes. Even the regimental British bands studied and played it. The Connacht Rangers marched to the battleground of Waterloo to the inspiring strains of "Garryowen" and "St. Patrick's Day"—and history does not record that any of them fell from shots in their backs in that memorable conflict.

Overcoming prejudice, Moore's *Melodies* were sung in every drawing-room and charmed every circle; and it is no exaggeration to say that their instantaneous and enduring popularity has had no parallel in musical history.

Oblivious of the swelling tide of Irish tunes and airs, the Edinburgh publisher, George Thomson, compiled and printed in expensive style *A Select Collection of Original Irish Airs* in two folio volumes, 1814-16. For this work *Symphonies and Accompaniments for the Pianoforte, Violin & Violoncella* were composed by Beethoven. Many of the so-called original airs had been previously printed in Burk Thumoth's *Irish Airs, The Hibernian Muse,* and in Bunting's First and Second Collections. It is doubtful if more than one-half of Thomson's sixty airs were new to students of Irish melody.

Fitzsimon's *Irish Minstrelsy,* edited by Dr. Smith, came from the Dublin press in 1814-16, also.

The good work continued to prosper, for an enthusiast named Kinloch produced his contribution to the cause— *One Hundred Airs, Principally Irish*—in 1815-17.

A Selection of Irish Melodies, which, we are informed by an antiquarian bookseller, was called *The Bee,* was printed in Dublin, without date. The title-page of the writer's copy of this interesting little work is missing, but the contents are diversified and include the music of many songs by Lover and other noted writers. Altogether, this is a most attractive publication; but, from its containing exactly two hundred tunes, and from other circumstances, I am inclined to believe it is Clinton's *Two Hundred Irish Melodies for the Flute,* printed in 1840.

After a delay of ten years, Holden again woos the public favor with a third collection of *Favorite Irish Airs,* Dublin, 1818.

An examination of McCullagh's compilation, *A Collection of Irish Airs for the Flute, Violin and Flageolet,* three volumes, 1821, reveals nothing but the airs in Moore's *Melodies* arranged in duets.

In the same year O'Callaghan's *Collection of Irish Airs* first appeared, but as writers on Irish minstrelsy make no allusion to the work, its value is problematical.

In the year 1825, *The Irish Minstrel; or a Selection from the Vocal Melodies of Ireland,* containing one hundred three numbers with songs by contemporaneous poets, was published in Edinburgh by R. A. Smith.

Departing from tiresome yet time-honored precedent, the editor introduced many nice Irish airs not included in Moore's *Melodies.* Powers, the Dublin publisher, caused the work to be suppressed for an infringement of copyright. The copy in my library is highly prized—not for its rarity alone, but for its intrinsic merit.

Egan's *National Lyrics* appeared in 1826, and from that date until 1840, when Bunting's last collection was printed, nothing new in the way of Irish music was introduced to the public except the final number of Moore's *Irish Melodies.*

The year 1840 was prolific in the publication of collections of Irish Folk Music. Besides Bunting's work, which has been previously discussed, Clinton's *Two Hundred Irish Melodies for the Flute* and Alexander's *Flowers of the Emerald Isle* came from the press.

In the following year, Frederick Nicholls Crouch, the

composer of "Kathleen Mavourneen," published *Celebrated Songs of Ireland,* and Clinton again came out with an additional volume entitled *Gems of Ireland—Two Hundred Airs Arranged for the Flute.*

This neat volume, while reprinting many airs from Moore's work, is redeemed from monotony by the inclusion of selections from O'Carolan's and O'Connallon's compositions, as well as many nice tunes not generally known.

Dr. W. E. Hudson edited forty-three airs and dance tunes from his own private collection, printed in volumes 3 and 4 of *The Citizen,* a monthly magazine published in Dublin in the years 1840 and 1841. A technical and instructive sketch of each tune is given, and it is much to be regretted that lack of public support ultimately forced a suspension of his praiseworthy undertaking.

Presumably impelled by sincere love of the native music of his country and zeal for its preservation, Dr. Hudson essayed to continue the publication of the periodical under a new name, viz., *The Dublin Monthly Magazine.* The same fatal apathy of the people rendered abortive his commendable effort, after an issue of eight numbers—January to August, 1842, inclusive. Twenty-nine melodies were printed with this set, among them being "O'Connell's Welcome to Clare," "The Leaves So Green," a quaint version of "The Wild Irish Boy," and several others to be found only in this volume.

In the writer's library, besides a complete set of the periodical mentioned, there is an oblong volume of manuscript Irish music, on the fly-leaf of which is written the compiler's name and address, "Henry Hudson, 24 Stephen's Green." The volume, which contains one hundred thirty numbers, is neatly written, with most of the names in English and Irish. Although microscopic, the writing is distinct and legible, and an index, in the same diminutive hand, meets all requirements. From the identity of the surname and tunes, close relationship must exist between the compiler and Dr. Hudson, the musical editor of *The Citizen*.

Fitzgerald's *Old Songs of Old Ireland* was published in 1843, and in 1844 Frederick William Horncastle favored us with *The Music of Ireland,* a work of considerable importance, often referred to by Alfred Moffat in his *Minstrelsy of Ireland*.

Horncastle has been mentioned as an English musician, on account of his being the leader of Queen Victoria's Sacred Choir; but in *British Musical Biography* we find that he is an "Irish composer and organist of Armagh Cathedral, and afterwards a Gentleman of the Chapel Royal." We are further informed that "He compiled *The Music of Ireland* as performed at Horncastle's Irish Entertainments." The renown which he won by his talents in this field of endeavor can be judged by the following extract from the *London Sun* of October 18, 1844:

"Mr. Horncastle, of the Queen's Chapel Royal, has published a volume entitled *The Music of Ireland,* a collection of beautiful, perhaps matchless, melodies. The service which the composer has rendered to music, and even to ethnology, by the preservation and publication of those exquisite relics of ancient science and refinement, is enhanced by his judicious as well as reverential abstinence from attempts at improving perfection. In this respect he stands very much above his predecessor in the same field, Sir John Stevenson, for he at once admits that the old music of Ireland as it is found is not the wild effusion of a rude and simple people, but is the production of a school in a high degree methodized, skillful and cultivated. The Irish *caoine,* according to Mr. Horncastle, is a noble

LATER AND MISCELLANEOUS COLLECTIONS

and most expressive piece of music. Those *caoines* serve as examples of the most beautiful harmonic composition, and prove beyond doubt that music in those early ages was in the highest state of cultivation."

Lynch's *Melodies of Ireland* appeared in 1845. This thin folio volume is elaborately arranged, yet scarcely anything new or novel can be found among its one hundred twenty numbers. The index differs but little from that of Moore's *Melodies*.

Henderson's *Flowers of Irish Melody*, in two volumes, followed in 1847.

The first edition of that highly interesting work, O'Daly's *Poets and Poetry of Munster*, was published in 1849. This popular production, including songs in Irish and English, with music, was the result of painstaking and intelligent research in a long-neglected field, and public appreciation is well exemplified by the rapidity with which three editions were disposed of in two years. Equally gratifying was the popularity of a new and enlarged edition which appeared in 1860.

Surenne's *Songs of Ireland, Music Without Words*, printed in 1854, is practically a compilation extracted from Moore's *Melodies,* although it contains a few tunes not included in that work.

An exceedingly rare and curious little book is *The Emerald Wreath,* by Professor White, Mus. Doc., printed by subscription in Dublin, 1852, but the number of tunes printed therein (in green ink) is very limited.

Having accumulated about two thousand traditional Irish airs, marches, jigs, reels, hornpipes, laments, lullabies, etc., including duplicates and variants, while traveling through Ireland in the performance of his professional avocations, George Petrie, LL. D., R. H. A., V. P. R. I. A., foreign member of the Imperial Society of Antiquaries of Scotland, Copenhagen, etc., etc., was elected president of a

"Society for the Preservation and Publication of the Melodies of Ireland," founded in Dublin in the year 1851. The list of officers of this imposing organization included one "Most Noble Marquess" and six Right Honorable Lords and Earls. All of the twenty-three Council members were distinguished gentlemen, titled to the point of distraction, and so were the "Honorable Treasurer" and "Honorable Secretaries."

A splendid folio volume, the result of Dr. Petrie's four years of incessant labor, entitled *The Petrie Collection of the Ancient Music of Ireland, Volume 1*, appeared in 1855. The music was harmonized and the text descriptive of each of the one hundred forty-seven tunes in this welcome volume was of absorbing interest to the musical student. Yet this work, originated under such auspicious circumstances, fell far short of the success anticipated by its promoters. Why? The answer is simple: Public indifference, the blight of all such undertakings.

Pianofortes were not numerous in Ireland in those times; therefore harmonized music was not in phenomenal demand. The great majority of musicians among the peasantry were either self-taught or received instruction orally instead of from printed music; consequently the publication of Irish music has seldom been a profitable enterprise, and it is only the irresistible fascination of the subject which sustains those who devote much valuable time to the indulgence of a hobby which, like virtue, is predestined to be its own and oftentimes its only reward.

A small supplement comprising thirty-six airs was issued in 1882, long after Dr. Petrie's death, which occurred in 1866, but there was never a second volume.

It was left for the "Irish Literary Society of London" to revive the project and accomplish the publication of the Complete Petrie Collection, at the instigation of Alfred

George Petrie

LATER AND MISCELLANEOUS COLLECTIONS. 253

Perceval Graves, a forceful member of the organization and the son of Rev. Charles Graves, D. D., F. T. C. D., V. P. R. I. A., one of the original Council in 1851.

In the meantime Dr. Petrie's manuscripts had been lost sight of, and only by diligent search on the part of Sir Villiers Stanford were they discovered. The total number of tunes amounted to two thousand one hundred forty-eight, of which more than five hundred are duplicates or slight variants, according to Dr. Stanford. Besides those tunes, there are scattered references in the manuscripts to eighteen other pages, of which no trace can be found.

No inconsiderable portion of the Petrie collection was made up from private collections, whose owners unselfishly permitted him to copy.

New editions of the popular favorite, Moore's *Irish Melodies,* arranged by Glover, and by Balfe, came from the press in 1859; but this did not deter other modest enthusiasts from contributing their mite to the cause.

Gems from Ould Ireland, by Ogden, and *Old Songs of Old Ireland,* by Wellington Guernsey, appeared in 1860. Born at Mullingar, County Westmeath, Guernsey was also a poet and composer. The old-time favorite, "I'll Hang My Harp on a Willow Tree," was one of his productions.

Davidson's *Irish Melodies* and Hughes' *Collection of Irish Airs* followed in 1861, and in 1865 Arthur O'Brien published *Old Songs of Ireland.*

It will be noticed that the titles of all collections or publications mentioned so far indicate the nature of their contents. Melodies, Airs, Songs, etc., monopolize their pages to the almost utter exclusion of Dance tunes which are no less characteristically Irish and popular.

In looking over Bunting's three volumes of nearly three hundred numbers, covering a period of forty-four years, we find but three jigs, so called. No mention is made of either reel or hornpipe, or even the ancient *Rinnceadh Fada,* or Long Dance. Lamentations there are in plenty, and an occasional lullaby adds a little variety to the gloom.

The tone of Dr. Petrie's collections made among the peasantry is more cheerful and optimistic. His pages are happily diversified with all varieties of Dance tunes, but not by any means to the extent one would expect to find in collections of Irish music assembled under such favorable conditions. We must not overlook the fact, however, that much of our Dance music is not ancient, but a development having the old airs and marches for its basis.

It is worthy of remark that this apparent neglect or indifference on the part of Irishmen in Ireland was first remedied by an Irishman settled in London. His baptismal and ancestral name was Richard Michael O'Shaughnessy, and "his father before him" was a famous musician.

R. M. Levey's *Collection of the Dance Music of Ireland,* comprising two hundred tunes, unclassified, in two volumes, were published in London in the years 1858 and 1873, respectively. The tunes were obtained from street players, mainly, and the extent of supervision or discrimination exercised in their arrangement can be judged from a footnote: "This is the only tune I have at all interfered with. Three different fiddlers persisted in ending in the major key. When I played it as it is now set, ending in the minor, they were very much shocked, and I confess I made the change unwillingly."

This work is well printed, harmonized, and certainly "filled a longfelt want."

But what, in the name of all that is good and patriotic, could have induced the talented editor to substitute the Hebrew cognomen Levey for O'Shaughnessy, the grand old patriarchal surname of his ancestors in Iar Connacht? Perhaps, after all, like many another Irishman, he found it advisable, in the chilly atmosphere of Cockneydom, to sacrifice pride to expediency.

Coincident with Levey's first collection, another Irish exile, P. M. Haverty, of New York, who by the force of his talents added to the lustre of his patronymic, began the publication of the notable work, *Three Hundred Irish Airs.* They were issued in three parts of one hundred numbers in each, and included also marches, lullabies and dance tunes. Neither preface nor classification was attempted— a strange omission for a work so expensively printed and bound. Much of the contents was derived from *Moore's Melodies.*

In the year 1873, P. W. Joyce, LL. D., M. R. I. A., published his *Ancient Music of Ireland,* a volume consisting of one hundred folk tunes, with descriptive text, not included in previous publications.

This was followed in 1887 by *Irish Music and Song,* a collection of songs in English and Irish, set to well-known airs.

Dr. Joyce's last and greatest work, *Old Irish Folk Music and Songs,* came from the press this present year, 1909. It was published under the auspices of "The Royal Society of Antiquaries of Ireland," of which he himself is president. Besides his own collections it includes the *Forde* and the *Pigot* collections, which each had compiled and hoped to personally publish, when death intervened to prevent the fruition of their purpose. Although purporting to be entirely new, it is no reflection on the work to remark that a sixth of its contents, more or less varied and mostly under different titles, had been previously published.

Molloy's Songs of Ireland appeared also in 1873, and Hoffman's *Selections from the Petrie Collection,* arranged for the pianoforte, were published in 1877.

It is with pleasure we enumerate the productions of

Alfred Perceval Graves, that charming poet and literary leader in Ireland's regeneration, viz.: *Songs of Old Ireland*, 1882; *Irish Songs and Ballads*, 1873; *The Irish Song Book*, 1895; *Irish Folk Songs*, 1897; and *Songs of Erin*, printed in 1901, all with music little of which had been previously published.

Of the great work done and being done by Joyce and Graves in bringing to light and wedding to worthy songs so many of our neglected melodies, in a series of books, only limited mention can be made in a sketch of this character. It is quite probable that, like their predecessors in this line of human endeavor, the birth of due appreciation will succeed their death, when some later Boswell will arise to do them justice.

One of the most interesting collections of Irish songs with music is *The School and Home Song Book* for use in Irish schools, selected and arranged by P. Goodman, Professor of Music in Central Training College and Model Schools, and St. Patrick's Training College, Dublin, published without date.

More than ordinary interest attaches to Professor Goodman on account of his being the son of the amiable and respected Rev. Canon Goodman, of Skibbereen, County Cork, a famous Irish piper. Manuscript collections of local melodies and tunes made by the revered musician during a long life have been deposited in some museum in Dublin.

A very creditable and unique undertaking, which should encourage imitation, is *Songs of Uladh*, printed in Belfast in 1904. An advertisement on the fly-leaf tells the whole story: "These old airs were collected in Ulster, the words written, and the illustrations drawn in the same province by three Ulster youths. The printing has been done in Belfast, and all the blocks made there. The paper was made at Ballyclare, in the County of Antrim. The work is, therefore, essentially a home product."

Few collectors of Irish music knowingly included the melodies of other countries in their published works. Whether this exclusiveness was a matter of principle or resulted from a superabundance of native material, the fact remains that Irish collections are singularly free from foreign compositions. Our canny kinsmen on the other side of the North Channel have been admittedly acquisitive in appropriating Irish tunes which took their fancy.

As accusations of this nature invite resentment, it may be just as well to produce at least some evidence in support of the statement. From Chappell's *Old English Popular Music*, volume 2, page 210, the following is extracted:

"Burns and George Thomson confess in their published correspondence to have taken any Irish airs that suited them."

The author in a paragraph too long for quotation condemns the Scotch writer Stenhouse for his plan of claiming "as Scotch every good tune that had become popular in Scotland."

In correspondence with his publisher, George Thomson, in the year 1793, Robert Burns, the Scottish poet, says: "Your Irish airs are pretty, but they are downright Irish. If they were like 'The Banks of Banna,' for instance, though really Irish, yet in the Scottish taste, you might adopt them. Since you are so fond of Irish music, what say you to twenty-five of them in an additional number? We could easily find this quantity of charming airs. I shall take care that you shall not want songs, and I assure you that you would find it the most salable of the whole."

Mr. Thomson admits the desirable qualities of the Irish airs in his reply to the celebrated poet. "We have several true born Irishmen on the Scottish lists," he confesses, "but they are now naturalized and reckoned our own good subjects. Indeed, we have none better."

Farquhar Graham, editor of Wood's *Songs of Scotland*, concedes the Irish origin of many of the airs to the songs in that work.

Although risking the possibility of exhausting the reader's patience, the writer would not be justified in bringing this article to an end without some allusion to other English and Scottish collections of music in which Irish airs or tunes were also included.

Playford's Dancing Master, a work commenced by John Playford, a London publisher, in the year 1650, continued to be printed in editions of great variety until the year 1725. A wonderful work for those times, it included many Irish tunes and is an enduring monument to its founder. Playford issued several other musical publications, but none achieved more lasting fame than *Wit and Mirth, or Pills to Purge Melancholy*, first printed in 1699. Several successive editions appeared before 1719, when Tom D'Urfey took charge and published an edition in five volumes. It was in the enlarged work that Irish tunes first appeared, and it was known thereafter as D'Urfey's *Pills to Purge Melancholy*.

Names of a strikingly grotesque phraseology were much in vogue in those days.

A few years before, in 1716, J. Walsh published the first volume of *The Merry Musician, or a Cure for the Spleen—Being a Collection of the most diverting Songs, and Pleasant Ballads set to Musick*. The fourth and last volume of this famous work was issued in 1733.

The first volume of Oswald's *Caledonian Pocket Companion* appeared in 1743, and the twelfth and last in 1764. Oswald, who was a music teacher, compiled other collections, but the *Pocket Companion,* which was in thin octavo books, included many vagrant Irish tunes.

A work entitled Rutherford's *Two Hundred Country Dances* was published in 1748-9, and Thompson's *Two Hundred Country Dances* followed in 1765. McDonald's *Collection of Highland Airs* appeared in 1784.

A work called *The Musical Miscellany, a Select Collection of the Most Approved English, Scots and Irish Songs, Set to Music,* was first printed at Perth, Scotland, in 1786. Two years later a new and enlarged edition of it was printed at London in which a new name, *The Calliope,* was prefixed to the original title.

One of the most important and comprehensive collections of music ever printed is known as *Aird's Selections,* the full title being *A Selection of Scotch, English, Irish and Foreign Airs.* This work consisted of six small oblong volumes of 200 tunes each, issued serially from 1782 to 1797. Some choice Irish airs as well as a large number of Irish jigs, reels and hornpipes, many of them unknown to the present generation, are to be found scattered through the pages. While I have seen no mention of the work except in *British Musical Biography,* 1897, I possess two volumes of this collection, "Humbly Dedicated to the Volunteer and Defensive Bands of Great Britain and Ireland, printed and sold by John McFadyen, Glasgow."

The *Edinburgh Musical Museum,* two volumes, 1792-3, is *A Collection of the Most Approved Scotch, English and Irish Songs Set to Music.*

The *Vocal Magazine,* 1797-9, is said to contain some Irish airs, and so does *The Scots Musical Museum,* published 1787 to 1803.

All of the various Collections of Country Dances issued almost yearly up to the beginning of the nineteenth century contained Irish tunes.

A few years ago the writer secured from an 'antiquarian book-dealer in the City of Cork a valuable work named *The Repository of Scots and Irish Airs, Strathpeys, Reels, etc.* Printed and sold by A. McGoun, Glasgow. In general character, variety, and excellence of its contents, it is decidedly superior to all others of that period, at least. One of the Irish airs has as many as nine variations and several have four and even more. A remarkable circumstance is the fact that no mention is made of the collection by writers, who so frequently allude to other similar works of far less importance. The date of publication is said to be 1799 or 1800.

Another extremely rare work not mentioned by musical writers is, *A Pocket Volume of Airs, Duets, Songs, Marches, etc., Selected from the Works of Eminent Masters and Carefully Adapted to the Flute or Violin*, Dublin, published by Paul Alday, two volumes, *circa* 1800. Many of the Irish airs are extended to pages of variations.

That the gentle art of advertising was not unknown in those days is well illustrated by the publisher's note at the end of the index to the first volume. "P. Alday, at his Musical Circulating Library, No. 16 Exchange Street, is at all times provided with Flutes and Violins of every description by the most approved Makers, and is constantly assorted with every Musical Publication, and all things in the smallest degree appertaining to the Business. Likewise hires out, tunes and repairs All Instruments with the utmost care and dispatch."

A nameless collection of forty-eight pages which includes sixteen Irish airs is bound in with Alday's volumes.

Crotch's *Specimens* appeared in 1801; *The Musical Repository of Scotch, English and Irish Songs, Edinburgh*, in 1802; Abram McIntosh's *Collection of Airs* in 1807; Fraser's *Highland Airs* in 1808 to 1812; *The National*

LATER AND MISCELLANEOUS COLLECTIONS 261

Melodies of England and Ireland in 1812; and Campbell's *Albyn's Anthology* in 1816-18.

There is but one Manx collection which includes Irish tunes, viz., *Mona's Melodies*.

A rare and interesting work is, *A Companion to the Ball Room, Containing a Choice Collection of the Most Original and Admired Country Dances, Reels, Hornpipes, Waltzes and Quadrilles, &c., &c., with Appropriate Figures to Each—The Etiquette—And a Dissertation on the State of the Ball Room*. By Thomas Wilson, Dancing Master from the King's Theatre—Opera House, London, 1816. This work contains many old Irish jigs, chiefly of the variety called Slip Jigs or Hop Jigs, although jigs are not mentioned in the phenomenally long title. A frontispiece displaying the positions of the dancers in the various dances is no doubt of considerable historical interest.

The Thrush and *The London Minstrel*, published in 1820 and 1825, respectively, are small but neat volumes, each containing "A Collection of Esteemed English, Irish and Scotch Songs, Glees, Duets, etc., Set to Music."

In the same class may be placed Plumstead's *Beauties of Melody, a Collection of the Most Popular Airs, Duets, Glees; Also a Collection of the Best and Most Approved Irish Melodies, Interspersed With Many of the Beautiful Scotch, Melodies, etc., etc., Words and Music, London, 1827*.

Two magnificently engraved large paper volumes entitled *Alexander's Select Beauties for the Flute* and *Alexander's Miscellaneous Beauties for the Flute,* published in London, no date, include many Irish airs, some of which are embellished with variations.

The last compilation which will be considered under this classification is R. Cocks & Co.'s *Encyclopedia of Melody. One Thousand and Twenty-one Airs Selected from the*

National Music of All Countries, etc., etc. Arranged by William Forde, two volumes, London, no date.

In this tastefully engraved work, Irish Music is generously represented, and it is not easy to understand why a publication of such scope and merit should remain hitherto unnoticed in musical literature.

Private collections of Irish tunes no doubt existed before J. & W. Neale published the first printed collection, and the practice of accumulating compilations of that nature has been a favorite hobby with some musicians down to the present day. Almost every musician, and particularly those who taught others, rejoiced in the possession of collections of manuscript music, often heirlooms in the family. Many such collections are mentioned by Dr. Petrie as the sources from which a great number of his tunes were obtained.

An enormous, well-bound volume of that character was submitted for inspection to the writer recently as a special favor. Of folio size and hefty bulk, its contents numbering many hundreds included Irish, Scotch and English tunes. Though browned by age, the compiler's name and address, "John O'Brien, Dublin, 1798," were distinctly legible. By the compiler's granddaughter, Mrs. Scott, born in West Virginia, it is treasured as the most precious of her possessions.

It must not be assumed that the works mentioned in this article (though the list is a long one) are all that include Irish music among their contents. Surprises may always be expected, for books of which we had not previously heard are still being discovered and brought to our attention.

We can claim with confidence, however, that no important collection of Irish music has been overlooked, and when we come to consider the immensity of Hibernia's musical remains embalmed in scores of publications, the reason why Irish collectors and publishers refrain from trespassing on the musical preserves of other nations ceases to be a matter for surprise or speculation.

> "Angel of music, when our finest speech
> Is all too coarse to give the heart relief,
> The inmost fountains lie within thy reach,
> Soother of every joy and every grief;
> And to the stumbling words thou lendest wings
> On which aloft the enfranchised spirit springs."

CHAPTER XIV

THE DECLINE OF IRISH MUSIC AND CERTAIN CAUSES THEREFOR

"O wake once more! how rude soe'er the hand
  That ventures o'er thy magic maze to stray,
O wake once more! though scarce my skill command,
  Some feeble echoing of thine earlier lay;
Though harsh and faint, and soon to die away,
  And all unworthy of the nobler strain;
Yet if one heart throb higher at its sway,
  The wizard note has not been touched in vain;
Then silent be no more! Echantress wake again."

It has been shown in preceding chapters that many airs and tunes of Irish origin were included in Scotch and English collections of popular music long before the first collection of Irish melodies was published in Ireland. This circumstance cannot but be regarded as significant of the esteem in which Irish music was held beyond Hibernia's verdant shores centuries ago. The early appreciation of Irish music by other peoples, however flattering to our racial vanity, when contrasted with national neglect, may be construed as a serious reflection on our patriotism.

We have the testimony of Welsh historians as to the state of musical science in Ireland in the tenth and eleventh centuries. Giraldus Cambrensis, Brompton, and John of Salisbury, in the twelfth; John de Fordun, in the thirteenth; Friar John Glyn, in the fourteenth; Polydore, Virgil, and John Major, in the fifteenth; Galilei, Bacon,

ANCIENT IRISH MUSICAL NOTATION, WITH A TRANSLATION INTO THE MODERN SCALE.

Stanihurst, Spencer, and Camden, in the sixteenth centuries; besides, modern writers without number speak of the phenomenal development of music in Ireland, and the incomparable skill of her musicians in their day. As there seems to be no dissenting voice, it would be a waste of time to advance arguments to sustain an uncontested position; so the question naturally arises: what are the prevailing causes which led to the gradual decline of Ireland's musical eminence?

It will be remembered that in the early centuries the bards outranked the "principal nobility and knights," being permitted by law to wear six colors, which was only one less than that worn by the royal family. Many were attached to families of distinction, but wherever they were or went, they were the recipients of honors and gratuities. There came a time, however, succeeding the incursions of the Normans, when the bards and harpers were persecuted by the agents of the government, as inimical to English interests. The Statutes of Kilkenny, enacted in 1367, forbade the Irish minstrels to enter the Pale and made it an offence against the law to give them shelter or entertainment.

At the very commencement of the fourteenth century, they were subjected to persecution by Sir John Stanley, then Lord Lieutenant of Ireland. Intermittent persecution they suffered for successive centuries, ranging from confiscation of their property and belongings, with imprisonment for life, in the reign of Henry the Sixth, to hanging, by Lord Barrymore on the orders of Queen Elizabeth, who, by the way, kept an Irish harper on her staff for personal entertainment. Although she has been reprobated for bloodthirstiness in the suppression of the bards and harpers in Ireland, where their abundance it is claimed was not an unmixed blessing, she was at least consistent to the extent of suppressing them by less rigorous means in England as well.

Gosson, in his *Short Apologie of the Schoole of Abuse,* published in 1586, says: "London is so full of unprofitable pipers and fiddlers, that a man can no sooner enter a tavern than two or three companies of them hang at his heels to give him a dance before he departs." By an act passed in the 39th year of her reign "Minstrels wandering abroad" were held to be "rogues, vagabonds and sturdy beggars," and punished as such. As a result of these drastic methods of discouraging minstrelsy and music, the bardic order began to decline; and when their friends and patrons were impoverished by the confiscation of their lands, the condition of the harpers and minstrels who had escaped the gallows was far from enviable.

The feudal system which had so long prevailed in Ireland received a severe blow from Elizabeth, which was repeated by Cromwell, and fatally reiterated by William the Third. The pride of the chieftans was humbled and many of their castles razed. Some of these unfortunate men fled to the Continent; others submitted to the English yoke. In those halls which formerly resounded with the voice of minstrelsy and song and barbarous magnificence, Walker in his *Historical Memoirs of the Irish Bards* tells us, there reigned a death-like silence and a dread repose.

The adventurers upon whom the confiscated lands had been bestowed were indifferent, if not hostile, in most cases; and the bards were no longer entertained in the families of the great, nor treated with wonted respect. They degenerated into itinerant musicians wandering from place to place and offering to play for hire—sometimes sprightly tunes for a dance at a "Patron" and sometimes raising the solemn dirge at a Wake. Very naturally the decline of the harp kept pace with the fall of the bards, and the taste for the old airs embellished with graces and variations waned with it.

When the House of Hanover succeeded to the British throne, musicians were imported from Italy to London, and Italian music began to reign with despotic sway in the great city. Its influence reached across St. George's Channel, Irish music became deranged, and our sweet melodies and native musicians fell into disrepute; but as our musical taste is scientifically rectified, the pleasure we derive from pure melody is lessened, and the ear is so far removed from the heart that the essence of music cannot reach it.

The following extract from the Rev. Fordyce's *Sermons to Young Women,* early in the eighteenth century, may not be out of place in connection with this change in musical taste: "This wonderful charm of melody, properly so called, together with the whole merit of expression, is sacrificed as we frequently find, to the proud but poor affectation of mere trick and execution; that instead of rendering the various combinations of sounds, a powerful instrument of touching the heart, exciting agreeable emotions, or allaying uneasy sensations, as in the days of old, it should be degraded into an idle amusement, devoid of dignity, devoid of meaning, absolutely devoid of any one ingredient that can inspire delightful ideas or engage unaffected applause."

Italian music became the rage in the middle of the eighteenth century, and the fair dames of Dublin learned to expire at an opera. Concerts were the favorite amusements in the houses of the nobility and gentry, and musical societies were formed in all the great towns in the Kingdom. Walker tells us that "Politics, gaming, and every species of dissipation had so blinded the finer feelings of their souls that their warm devotion to music at length degenerated into cold neglect."

How true among the Irish today is that author's remark in 1786, "Music, however, is sometimes the subject of conversation amongst us, and is still cultivated by a few, but it is no longer a favorite topic, nor a favorite study."

After the death of O'Carolan, the last of the bards, and the subsidence of that enthusiasm which his charming compositions had produced, Bunting says the condition of the harpers had gradually declined. Persons of the better class had not for a long time adopted native music as a profession. Still the harpers of the genuine old school had not altogether disappeared from the tables and entertainments of the gentry of native Irish family, but the decadence of music and the decrease in musicians awakened regret and aroused a desire to restore both to their due place in public esteem.

Four distinct efforts with this commendable object in view were undertaken within a term of fifty years. The first was originated by a patriotic Irish gentleman residing in Copenhagen, named James Dungan, who had conceived the idea of instituting annual meetings at his native town Granard in the County of Longford. For this purpose he remitted sufficient funds to defray expenses and award premiums at the first meeting, which took place in 1781. Seven harpers only attended in this instance. Nine responded in the succeeding year, and two new names were among the competitors at the third and last meeting, which Mr. Dungan himself came all the way from Denmark to attend.

His presence attracted a large audience, including many persons of rank, from forty miles around, but the meeting appears to have been marred by private jealousies, which so disheartened the generous originator and patron, that he did not afterwards attempt a renewal of those interesting assemblies.

A few years later, 1791, some prominent music-loving inhabitants of Belfast issued a circular, inviting subscriptions to be applied to the promotion of an attempt to revive and perpetuate the ancient music and poetry of Ireland. How pathetic was the language of their address can be judged from the following extract: "They are solicitous to preserve from oblivion the few fragments which have been permitted to remain as monuments of the refined taste and genius of their ancestors."

Ample funds were contributed and ten harpers responded to the call to assemble at Belfast in July, 1792. Edward Bunting, organist of St. Stephen's Chapel, Belfast, was selected to note down as many as possible of those musical treasures which might perish with their venerable repositories. Prizes were awarded and all competitors were lavishly entertained by Dr. McDonnell, the prime mover of the enterprise.

The third attempt at reviving Irish music was initiated by the formation of the Belfast Harp Society in 1807. This organization engaged Arthur O'Neill, a prize winner at all contests, to instruct a number of indigent and blind boys, who were supplied with board and lodging. Like many modern undertakings of a patriotic and philanthropic nature, the harp school flourished—for a time—but in consequence of the decline of pecuniary supplies it came to an end in 1813; but Arthur O'Neill, the blind teacher, was paid a liberal annuity until his death by a few generous members of the society, in consideration of his abilities and creditable conduct in the school.

A considerable fund had been collected for the founding of a harp society in Dublin some time previously, but nothing else was accomplished. The disposition of said fund is not a matter of record.

A fourth and final effort to rescue the national instrument from extinction was strangely enough made by a number of spirited noblemen, mainly of Irish birth, residing in India. Remittances amounting to eleven hundred pounds, or fifty-five thousand dollars, were forwarded to Ireland for the establishment and maintenance of a school for harpers.

Rainey, nephew of Robert Burns, the poet, one of Arthur O'Neill's pupils, was placed in charge and the school prospered for a few years, but the death of the teacher and the exhaustion of the funds hastened the inevitable ending, early in the year 1840.

In commenting on the deplorable outlook for the continuance of the harp school, John McAdam says: "We might probably keep up the society for a few years longer by private subscription. Our gentry in Ireland are too scarce and too little national to encourage itinerant harpers, as of old; besides, the taste and fashion of music no longer bears upon our national instrument; it had its day, but, like all other fashions, it must give way to novelty." Well said and truly. The passion for discarding the old, and taking up the new in music, operates as persistently today as in 1839, when McAdam penned those lines.

English state papers abound with records of pardons granted to imprisoned pipers who had been as assiduously jailed under Elizabeth and her royal predecessor as they have been inconsiderately discountenanced and suppressed by the clergy in the nineteenth century. Severe measures in dealing with certain abuses and excesses were no doubt justifiable and necessary in some cases. Yet the wisdom of indiscriminate suppression of music and dancing is open to question; and there be many even among clergymen, who, at this late day, are decidedly favorable to the regeneration of both.

It is at least a hopeful sign, when a Jesuit father presides at an entertainment given by juvenile classes of dancers and choral singers, at the Moore anniversary in Chicago, in 1910. Their performance was appreciated and applauded by an audience which taxed the capacity of Orchestra Hall, and so favorable was the impression made on clerics and laics, that the movement first encouraged by Father McNulty bids fair to extend.

However much we may be inclined to criticize and deplore the result, we must allow that the policy of the Irish clergy was extremely moderate, as compared with the drastic methods of certain Scotch divines, who proclaimed with pride that they had "burnt the last bagpipe or fiddle in the parish."

In the language of Duncan Fraser, "The attitude of the Free Church in the Highlands towards all forms of innocent amusements, including piping and dancing, has much to answer for. It has taken all the color out of the people's lives, and at the close of the day the tired workers have nothing to look forward to but dreary theological discussions, fittingly carried on in blinding peat-reek."

Almost every parish had its patron saint, whose birthday was in olden times a holiday, celebrated with great festivity. Those days, in time, came to be called "Patrons." On such occasions it is recorded that not only the people of the parish, but the neighbors far and near, assembled together dressed in their very best clothes. The older people never failed to enter the church yard and offer up prayers for the dead, particularly if any among their own connections happened to be buried there. The place selected for the festivity was usually a large common, about which tents were erected, and there was plenty of eating and drinking, with an accompaniment of fiddling, piping and dancing.

Mrs. Anne Plumptre, who traveled in Ireland in 1814-16, says these meetings sometimes ended in scenes of riot and disorder, when ancient quarrels which had been slumbering broke out again. For this reason, the attendance of the priests was discontinued in the year 1780, but the "Patrons," much changed in character, were maintained for nearly a century thereafter.

The original festivities were of a very ancient date, religious in character, and bore little resemblance, except in name, to the Sunday afternoon diversions of later years, in which athletics had its votaries, as well as music and dancing. I may be pardoned for digressing from the subject to state that many of the world's most famous athletes had their mettle tested at those weekly contests among the peasantry; and it is a noteworthy coincidence that the majority of the record makers were born and bred in the southern provinces, where their prowess was discovered and developed at the Sunday "Patrons."

In considering the diverse causes which contributed to the decadence of national music and customs in Ireland, we must place no little responsibility on the ravages of famine, which devastated the country for years in the middle of the nineteenth century. Musicians and their friends alike were swept away by starvation and pestilence, and those who survived were in no frame of mind to play or appreciate any strains but those expressive of despair or lamentation.

At least two bishops and certainly many of the clergy, both Catholic and Episcopal, bore enviable reputations as pipers. Disguised as Irish pipers or Highland pipers, priests, in the Penal days, evaded the bloodhounds of the law, visited their scattered flocks and administered extreme

THE PIPER.
Without Patronage.

unction to the dying. Revd. Charles Macklin was described by Lady Morgan as "a marvellous performer on the Irish bagpipes—that most ancient and perfect of instruments." From Grattan Flood we learn that the reverend musician was dismissed from his curacy for playing a solo on the pipes while his congregation was filing out of church after the service. The late lamented Canon Goodman of Skibbereen, in the County of Cork, was a piper of note; and such was his love of the music of his country, that he devoted much time to forming a manuscript collection of it. Among the clergy are many proficient musicians, and, by the way, such a thing as footing a neat step or two, learned before ordination, in the seclusion of the home of intimate friends, is not an unheard of proceeding.

Irish literature abounds with passages illustrating the friendliness existing between the priests and the people in their social relations in former times. Whence came the changed attitude of the clergy to those simple entertainments, which may be regarded a national institution? No one at this day seems to be able to tell. The poor musicians, blind or crippled, deprived of their livelihood, became a burden on their friends, or took final refuge in the poorhouses. Their calling is now nearly obsolete and it can be easily perceived that many of their tunes did not long survive them.

No defensible reason has been assigned for the hostility of the Irish priests to music and dancing, as practiced for centuries, but the interests of morality. The millennium is not yet here, and we are still far from the attainment of human perfection. The Irish are a moral race at home and abroad, but their reputation for virtue has not been acquired in the nineteenth century. Neither is there any such noticeable change in Irish character as would justify the suppression of the time-honored pastimes of a whole people, on the score of improved moral conditions, when we take into consideration that all such festivities were conducted publicly in the open fields, or among friends and neighbors, at the farm houses. It is not apparent what objectionable features could have been connected with such diversions, seeing that the waltz and other grappling dances, discountenanced by the church, were not in vogue in Ireland.

After all, the commendable qualities of the Irish were at least as pronounced when music and song throughout the length and breadth of the land served to punctuate and relieve the weary monotony of peasant life, as they are now, after the harper and piper, and it may be said fiddler, have followed the Irish elk and wolf dog into extinction.

Who can read the impassioned and despairing appeal of the learned Eugene O'Curry, author of the *Manners and Customs of the Ancient Irish*, and other works, without feeling that the Irish people by their exasperating indifference have also much to answer for.

"Oh! why do not Irishmen cultivate, encourage, cherish and hoard up in their innermost souls, the priceless treasure of never-failing consolation and delight afforded by their matchless music, if but worthily understood and performed? Why have we banished to contempt, to poverty, and to the pauper's grave, the ever good-humored and often talented, though in their neglected state, but too ill-instructed, wandering professors of this, the proudest remnant of our ancient inheritance? And why, may not I also ask, has not Dr. Petrie been supported in the effort lately made to bring out his great collection of ancient airs? How is it that there could not be found in all Ireland, as many subscribers of a pound a year, for two or three years, as would bring out a yearly volume of this splendid collection? Oh, while it is not yet too late, let me even here entreat the co-operation of my countrymen in securing its completion before that peculiarly gifted man, who has spent the greater part of a long life in collecting it, is snatched away from us forever. It is little you know him, but I know him well, and I do not hesitate to say that when you have once lost him, you shall never again look upon his like. How unlike the English! How immeasurably unlike the Scotch! There is scarcely in all Scotland, from the thrifty and well taught laborer and mechanic, up to the lordliest duke, a man in whose home volumes of the noble music of his native country, as well as of every scrap of national poetry or song, in Gaelic and English, that from time to time issues from the active press of his country, may not be found."

It was all in vain. Dr. Petrie was not sustained in his efforts. After the publication of one volume, in 1855, the undertaking was abandoned. He died in 1866, and no one at all comparable to him in versatility of talent, and unselfish devotion to the intellectual interests of his native land, has since appeared to take his place, and it is extremely doubtful if there ever will.

Although the race of pipers is evidently doomed, the fiddler family, which continues to thrive and multiply, occasionally produces a real genius, who, overcoming the limitations of modern musical training, develops a taste for Irish music with the ability to give it proper swing and expression. Instead of the aid and encouragement, which talented novices have a right to expect from Irish musicians of mature years and more or less prominence, who loudly bewail the decline of Irish music, they are unfortunately treated with indifference if not open hostility as possible rivals.

In their little fools' paradise of self-conceived superiority, most self-taught or untaught Irish pipers and fiddlers look with disdain—nay, even scorn, on aspiring students of Irish music who have had a modern musical education.

This illiberal attitude which chills ambition and paralyzes effort, is to no inconsiderable degree among the chief agencies responsible for the decline of Irish Folk Music, at least in modern days.

> "Mute, mute the harp—and lost the magic art,
> Which roused to rapture each Milesian heart,
> In cold and rust the lifeless strings decay,
> And all their soul of song has died away;
> Fallen is the bard, his glory prostrate lies,
> Crushed in the wreck of years, no more to rise,
> Oft on these shores they bade the youth advance,
> With measured footsteps to the martial dance;
> Or with solemn slow majestic tread,
> The holy circuit of the round tower led,
> Or when the hills with sacred splendor bright,
> Hailed every star, and bless'd the God of light;
> In loftier tone their hallowed numbers flow'd,
> And poured to Heaven the spirit-breathing ode,
> Love, pity, rapture, all the world of soul,
> Dwelt in their touch and owned their bland control.
> Then first in glory, as in worth, they moved,
> By nations honored, and by monarchs loved;
> E'en kings themselves have mixed the bards among,
> Swept the bold harp, and claimed renown in song."

CHAPTER XV

THE PAST AND FUTURE OF IRISH MUSIC

"From the pastoral cot and shade
Thy favorite airs, my Erin came,
By some obscure Beethoven made,
Or Handel never known to fame!
And hence their notes, forever warm,
Like nature's self, must ever charm."

NOTWITHSTANDING the many evidences of a growing interest in the revival of Irish music coming to our notice in recent times, it may be well to inquire whither are we drifting, and to consider if there is really any future for distinctively Irish music. It has had unquestionably a glorious past—a renown unequaled by the music of any other nation from the early centuries until comparatively recent times. It had a character and an individuality all its own. To describe in words its peculiarities has often foiled the most skilful pen, yet to anyone having an ear for music, the recognition of an Irish strain presents no difficulties.

"The Irish music is in some degree distinguished from the music of every other nation," remarks Walker in his *Historical Memoir of the Irish Bards*, "by an insinuating sweetness which forces its way irresistibly to the heart, and then diffuses an ecstatic delight that thrills through every fibre of the frame, awakens sensibility and agitates or tranquilizes the soul. Whatever it may be intended to excite, it never fails to awaken."

After quoting the above in the introduction to *The Hibernian Muse*, printed in 1787, the Thompson Brothers (publishers also of *The Caledonian Muse*) add for themselves: "Abating something for national partiality, a great degree of excellence must be allowed to the plaintive airs, and a wonderful glee and vivacity to the jigs. We have hinted on a former occasion that the Scots probably derived a great part of their music from the Irish, and there is reason to think that the Welsh were indebted to the same masters."

Since the extinction of the bardic order, Irish music has stagnated or declined, while the cultivation and development of music in Continental Europe, and particularly in Germany, has made tremendous strides. "A people hunted like wolves, as the Irish have been by their barbaric neighbors, for the last three hundred years," says Mooney, the historian, "could not have practiced the nice and minute rules necessary to keep up a good musical school; they were not able to progress according to the rapid development of musical science in other happier nations." Modern music has overshadowed and practically obliterated the music of the olden time, and to such an extent has musical taste changed that aspiring musicians of the rising generation look with indifference, if not disdain, on the Folk Music which fascinated their parents. Ireland from a remote period had been celebrated for its cultivation of music. One of the most certain criteria of the antiquity of a nation is its being possessed of a native or original music. Dr. Brown in his famous essay on *Poetry and Music* says, "Most countries peopled by colonies which after a period of civilization have issued from their native soil, possess no characteristic music of their own; that the Irish, Welsh and Scotch are strictly natives, and accordingly have a music of their own; that the English, on the contrary, are a foreign mixture of lately established colonies and in consequence of this have no native music."

Giraldus Cambrensis, a Welsh prelate, familiar with the music of his country and intimately acquainted with the fine arts in general, writing in the year 1185, gives a striking account of Irish music at that period. "The attention of this people to musical instruments I find worthy of commendation, in which their skill is beyond comparison, superior to that of any nation I have seen; for in these the modulation is not slow and solemn, as in the instruments of Britain, to which we are accustomed, but the sounds are rapid and precipitate, yet at the same time sweet and pleasing." The above is but a mere extract from a comprehensive description of Ireland's superiority in music.

With respect to the musical compositions of the Irish bards, an ingenious critic and antiquarian, Dr. Ledwich, has observed: "The incomparable skill allowed to the Irish in music could never be predicated of unlearned extemporaneous bardic airs, that it implies a knowledge of the diagram and an exact division of the harmonic intervals, a just expression of the tones, and, in the quickest movements, a unity of melody."

Why the Irish harp received such unvarying praise, while the tones of our modern improved instrument, while pleasing, are not of exceptional brilliancy, may be explained by what follows:

Lord Bacon in his *Sylva Sylvarium* says: "No harp has the sounds so melting and prolonged as the Irish harp." John Good, a priest educated at Oxford, on the request of Camden, wrote a description of the "Wild Irish" in 1566. "They love music mightily," he says, "and of all instruments, are particularly taken with the harp, which, being strung with brass wire and beaten (plucked) with crooked fingernails, is very melodious." The last of the harpers who played in this manner was Denis Hempson, or

O'Hempsey, who died in the year 1807 at the extraordinary age of one hundred twelve years.

Fuller, in his account of the Crusade conducted by Godfrey of Boulogne in the last of the eleventh century, says: "Yea, we might well think that all the concert of Christendom in this war would have made no music if the Irish harp had been wanting."

The Irish were in their day what the Germans are now in the world of music. Dr. Campbell in his *Philosophical Survey* confidently asserts that "The honor of inventing the Scots' music must be given to Ireland." The Scottish historian, John de Fordun, who went to Ireland in the fourteenth century to collect materials for a history of Scotland, expressly states that Ireland was the fountain of music, whence it began to flow into Scotland and Wales. "Every research connected with the Highlands leads to their Irish origin," wrote Gunn, a Scotchman, in 1807. "The gentlemen of note were educated in Ireland, to which country all who adopted poetry or music as a profession were uniformly sent to finish their education."

Jamieson, another Scotchman, informs us, in 1822, that "till, within the memory of persons still living, the school for Highland poetry and music was Ireland, and thither professional men were sent to be accomplished in those arts." Even Lord Kames is positive that those airs designated "The Old Scots Tunes" were originally Irish compositions, and their structure and tonality fully corroborate his opinion.

The harp has been for ages the national instrument—the instrument of the native princes and their bards; and even in the decline of ancient manners and so late as the eighteenth century itself, national habits had sanctified a custom which tended to insure its cultivation. The professional harper, and even piper, was reserved as a humane provision chiefly for those who happened to be born blind or had the misfortune to lose their eyesight in early youth. The principal families were everywhere in the habit of entertaining those musicians whose custom it was to travel about from house to house, remaining from a week to a month in each, and renewing the visit every few years.

From the habit of wandering, their compositions and tunes were disseminated and perpetuated in the memories of the people, to be handed down traditionally from one generation to another. This accounts for the many variants or settings of old tunes to be heard all over the country, and refutes the contentions of persons who condemn all settings that vary from those with which they are themselves familiar.

The race of harpers has now passed away, but, happily, memorials of their skill and music have been preserved. Considering what persecution and privation they suffered at times, it is little short of miraculous how so many of them survived up to the beginning of the nineteenth century. The last, and in many respects the most noted, Arthur O'Neill, died in 1818, aged eighty-five years.

The enthusiasm and industry of Edward Bunting at the great Belfast harp meeting in 1792, and for nearly half a century thereafter, preserved for posterity hundreds of inimitable melodies, many of which but for his zeal and skill would have passed into oblivion. What kept alive his ardor was a strong innate love of those delightful strains for their own sake, which neither the experience of the best music of other countries, nor advancing years, had ever been able to alter or diminish.

Moore's *Melodies* were founded on Bunting's success, and, although the nation owed him an inestimable debt, his mortal remains were allowed to be carried to the grave in Mount Jerome Cemetery, Belfast, and to slumber there without even the tribute of a newspaper paragraph to do his memory honor! And this was in 1843, barely three years after the publication of his great work, *The Ancient Music of Ireland.*

Our Scottish cousins, and even some Englishmen, have been no less active in the publication and preservation of Ireland's melodies than the Irish themselves—notably, John Playford, the three brothers, S., A. and P. Thompson, B. Crosby, George Thomson, R. A. Smith, and Alfred Moffat, whose collections have been discussed in preceding chapters.

Ireland had at all times, and still has, indefatigable collectors of her Folk Music, sustained in their arduous and expensive hobby by an inborn love of the strains which for them possess an undying fascination. Neither class nor creed has been exempt from its thraldom. The assiduity of collectors has safeguarded the preservation of Irish music in all its varieties, as far as printer's ink can serve the purpose. Tunes by the thousand, the reader realizes, have been collected and published—but what use are we making of them? To be regaled with vocal and instrumental "chestnuts," in monotonous repetition year after year, is, to say the least, a severe test of our patience, if not a reflection on our intelligence.

Not a few of our people, including professional vocalists and musicians, are seemingly unaware of the existence of any Irish music except what is included in Moore's *Melodies*, when in fact the poet by his matchless lyrics made known to the world but a fraction of the airs which Bunting, Petrie, Holden and others liberally offered him. With all their charm and beauty, Moore's *Melodies* are in real danger of palling on our ears. A few of them appear to monopolize all our programmes. A change of musical diet occasionally would not be unwelcome, and it may not be presumptuous to call the attention of our Irish Choral Societies to the several volumes of songs by another native-born Irishman, Alfred Perceval Graves, set to old Irish airs and arranged for the voice and pianoforte.

It is little wonder that a vein of diffidence and pessimism occasionally obtrudes in the author's introduction to *The Petrie Collection of the Ancient Music of Ireland*, published in 1855. Following is an instance: "I cannot but confess, I could not suppress a misgiving that, let a work of this nature possess whatever amount of interest or value it may, there no longer existed amongst my countrymen such sufficient amount of racy feeling of nationality and cultivation of mind—qualities so honorable to the Scottish character—as would secure for it the steady support necessary for its success, and which the 'Society for the Preservation and Publication of the Melodies of Ireland,' as I thought, somewhat too confidently anticipated."

The aged antiquarian's misgivings were prophetic. Only forty-eight pages of a supplement, instead of volume 2, came from the press, sixteen years after his death.

About this time also, Conran, in the last chapter of *The National Music of Ireland*, alive to the musical degeneracy of the times, calls attention to the necessity for concerted effort and suggests certain means to be employed to regain that artistic excellence in music which had been so universally acknowledged.

The author's sentiments are best expressed in his own language, which follows: "I may venture to remark that as our continental neighbors have ascribed to us the merit of an early familiarity with the effects of sweet song, and as the beautiful native charms of Ireland's melody are heard in agreeable contrast with the concerted music of other countries, should we not endeavor to regain something of that early artistic excellence for which our country was formerly remarkable, now that many of those uncongenial measures which retarded the development of art have passed away?"

Evidences of Ireland's musical decadence were recognized on all sides and many of her most loyal sons deplored the listless apathy of the people, who were discouraged and stupefied by famine's dire afflictions. The characteristic optimism of the race would soon overcome despondency, however, had not other well-understood influences supplemented famine's blight by enduring hostility.

Encouragement and patronage are what are needed in our day in Ireland, and not suppression or indifference, if the music of our forefathers is to be preserved as a living entity. The zeal and labors of the "Irish Folk Song Society" of London and the "Royal Society of Antiquaries of Ireland" will count for little unless the Irish race, particularly in Ireland, displays a more lively and practical interest in the regeneration of their musical heritage.

"It is indeed high time for us to restart a school of national Irish music," writes Perceval Graves in the introduction to his delightful little volume, *The Irish Song Book*. "If not, we shall assuredly forfeit our national birthright of song; for, Antæus-like, our musicians have lost their power since they have been lifted from the touch of their native earth."

Through the Gaelic League crusade in the last few years the revival of traditional Irish music is being encouraged, but not in the sense suggested by Mr. Graves. Although a healthy sentiment has been aroused, the absence of great traditional musicians, whose example and performance would be an inspiration and incentive to ambitious youth, is a lamentable drawback. They are gone beyond recall and have passed on to heaven and history. To insure its permanence as a living study on an equality with the music of other nations, nothing but a national movement reinforced by unselfish co-operation can hope to check the prevailing demoralization. Spasmodic attempts to revive Irish music and dancing are not infrequent in American cities, but the fatal faculty of inharmonious management too often leads to disintegration and failure.

More pretentious in their projects are the sporadic Irish Choral Societies, from which much had been hoped for. A very limited number of threadbare Irish melodies, scarcely enough to justify the name, are presented with persistent monotony. Modern compositions constitute the more ambitious part of their programmes.

The Irish are not afflicted with any stubborn prejudice against music not their own. As a people they are ever ready to recognize and applaud conspicuous merit, for did they not glorify Handel's *Messiah* and other compositions in Dublin and Cork in 1742, after their failure in London, and are they not singing their national anthem, "God Save Ireland," to the air of the American song, "Tramp, Tramp, the Boys Are Marching," in our day?

Taste in music is largely a matter of environment and training. Our ears are attuned to the tones and themes which pleased us in our impressionable youth, and the love of such strains is imbedded in the very nature of all races. The world moves, and musical taste and fashion move with it, we must admit. Some Irish music can never die, but the short strains and fragments of pastoral melody which swell the totals of certain publications, have had their day, apparently, for the rising generation of musical proclivities will scarcely pay them even the courtesy of more than a passing glance.

Some musical authority has well said that the ear for music is not what it once was; it undergoes an imperceptible but gradual change. We now take exception to a great deal that in former times was universally accepted. Davey, the avowed eulogist of English music, says: "Not a piece of music endurable by modern ears existed in England before the commencement of the fifteenth century."

As far as change of taste and the gradual devolution from ancient ideals in music are concerned, Ireland is not exceptional; for an examination of the pages of Chappell's *Old English Popular Music* will show to what extent time and taste have affected the music of England also, the only difference being that while Irish music has stagnated or deteriorated, English composition has improved.

Rivalries based on the respective merits of vocal and instrumental music in modern times, as compared with traditional music and singing after the manner practiced by our ancestors, have engrossed the attention of some really able minds in Ireland of late years; yet when the verbal storm subsided and the battle of the pens came to an end, what had been accomplished? Nothing.

The result reminds us of the indignant rejoinder of the lady who had been accused by a disputant that she was not open to conviction. "I scorn the imputation, sir," she warmly replied, "but show me the man who can convince me."

Although it no longer holds exalted sway in the land of its origin and development, the insinuating charms of Irish music are admitted by all. Writers of distinction, unbiased by racial ties, have descanted on its excellence for a thousand years, and no dissenting voice invites a plea to uphold its fame. Such were its beauties, that other peoples appropriated its strains to flavor their compositions, and yet Ireland, seemingly unappreciative of her musical treasures, ignored the brightest jewel in her diadem.

Regardless of what causes led to its decadence, or on whom may be placed the responsibility for unwise hostility to the agencies for its perpetuation, there can be no difference of opinion as to the urgent necessity for its revival and encouragement. No one returning to Ireland after the lapse of years can fail to notice the subdued demeanor of the peasantry, compared with their former vivacity; and this change can be safely attributed in no small degree to the monotony of their lives under existing conditions.

A quotation from a recent work, *A Handbook of Irish Dance*, by O'Keeffe and O'Brien, so accurately expresses the views of a growing majority of the Irish people, that it is given preference in expressing the sentiments entertained by the writer on that vital question:

"No country, and least of all Ireland, can afford to ignore its pastimes. Besides, it would be impossible to detach the magnificent body of Irish dance music from the dances themselves. We are concerned today, all of us, with the study of old Irish music; it would be incongruous if we were not concurrently interested in the dances to which so much of that music pertains. If we are to have a revival of things Irish, we cannot in reason pass by the dances. This, however, is only the academic view of the question. The study of Irish dances can well afford to be put on a higher plane of consideration. No one who has given any thought to our town and village, and, above all, to our rural life, can deny that it is sadly lacking in the most elementary resources of pleasure. This dullness, this death in life, has often been advanced, and surely with justice, as one of the many reasons for the terrible drain of emigration from our country. Everywhere people tell you that beyond the daily round of labour, there is nothing to look forward to in Irish provincial life. Can it, therefore, be a matter for surprise that the noisy streets and music-halls of foreign cities allure our people? It was not so at any time, so far as we are aware, in Irish history down to the end of the eighteenth century. Town and country life in Ireland, for many centuries, within the ken of observant travelers, appears to have resounded with the music of the pipes and the accompanying movements of the dancers. We would desire to see once more the village crossroads peopled with merry groups of dancers; to hear the music of the pipes borne down the lanes between the whitethorn trees, in the interval between the long day of labor and the night of rest."

Where a generation ago a wealth of folk music was the common possession of the peasantry, now scarcely a fraction of it is remembered. We are told by our optimistic orators and rhymers that Irish music will speedily resume its sway when Irishmen govern Ireland. Let us hope so—but how? when? where? Who is to teach? Have those optimists any assurance that the clerical ban on the "Patrons" and "Mehils" and other national festivities has been raised when music and dancing constitute an especial part of the entertainment? It is true that a few of the younger clergy are well disposed, but we must not forget that the frown of the prelate will dampen the ardor of the most enthusiastic.

A six weeks' trip through Munster and Leinster, a few years ago, after an absence of over forty years, disclosed nothing which afforded much evidence of a musical regeneration. Not a piper nor a fiddler was encountered at the five fairs attended, and but one ballad singer. The competitors at the *Feis* at Cork and at Dublin were amateurs, except one or two fluters. Their very best performers on any instrument at either *Feis* are easily outclassed here in Chicago. The youthful dancers in groups from far-off

Kerry and West Cork, trained largely by John S. Wayland and judged by the magnificent Conor O'Mahony, of Tralee, were a revelation. Such grace, rhythm, precision and uniformity in the most intricate evolutions of the eight-hand and sixteen-hand reels, by boys and girls, excelled anything of the kind ever witnessed by the writer.

After hearing several of the prize-winners at former musical competitions play, the conclusion was irresistible that the judges were certainly men of very liberal and generous impulses.

Such is the indifference of the well-to-do, that in response to hundreds of circulars printed and mailed at the personal expense of Mr. Wayland, the founder and secretary of the "Cork Pipers' Club," appealing for financial aid to defray overdue hall rent, not one penny was received. It is but simple justice to a whole-souled, generous man to acknowledge that the club has been extricated from financial difficulties more than once by Alderman William Phair, of Gill Abbey House, who is an enthusiastic performer on the Union pipes himself.

Instead of receiving encouragement and substantial support other than hand-clapping at home, musicians of talent found it necessary to seek recognition and patronage in London; while their humbler fellows are obliged to obtain a livelihood by playing on the highways and in public houses (saloons), where their reward is too frequently in that which leads to disaster instead of prosperity.

That it is not the decline of musical talent which brought about this lamentable state of affairs, is evidenced by the fame of such Irishmen as Michael Kelly, Henry Purcell (born in England, of Irish parents), John Field, Michael Balfe, William Vincent Wallace, Arthur Sullivan (the son of a Kerry bandmaster), Villiers Stanford, Victor Herbert and Grattan Flood. Their compositions, however, are of the modern school. The composition of airs in the ancient style ceased on the death of Parson Stirling, of Armagh, and "Piper" Jackson, of Limerick, late in the eighteenth century.

Kelly, who was born in Dublin in 1762, wrote the music of sixty English operas and burlettas, a list of which is given in his *Reminiscences*, published in 1825, the year preceding his death. A prolific genius, he also wrote the music of at least five hundred standard songs, including Dibdin's famous compositions.

Even in our own time we find the airs from Balfe's and Vincent Wallace's operas complacently included in the *Minstrelsy of England*, fresh from the press. Just think of it—the musical talents of Ireland's famous sons diverted to the glory of England!

American anthology and popular music has been liberally enriched by Irish-Americans such as Dan Emmett, Harrington, Stephen Collins Foster, Henry McCarthy, Charles Carroll Sawyer, Patrick Sarsfield Gilmore, D. K. O'Donnell, Father Abram Ryan, Rose Carey, and many others. How many are aware that the immortal "Old Folks at Home" and "My Old Kentucky Home" were produced by Stephen Collins Foster, to whom monuments have been erected in two states of the Union?

"No enemy speaks slightingly of Irish music and no friend need fear to boast of it." So spoke the poet patriot, Thomas Davis, some seventy years ago. Had he lived in our time he would have found it neglected, aye, despised by certain swallow-tailed Irishmen as being too vulgar and frivolous for people of their cultivated tastes. It has been found worth appropriating by other nations, however, and in the course of time being regarded as the property of the purloiners. Our old friend, "The Groves of Blarney" (Moore's "Last Rose of Summer"), is now being claimed by the Germans because Flotow incorporated it bodily in his opera of *Martha*. Neither can it be said that Irish music is unpopular, when Orchestra Hall, the Coliseum Annex and other halls are repeatedly filled to overflowing when the semblance of an Irish entertainment is given. The same halls yawn with empty seats when the colorless compositions of a naturalized Irishman like Esposito are elaborately rendered.

It would be disconcerting were it not amusing to listen to guileless but well-meaning speakers on special occasions eulogizing certain vocalists as being engaged in the sublime work of rescuing our melodies from oblivion, when the facts are that those selfsame vocalists could not be induced for love or money to entertain us with anything but a few threadbare selections from Moore's *Melodies* and possibly one or two nondescript airs which possess no trace of Irish feeling whatever.

We cannot expect German, French, Polish or Scandinavian music teachers to promote the study of Irish music. To their credit be it said, they are loyal to their own. When those to whom we entrust the education of our children, discourage the study of or refuse to teach Irish music, we must confess the outlook is anything but encouraging.

Few musicians of any nationality find difficulty in playing Irish airs, but many appear to have little conception of that peculiar rhythm or swing without which Irish dance tunes lose their charm and spirit. We cannot justly criticise others for shortcomings in this respect when musicians of more than local repute, of Irish birth or ancestry, give public exhibitions of frenzied execution in dance music inconceivably beyond the capacity of the most expert dancer. The jig and reel, at their hands, become a mere jumble of sounds, disappointing to the ear and disqualified for the dancer. No Irish music, as played in Ireland or elsewhere, for a skillful Irish dancer, is livelier than quickstep time. Such favorites, for instance, as "Garryowen" and "Rory O'Moore," served equally well as jigs or marches. The prestige of Irish music has suffered incalculable loss by disregard of the old Irish time, by many of its admirers and would-be friends, who no doubt obtained their erroneous ideas from the frantic contortions of vaudeville entertainers. Irish dance music was intended for Irish dancers, and neither the fancies nor the vagaries of musicians, humble or famous, will justify any faster time than a dancer requires.

In deploring the decline of the once renowned music of Ireland, no reflection on the music of other countries is intended. To paraphrase a saying concerning a certain cheering beverage, "All music is good, but some music is better."

Viewing the entire subject in perspective, from the extinction of the harpers to the present, are we giving way to unwarranted pessimism when impelled to ask: Has Irish music any future as a vital, distinct entity? Or shall it be classed with the antiquities and referred to the musical archæologists? Let those answer who, while professing or pretending to encourage its cultivation, inspire doubts of their sincerity by persistent worship at the shrine of false gods.

> "Oh, Erin! Blest shall be the bard,
> And sweet and soothing his reward,
> Can he but wake, one patriot thrill
> For days, though gone, remember'd still;
> Whate'er may be his humble lot,
> By foes denounced—by friends forgot,
> Thine is his soul—his sigh—his smile—
> Gem of the Ocean! Loved Emerald Isle!"

CHAPTER XVI

DR. P. W. JOYCE'S ESTIMATE OF THE TOTAL NUMBER OF IRISH AIRS QUESTIONED

In estimating the number of different Irish airs or tunes accessible in print, excluding duplicates and slight variants, Dr. P. W. Joyce, president of the "Royal Society of Antiquaries of Ireland," places the total at approximately three thousand one hundred, and in doing so credits the writer with procuring and publishing five hundred of them not previously in print. To be given credit for the preservation of nearly one-sixth of the whole, by such distinguished authority, is no small honor indeed; still, I trust I may be pardoned for not agreeing with his conclusions in some respects.

Of his late work, *Old Irish Folk Music and Songs*, the learned Doctor says in his introduction, "This present book of mine contains eight hundred forty-two not previously published." Elsewhere he adds: "I have examined the collection lately published by Captain Francis O'Neill, of Chicago, *The Music of Ireland*, and I do not think I have reproduced any of his airs. But it was only when a good part of this book of mine was printed that his second volume, *The Dance Music of Ireland*, came into my hands, and I find that one or two of his dance tunes have been repeated here, though in different versions."

Had the celebrated antiquarian examined O'Neill's collections more carefully he would have found that he had repeated at least eighty of his dance tunes and thirty-five of his airs, more or less varied in names and settings.

Coming from a man of such prominence, Dr. Joyce's figures will be regarded as authoritative, and it is for that reason alone that the writer begs leave to submit to the general reader a modified view of the question.

Dr. Joyce bases his conclusions on the following figures: Bunting's three collections— dated 1796, 1809, 1840—sum up about two hundred ninty-five numbers; various Petrie collections, viz., *Ancient Music of Ireland,* Hoffman's edition of another part of the Petrie collections, and the Stanford-Petrie edition, in all about one thousand tunes not printed elsewhere; Joyce's *Ancient Irish Music,* one hundred. "Making allowance for some overlapping in those five collections," he says, "we may take it that they contain at least sixteen hundred airs." To this estimate he adds eight hundred forty-two, the entire contents of his late work, as being previously unpublished, five hundred from my collections, and to the ninety minor publications referred to by Grattan Flood, a vague allowance of "two hundred airs not found duplicated elsewhere."

It will be noticed that all the principal collectors devoted their attention mainly to the accumulation of airs, evidently regarding dance tunes as of minor importance. This circumstance directed attention to a long-neglected field, and the results achieved fully justified the effort, and exceeded by far my most sanguine expectations. It is in no spirit of criticism that I invite attention to the following comparative figures:

Bunting's collections contain but three jigs. No mention is made of reels or hornpipes, or even long dances. Yet although not so designated, we may allow ten as being of the dance tune class. From the index to the *Complete Petrie Collections* we extract a total of one hundred thirty-eight dance tunes, although on a liberal examination of the contents, including duplicates and variants, the number may be increased to one hundred sixty-nine. Dr. Joyce's *Ancient Irish Music* includes but twenty-four of that class, while his latest and most important work, *Old Irish Folk Music and Songs,* contains but one hundred ten dance tunes. Now, taking into consideration the most liberal figures, the total dance tunes in the Bunting, Petrie and Joyce collections amounts to but three hundred thirteen. Their own estimate would make it thirty-eight less. On the other hand, O'Neill's *Music of Ireland* contains eleven hundred classified dance tunes, omitting a score or more scattered through the volume. To this number we must add one hundred forty-six tunes from the *Dance Music of Ireland* not included in the larger collection. This makes the respectable total of one thousand two hundred forty-six, as compared with three hundred thirteen dance tunes in all of the other publications mentioned by Dr. Joyce. Among the seven hundreds airs, marches, etc., in O'Neill's *Music of Ireland* there are unquestionably many not previously printed; but, ignoring those altogether, my two volumes named by Dr. Joyce contain at least nine hundred thirty-three tunes not included in the Bunting, Petrie, Joyce, and minor collections.

If I have printed occasionally two versions of one tune, so have they, quite as frequently, but, as a rule, anonymously or under different names. On that score we are about even; and as figures can't lie, in this case at least, are we presumptuous in claiming that Dr. Joyce's estimate of five hundred previously unpublished tunes to my credit is at least one hundred per cent too low?

CHAPTER XVII

REMARKS ON IRISH DANCES, ETC.

"When Felix Magee puts his pipes on his knee,
  And with flourish so free
  Sets each couple in motion;
With a cheer and a bound the lads patter the ground,—
  The maids move around,
    Just like swans on the ocean.
Cheeks bright as the rose, feet light as the doe's,
  Now coyly retiring,
  Now boldly advancing,—
Search the world all around from the sky to the ground,
  No such sight can be found,
    As an Irish lass dancing."

FOR nearly a thousand years Irish music has been the subject of unstinted praise by all writers who happened to come within the sphere of its fascinating influence; yet allusions to dances or dancing, popularly assumed to be coexistent with it, are both meager and ambiguous in Irish literature until comparatively recent times.

The cultivation and practice of poetry and music were chief amusements of the Gael, and connected with them was dancing, a form of entertainment or ceremonial in vogue with almost all races.

Everyone knows that the jig, reel and hornpipe are so associated with Irish festivities in the past few generations as to be regarded as national dances. When we fail to find Irish words for those names in dictionaries of the Irish language we can hardly escape the conviction that those dances are not of very ancient origin.

On concluding an exhaustive essay on "Music and Musical Instruments in Ancient Erinn," in his great work, *The Manners and Customs of the Ancient Irish,* Professor Eugene O'Curry remarks: "It is strange and will, I am sure, appear to my readers almost incredible, that as far as I have ever read there is no reference that can be identified as containing a clear allusion to dancing, in any of our really ancient manuscript books." Further on he continues: "The ordinary native name now known in Ireland for singing music is *Fonn* and for dancing music *Port.* The former is a very old word; but I have never met an instance of the latter in the older writings, though it occurs in mediæval tales. Father Michael O'Cleary in his Glossary, published in 1643, applies the term to lyric music in general.

"In some of the middle age tales we meet with descriptions of social assemblies in which the phrase occurs, '*Ports* and *Cors* were played for them.' Now, this word *Cor* is an old Irish word for music, and wherever or whenever I met these two words, *Ports* and *Cors,* I understood them as signifying, if not dances, at least merry dancing tunes, such as we are now acquainted with.

"If I were to indulge in a little etymological speculation, I would venture to say that the *Port* was as it now really is, the same as our jig; while the *Cor,* which in Irish means a twist, a turnabout, or out of a direct line, would very well describe the character of the dance now called a reel." The older Scotch dictionaries have the word reel as merely a *Rinnceadh,* or dance without distinction from a jig.

"The term *Rinnceadh Fada,* or Long Dance, which is so often introduced by modern writers, is not to be found in any manuscript of Irish writing that I have ever seen," the learned author informs us. "It appears to be a modern descriptive name for what is called a Country Dance, which is itself but a corruption of the French words "Contre Danse," a name merely descriptive of the simple arrangement of the dancers in two lines opposite to another."

O'Curry is of the opinion that the modern term *jig* is derived from the French word *gigue* or the Italian word *giga*, although we know that jig tunes were by no means scarce in English and Irish printed collections of music before the influence of Italian music was felt in Ireland.

Besides its use as descriptive of any kind of lively music, the term *jig* was applied to any light metrical composition. The quotation, " 'Tis one of the best jigs ever acted," from the writings of Chapman, illustrates the application of it in this sense.

As a matter of fact, the terms *jig, reel, hornpipe* appear to have been interchangeable in the seventeenth, eighteenth and even in the early part of the nineteenth century, as the following examples will show: That old favorite jig, "The Priest in His Boots," is included in C. & E. Thompson's *Compleat Collection of 120 Favorite Hornpipes*, published 1765-77; the ninth number in *The Caledonian Muse*, published about 1785, is a tune in six-eight time, called "A Highland Reel"; while as late as the year 1840, Bunting published a tune, which he names "The Chorus Jig," in two-four time in *The Ancient Music of Ireland*. A dance tune, called "The Cobbler's Jig," in common time was printed in Playford's *Dancing Master* in 1686, as well as jigs in six-eight and nine-eight time. One of the tunes in the opera *Love in a Village*, 1762, named "Nancy Dawson, or Miss Dawson's Hornpipe," is also written in six-eight time. Further comment on this feature of the subject is unnecessary.

The etymology of the term *reel* is no less obscure and uncertain. Webster tells us that *reel* is from the Swedish *ragla*—to stagger, to incline or move in walking, first to one side and then to the other. The earliest mention of the term in English dates from the year 1598, when as "Reill" it appears in a rare work entitled *News from Scotland*.

Neither can the history or origin of the hornpipe be definitely traced, but we know that tunes of that name were popular in England since the sixteenth century. In Chappell's *Old English Popular Music*, volume 1, we find a tune in six-two time, entitled "A Hornepype," the composition of Hugh Aston in the reign of Henry the Eighth.

While admitting that the origin of the hornpipe is open to much doubt, J. G. O'Keefe, in an article on Irish Dances, published in the *Gael*, September, 1902, says "there are many evidences, however, that the hornpipe is of Irish origin, and that in fact it is the earliest Irish 'step' as distinct from 'figure' or 'round' dances"; yet in neither his article nor in *A Handbook of Irish Dance*, of which he is one of the authors, does he adduce any specific evidence to sustain his opinion.

In a scarce work called *The Ball; or A Glance at Almack's*, published anonymously in 1829, we are told that in Britain the hornpipe is a dance "held as an original of that country." Some of the steps have been used in the English Country Dance, particularly at village fêtes; and few English seamen were to be found that were not acquainted with the hornpipe.

The origin of the name is no less a matter for speculation than the dance. The name has been equated with *crannciuil*, that is, tree or branch music, and *corna-piopa*, or pipe-horn. Hence hornpipe. This derivation seems, at least, plausible, and it may be safely assumed, in the absence of evidence to the contrary, that the word hornpipe as a tune or dance was in some way connected with the ancient trumpet or instrument made from the horns of cattle.

In addition to the Double Jig, Single Jig, Slip or Hop Jig, the Reel, Hornpipe and Long Dance, there were also Figure Dances, Pantomime Dances and Cake Dances; but as this sketch is intended to deal only in a general way with features of the subject not generally understood, I will refer the interested student to O'Keefe and O'Brien's work, *A Handbook of Irish Dance,* for more detailed information.

In briefly alluding to peculiar Irish dances, perhaps it would not be out of place to describe a rather obscure one called "Cover the Buckle." Whether this name was applied to a tune or a dance, was not clear, and, strangely enough, an examination of the pages of O'Keeffe and O'Brien's work, before mentioned, shed no light on the subject. The name is merely included in a list of "Figure" or "Set" dances and tunes, without comment.

Fortunately, an interesting description of this dance—for dance it is—was unexpectedly discovered in Shelton Mackenzie's *Bits of Blarney*. It appears that when a dancing master was prevailed upon to "take the flure" to give his admiring pupils "a touch of quality," a door would be lifted off its hinges and placed in the center of the floor as a platform. For the occasion a piper would "discourse most excellent music," and on the door would commence that wondrous display of agility known as "Cover the Buckle." This name, the author says, was probably derived from the circumstance that the dancing master while teaching always wore large buckles in his shoes and, by the rapidity of motion with which he would make his many twinkling feet perpetually cross, would seem to cover the appendages in question.

The great effort was to exhibit all varieties of steps and

dances without once quitting the prostrate door on which the exhibitor took his stand. The jumps and "cuttings" in the air, the bends, the dives, the wrigglings, the hops,— these were all critically regarded by the audience, and sometimes rewarded with such exclamations of approval as "That's the way," "Now for a double cut," "Cover the buckle, ye divel," "Oh, then 'tis he that handles his feet nately," and so on.

It may not be inappropriate to give the reader the benefit of what little information is accessible in regard to "The Sailor's Hornpipe" also. Although there may be no evidence to sustain any claim to its Irish origin, we know at least that it was quite popular as a dance in Ireland, particularly in Munster, in the last generation. Every dancer in those days who made any pretentions to skill was expected to be able to enact that laborious piece of amusement called "The Sailor's Hornpipe," faint vestiges of which are still extant in nautical scenes as represented on the stage.

Words cannot describe the evolutions of this remarkable dance when exhibited with all the scientific varieties of which it is capable, says Shelton Mackenzie. The shuffles, cross-shuffles, jumps, hops, leaps, cuttings, slides, and so on, which were introduced, are impossible to picture accurately. The manner in which the "heel and toe" was employed and varied is left to some abler historian to record.

As danced on the stage, the "sailor" seems to be almost constantly engaged in his avocation of manipulating ropes —hoisting or coiling—with brief intermission to display his arms "a-kimbo." The music for this dance was discussed in Chapter VIII.

Dances of which the present generation know nothing are mentioned in Chappell's work, such as the Spanish

Pavan, the Galliard, Morris Dances, Fading, Trenchmore, the Irish Hey, Cushion Dance, Cheshire Round, and other Rounds—all popular in the sixteenth century. Only the Cushion Dance and some Rounds or County Dances survived to the beginning of the nineteenth century. The Trenchmore and Fading are believed to be identical with the Irish *Rinnce Fada* or *Long Dance*, which is being revived in Ireland and America again. The stately Minuet, another dance, quite popular in Colonial days, has been banished in favor of the cotillion and quadrille. As the dances changed, so did the music; and this reminds us of the paradoxical fact that there is nothing permanent in this world but change. While music may be changing in other countries, in Ireland it is dying out.

It may not be out of place to explain that the Country Dance, so popular in the days of our grandsires, is classed with the Long Dance, Set Dance and Figure Dances by O'Keeffe and O'Brien.

As the "Ring Dance," or "Rinka Dance," the Long Dance, or *Rinnce Fada*, of Ireland was well known in Scotland centuries ago. By those names it is described in a work entitled *The Complainte of Scotland*, published in 1549. Although then retained in the Highlands, it had been discontinued in the south of Scotland. Irish literature abounds with allusions to this oldest of Irish dances, and as the "Fading" it is mentioned in the works of Shakspeare and other English poets. In Cornwall it was termed "The Faddy."

"In this dance as performed today and for the past century," according to O'Keeffe and O'Brien, "the men all stand in a row, their partners facing them, forming another row. The dancing begins at one end and gradually works along through the whole line until all are stepping."

A more complicated and picturesque form of the *Rinnce Fada* had been practiced in more ancient times.

In a rare work entitled *Dissertations on the History of Ireland,* published in 1766, Charles O'Conor describes a dance performed by the ancient Irish in open spaces in the forest, during their hunting matches, as follows: "Their Rinkey or field-dance was generally performed in circles. Great agility as well as great skill was required of the performers, whether they broke or closed the circle. The action was governed by music. Each evolution had its stated time, till a new change in their *allegro* called for a change of action; and so on till a reiteration of the Dancing Port (as they termed it) relieved the dancer, and in their turn called out different actors."

The passion for dancing was strong in all the Celtic race, and it was employed in the service of religion, some remains of which practice long continued among the Welsh, who were accustomed to dance in the churchyard, according to James Logan, author of the *Scottish Gael*. *The Rinncefada* or field dance in Irish, he tells us, was performed to the *Cuisle Ciuil,* a simple sort of bagpipe, and used to conclude all balls. When James the Second landed at Kinsale in 1688 his friends received him with the *Rinnce Fada,* by which he was highly pleased. The manner in which it was performed is described as follows: "Three persons abreast, holding the ends of a white handkerchief, moved forward a few paces to the sound of slow music, the rest of the dancers following in couples, and holding also a white handkerchief between them. The music then changing to a quicker tune, the dance began, the performers passing successively under the handkerchiefs of the three in front; and then wheeling round in semi-circles, they formed a variety of pleasing evolutions, interspersed with occasional *entrechats*, finally uniting and resuming their original places."

It appears that the Irish had also a species of military dance, conducted by a *cathrinnee* or dancing master, but no details of it are now obtainable. Of such ancient Caledonian dances as the Dirk Dance and the Sword Dance, the latter still survives.

Sean Truis, so called from the name of the accompanying air, Logan tells us, is the native Highland hornpipe and is danced with much grace.

A writer in the *Gentleman's Magazine* of April, 1758, had the following to say concerning the Country Dance: "Now, sir, we have a species of dance amongst us which is commonly called country dancing, and so it is written, by which we are led to imagine that it is a rustic way of dancing, borrowed from the country people or peasants, and this, I suppose, is generally taken to be the meaning of it. But, sir, this is not the case; for as our dances in general come from France, as does the country dance, which is a manifest corruption of the French *Contredanse,* where a number of persons, placing themselves opposite one another, begin a figure. This, now, explains an expression we meet with in our old country dance books, 'Long ways as many as will.' As our present country dances are all in that manner, this direction appears to be very absurd and superfluous; but if you have recourse to the original of these dances, and will but remember that the performers stood up opposite one to another in various figures as the dance might require, you will instantly be sensible that that expression has a sensible meaning in it and is very popular and significant, as it directs a method or form different from others that might be in a square or any other figure."

From this description it appears that there was no

"Gillie Callum" or Sword Dance.

important difference between the *Rinnce Fada* or "Fading" introduced into England from Ireland and the *Contredanse* derived from France. In the dancing as described by Mrs. Anna Plumptre in her *Narrative of a Residence in Ireland* in the years 1814 and 1815, each lad dressed in his best clothes, selected his lass, who was equally adorned in all the finery she could muster. A circle was then formed and one of the couples danced a sort of a jig within the circle, neither of them taking their eyes from the ground the whole time, until the jig being concluded, the man took the woman round the waist, gave her a twirl, and snatched a kiss. Another couple then succeeded, and then another, continuing thus till all had taken their turns.

The Long Dance, given in honor of persons of distinction, described by Mrs. Plumptre in the work before mentioned, is headed by a lad and lass chosen for the occasion as king and queen and decked out with much ribbons and finery in their arms and sleeves. They carry a garland between them and walk or dance at the head of the troop. When they arrive at the house of the person they intend to honor, they stop before the door, and while the king and queen stand still, the rest of the dancers, linked together by handkerchiefs held between them, dance in a long string round and round them till they are completely encircled. The company then dances back in the same order till their majesties are completely disencumbered, when they in their turn dance. This done, the king invites any of the ladies of the mansion to come and dance with him, an invitation seldom refused. The queen then invites any of the gentlemen to dance with her, and this concluded, the whole company dances, according to fancy, or else one of the men dances a hornpipe. The company then linked together once more, encircle their sovereign, and, reversing, they dance off in the same order that they came.

Not until the decline of the artistic and picturesque Long Dance, and the Hey or Round Dance, did "step" dances come to be reduced to a system of fundamental movements, from which were developed innumerable steps suitable to the different varieties of modern dance music. O'Keefe ascribes the complex steps of the jig and reel to the dancing masters of the latter half of the eighteenth and the early part of the nineteenth centuries. Preeminent among them were the "Great O'Kearin," of Kerry, and after him Teig (Rua) O'Scanlan, of Limerick. Under their skillful tuition step dancing attained such method and precision that the Munster dancers were famed all over Ireland, a reputation which still clings to that province; for do we not find that most if not all who are now engaged in teaching Irish dancing, from London to Chicago, have been recruited from the Munster counties?

The example and teaching of such expert exponents of the nimble and rhythmic art as the Hennessy brothers, of Cork, John E. McNamara and James P. Coleman, of Limerick, and Dan and John Ryan, of Tipperary, have brought about a much appreciated revival of Irish national dances in the western metropolis.

Dancing of old had not been regarded so much an amusement as an agreeable system of physical training to acquire gracefulness of carriage, and all young people were expected to devote some time to the study and practice of the art.

Locke on Education says: "Nothing appears to me to give children so much becoming confidence and behavior, and to raise them to the conversation of those above their age, as dancing. I think they should be taught to dance as soon as they are capable of learning it, for though this

John Ryan.   John E. McNamara.   James P. Coleman.

consists only in outward gracefulness of motion, yet, I know not how, it gives children manly thoughts and carriage more than anything. Dancing is that which gives graceful motion through all our lives."

For ages, in the early stages of the world, dancing was exclusively a religious ceremony. The dance of the Jews established by Levitical law at the solemn feasts was perhaps the most ancient on record. The dancing of King David is frequently quoted, and there are other instances mentioned in the Scriptures. Stages were erected in many temples especially for those exercises.

The heathen also could "sport a toe" in the very earliest ages. Pindar calls Apollo "the dancer," and Homer tells us that this deity capered to the music of his own harp.

Much could be written of the dances of ancient Egypt, Greece, and Rome, and the story might be prolonged to include the many dances of more modern times in the different countries of Europe described by the author of *The Ball;* but as the dances of Ireland are mainly what concern us in this chapter, I must close the account and present instead an admonition appropriate to the subject.

> "Oh, may you walk as you advance,
> Smooth and erect as now you dance;
> May you on each important stage,
> From blooming youth to hoary age,
> Assert your claim to Merit's prize,
> And as at present charm your eyes;
> Observant of decorum's laws;
> And moving with the same applause,
> May you, through life's perplexing maze,
> Direct your steps with equal praise;
> Its intricate meanders trace
> With regularity and rhythmic grace;
> From the true figure never swerve,
> And time in every step observe."

CHAPTER XVIII

REMARKS ON THE EVOLUTION OF THE IRISH OR UNION PIPES

"Away with your fiddle and flutes,
  As music for wedding or ball,
Pianofortes, clarionettes, lutes—
  The bagpipe surpasses them all.

"For polkas, the waltz, the quadrille,
  There's naught with the pipes can compare;
An anchorite torpid 'twould thrill,
  And mingle its tones with his prayer.

"So tuneful, harmonious and sweet!
  The very perfection of art,
Lends wings to the tardiest feet,
  And joy to the sorrowing heart.

"Inspired the fair dancers would feel
  Like birds poising light on a twig,
As nimbly they trip in the reel
  And tip off the steps of a jig."

It would not be within the contemplated scope of this work to attempt a description of the musical instruments known to the Irish in ancient times, did there not exist a misconception concerning the character and compass of the Irish bagpipe in the minds of many. This most elaborate and sweet-toned instrument is commonly confused with the shrill Highland bagpipe and shares with it no little prejudice on that account.

Passing strange but no less true is the fact that many Irishmen of the present generation confess to having never seen a set of Irish pipes.

Not less than two centuries ago they became two distinct instruments, differing entirely in appearance, tone, compass and manipulation— so much so, in fact, that the great Highland bagpipe bears less resemblance to the Irish or Union pipes than it does to the bagpipes of Germany, Spain, Italy, Hungary, Bulgaria and Bohemia.

Some form of bagpipe was used by all nations from the most ancient times. Supplementing the statements of historians, sculptures prove indisputably that it was known to the Greeks and Romans. From the latter, who used it with the infantry, as the Scotch still do, it is supposed to have been introduced into Britain, although some historians contend that the bagpipe was brought in by the Scandinavians.

In a recent work, *Some Reminiscences, and the Bagpipe,* by Duncan Fraser, several varieties of Irish, Scotch, French, Italian and Northumbrian bagpipes are illustrated. There are also pictures of German, Bulgarian, Hungarian, African and East Indian bagpipes; and this does not by any means exhaust the list, for there were at the World's Columbian Exposition, at Chicago in 1893, performers on the double-chanter bagpipe of Hindustan and the harsh-toned, shrieking Berber bagpipe of Morocco and Algeria.

It is quite probable that some of those instruments are rare now, if not quite obsolete, and as they interest us only relatively, we will return to the consideration of the bagpipe of Ireland.

The earliest mention of pipers in Irish literature, according to Grattan Flood, occurs in the ancient historic tales of the fifth century. By Eugene O'Curry, in his lecture

On Music and Musical Instruments of the Ancient Irish, we are told that the Brehon Laws make mention of "*Cuislennach,* who played *the Cuislenna Ciuil* or musical tubes—whatever they were."

The piper and fiddler are both referred to by implication in the poem on the fair of *Carman* in the eight century, where pipes and fiddles are enumerated among the musical instruments. Pipers are more frequently mentioned thereafter; but from what we know authoritatively of the *Piob-Mor,* or Irish Warpipe, it was essentially the same as the Highland bagpipe of the period.

Giraldus Cambrensis, the Welsh prelate who wrote so approvingly of Irish music and musicians in 1185, omitted to refer to the bagpipe specifically as one of the musical instruments in use in Ireland in his time, unless, we identify it with the *Chorus,* which he enumerates as one of the native instruments. He does, however, classify the bagpipe as one of the musical instruments of the Welsh and Scotch; and from the frequent mention of it in English literature, we know that in some form it was extensively used in England also. In that country the bagpipe does not appear to have been held in such esteem as in Scotland and Ireland, judging by the shafts of ridicule and satire aimed at it by the poets.

At the Eisteddfod of Caerwys (in Wales) in the year 1100, King Griffith, in order to introduce the Irish bagpipes, gave particular prominence to pipe performances, Grattan Flood tells us, and we read in the Welsh Annals that "The prize was carried off by an Irishman, who received from the monarch a silver pipe as a reward for his skill."

Though the bagpipe was the pride and solace of the Scotch chieftain, and though the Scotch pipers studied under the best of tutors in a college for pipers in the Isle of Skye, yet this instrument never received any considerable improvement from the Scotch. In fact, they glory in their conservatism, and in justification thereof call attention to the undeniable reality that it has suffered less, in the decline of ancient musical instruments, than the improved bagpipes of other nations.

Still, from the primitive bagpipe of "Ane bleddir and ane reid," which had but five holes or notes in the chanter, like the Tibia of the Romans, and other ancient pipes, to the *Piob-Mor,* or Great Highland Bagpipe, was no small step in advance. It must not be supposed that the transformation was effected without many stages of development, for we learn from various writers that it was not until early in the sixteenth century that the second drone was added to the Scotch instrument. For about two hundred years thereafter the two-drone bagpipe was recognized as the standard form of the Great Highland Warpipe. Some time about the latter part of the eighteenth century a third drone was added, but its use did not become general for a generation or more. From this, however, we must not infer that a third drone was a novelty, because the Northumberland, Lowland Scotch, and the Irish or Union bagpipes were never equipped with less than three, while the French Musette of the seventeenth century had as many as five drones.

Unlike the custom existing in Scotland until the year 1747, when clanship was abolished by English law, hereditary pipers were unknown in Ireland. The Highland pipers were second only to the chiefs of their various clans, and stories of their fidelity, bravery and talents pervade all Scotch history.

Of this class, the MacCrimmons were the most eminent.

The first of them, *Iain*, or John, became piper to the MacLeods of Dunvegan Castle, Isle of Skye, in the year 1600. They became so famous that pupils came from far and near to study under them and no piper could possess a better certificate than the fact of having been taught by a MacCrimmon. So large grew the number of their pupils that they eventually opened a school or college for pipers in which seven years' study was prescribed as the regular course. This college was maintained until late in the eighteenth century.

It is worthy of note that *Domhnall Mor,* or Big Donald MacCrimmon, son of John, according to Manson, author of *The Highland Bagpipe,* was given special opportunities for learning by his chieftain MacLeod, by whom he was sent to a college for pipers in Ireland. The system in this institution, it appears, permitted but one pupil at a time to be in the presence of the master. So eager to learn was *Domhnall Mor* and so retentive was his memory that by hiding in a corner, where he could hear the other twenty-four students at their lessons he contrived to memorize the entire repertory of his master.

The MacCrimmons, being obscure before their musical talents made them famous, Scotch writers fancifully derive the alleged origin of the name from a tradition that the first of them came from Cremona in Italy! If the name is not Scottish, why not be candid and admit it is the Irish surname Crimmins or McCrimmeen of Munster —by no means a scarce one.

The fact that *Domhnall Mor,* or Big Donald, had a brother named *Padruig* and a son called *Padruig Mor* MacCrimmon adds somewhat to the probability of their Irish origin, especially as nothing definite is known to Scotch writers concerning their ancestry. *Padruig Mor,* who was the most famous piper of his day (the middle of the seventeenth century), was the composer of that classic, "Rory Mor's Lament."

From the following humorous story, as told by a Scotch writer in the eighteenth century, it can be understood that the music of the Highland bagpipe can inspire terror, as well as valor, and other emotions: "As a Scotch bagpiper was traversing the mountains of Ulster, he was one evening encountered by a hunger-starved Irish wolf. In his distress, the poor man could think of nothing better than to open his wallet and try the effects of his hospitality; he did so, and the savage animal swallowed all that was thrown him, with so improving a voracity as if his appetite was but just coming to him. The whole stock of provision, you may be sure, was soon spent, and now his only recourse was to the virtue of his bagpipe; which the monster no sooner heard than he took to the mountains with the same precipitation that he had come down. The poor piper could not so perfectly enjoy his deliverance, but that with an angry look at parting, he shook his head and said: 'Ay! are these your tricks? Had I known your humor, you should have had your music before supper.'"

That the bagpipes had not been transformed into the *Uilleann* or Union pipes at the end of the sixteenth century, as stated by Dr. Ledwich in *The Antiquities of Ireland,* Dublin, 1804, is apparent from the *Dialogue on Ancient and Modern Music,* by Galilei, published at Florence in 1589. "The bagpipe is much used by the Irish," he says. "To its sound, this unconquered, fierce and warlike people march their armies and encourage each other to deeds of valor. With it also they accompany their dead to the grave, making such mournful sounds as to invite, nay almost force, the bystanders to weep."

When the *Piob-Mor,* or Warpipes, inflated through a blowpipe from the mouth, were converted into the mild, modified and diatonic Union pipes, or by whom, is a matter of uncertainty. The general impression is, however, that the date was not much earlier than the beginning of the eighteenth century.

Judging from the illustrations in Dr. Ledwich's work before mentioned, the *"Piob Mala,* or Ancient Bagpipes," as he terms it, was of rather primitive construction. The oval bag, or skin, furnished with straps to buckle around the body, was held in front. Two tubes or drones of unequal length, set in a stock and held together, instead of being inserted separately in the bag, projected over the shoulder. The short chanter appears to have but seven instead of eight vents, while the blowpipe seems ridiculously short. Perhaps the manner in which the bag was to be held in front instead of under the arm, made a short blowpipe desirable. Its use, we are told, was confined to the peasantry even long after the Norman invasion, and it never shared in the popularity of the harp with the nobility. The set of Warpipes borne by the piper at the head of a body of native Irish warriors, as pictured in Derrick's *Image of Ireland,* published in 1587, is an infinitely superior instrument to that shown in the Antiquities of Ireland.

In the *"Cuislean* or Modern Bagpipe," as depicted in the plate, we see an early if not original type of the Irish or Union pipes blown or inflated by a bellows strapped under the right arm. As the performer is seated when playing, the four drones set in an ample stock rest across the knees. The chanter still retained something of the old form; that is, it "flares" or enlarges gradually towards the bottom, like in the Highland instrument, and therefore

IRISH WAR PIPER.
From Derrick's *Image of Ireland.* 1581.

could not be manipulated on the knee to pitch an octave, as in the modern Irish chanter. The engraving also shows it to have been a double chanter; that is, it had two tubes with two sets of holes for the notes, bored from one piece of wood. Two nicely matched reeds produced double tones, but the great difficulty of maintaining two reeds in identical pitch caused the double chanter to lose favor and the type is now rare if not obsolete. In the same plate is pictured a reed instrument called a *Feadan,* which closely resembles a musette or clarinet without keys.

The Irish or Union pipes from the first continued to be improved and developed until they became a complicated keyed instrument, capable of taxing the skill of the most capable performers.

Irish pipers entertained royalty in England and on the continent; they graced the London stage with their music, in certain operas, and became attached to the households of even English and Scotch nobility. King George the Second was so delighted with the performance of an Irish gentleman on the bagpipes that he ordered a medal to be struck for him. One of them, famed as a "musician and piper," compiled and published in 1809 a volume entitled *A Collection of Irish Airs and Jiggs with Variations, by John Murphy, Performer on the Union Bagpipes at Eglinton Castle.*

That the race was numerous and popular is well attested by an anonymous English traveler who contributed his views on Ireland to the *Gentleman's Magazine* in 1751. "Every village has a Bagpiper, who every fine evening after working hours, collected all the young men and maids in the village about him, where they dance most cheerfully; and it is really a very pleasing entertainment to see the expressive though awkward attempts of nature to recommend themselves to the opposite sex." Logan, author of *The Scottish Gael*, in describing the musical instruments of the Gaelic race, says: "The Union bagpipes that have been called the Irish organ, are the sweetest of musical instruments; the formation of the reeds and the length of the pipes increased by brass tubes, produce the most delightful and soothing melody, while by the addition of many keys and the capability of the chanter, any tune may be performed." To which may be added—it is now an elaborate concert instrument with a compass of at least two octaves of mellow tone, blending agreeably with flute, violin and piano.

The single regulator, with five keys, introduced by some unknown genius late in the eighteenth century, paved the way for the addition of several others, until during the present generation sets of Irish pipes manufactured by William Taylor, of Philadelphia, and William Rowsome, of Dublin, have as many as four and even five regulators, on which may be played in organ tones almost any air without the assistance of the chanter.

More than one hundred years ago, Miss Owenson, afterwards Lady Morgan, in a little work entitled *Patriotic Sketches*, noted that "the inordinate passion which the Irish have in all ages betrayed for music, must have eventually produced an eager pursuit of such means as would tend to its gratification. Musical instrument makers are, in fact, to be found in many of the smaller towns of Ireland and generally among men of the lowest professions." She gives many instances of untaught genius, among which that of John Egan, the famous musical instrument maker of Dublin, deserves special mention. Brought up from his earliest youth to the labors of the anvil, Mr. Egan was still serving his apprenticeship to a

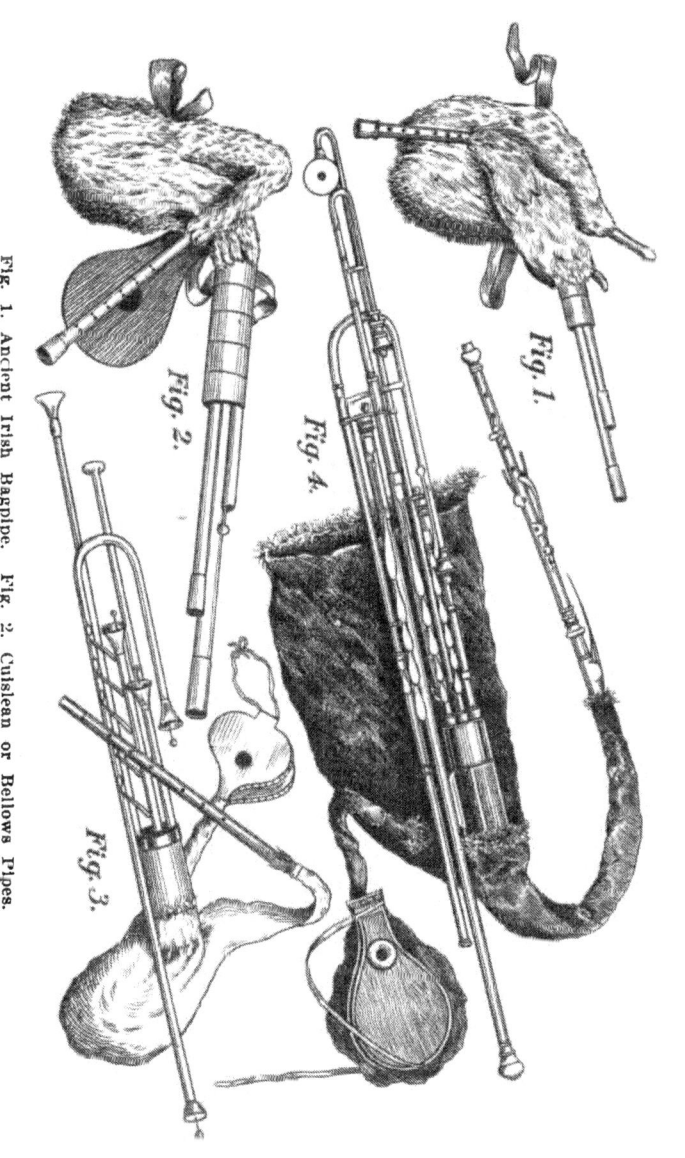

Fig. 1. Ancient Irish Bagpipe. Fig. 2. Cuislean or Bellows Pipes.
Fig. 3. Primitive Union Pipes. Fig. 4. Egan's Improved Union Pipes.

smith when chance threw in his way a French harp. A natural fondness for music, and the curiosity and admiration arising from the first view of the most beautiful and picturesque of all instruments, induced him to examine its mechanism. All the money he possessed in the world was shortly after laid out in the purchase of materials requisite for the construction of a pedal harp on an improved plan of his own invention. His success was immediate and his fame assured. Miss Owenson refers to Egan as ranking among the first in his profession in the kingdom. He improved and multiplied the concords or regulators of the Irish pipes, which up to his time were exceedingly limited. In short, he was to the Irish or Union bagpipes what Stradivari was to the violin; the master-maker of what John Gilmary Shea poetically termed "a hive of honied sounds."

A writer in *The Leader,* of San Francisco, February 26, 1910, borrowing some ideas from Grattan Flood's *A History of Irish Music,* credits "William Talbot, a Roscrea man," with having about the year 1800 improved and "perfected" the Union or Irish pipes "as we have them today."

Born in 1780, it seems, according to that story, Talbot was only twenty years old when he perfected the pipes. After voyaging to other countries for four years, he returned and became a professional piper in 1802. Some years later, through his experiments in building an organ, he acquired the skill to improve his favorite instrument.

Talbot was certainly a great piper and also a mechanical genius of a high order, who, though blind, used to employ his leisure hours in stringing and tuning pianos and repairing pipe organs, and he even constructed a set of "Grand Pipes" on an original plan of his own invention.

Following is what Carleton, the renowned Irish novelist, says of them: "His pipes indeed were a very wonderful instrument, or rather combination of instruments, being so complicated that no one could play upon them but himself. The tones which he brought out of them might be imagined to proceed from almost every instrument in an orchestra, now resembling the sweetest and most attenuated notes of the finest Cremona violin and again the deepest solemn diapason of the organ." These organ notes, every Irishman knows, are produced by the regulators, which had been invented long before Talbot's time—an assertion fortified by the fact that a system for their manipulation was included in O'Farrell's Treatise on pipe playing, published in London about the year 1797. (See Appendix A.)

Others beside Talbot, such as the Maloneys of Clare, constructed elaborate sets of Irish pipes which, though ingenious and impressive, proved impracticable as standard instruments.

Some idea of the magnificence of a set made by the latter for Col. Vandaleur, of Clare, two generations ago, but not used for the reasons stated, may be had from the frontispiece in O'Neill's *Dance Music of Ireland,* in which Professor Denis O'Leary, of Mount Melleray, the present proud possessor, shows them off to advantage.

Whether based on venerated memory, or on actual merit, the sentiment prevails among pipers to this day that it is doubtful if Egan's pipes have ever been equaled, not to say excelled, for mellowness of tone and adaptability as a parlor instrument. The music of lower than modern concert pitch was sweet and soothing, and on certain temperaments it exercised a peculiar fascination not easily explained.

The instruments now being manufactured by Mr. Rowsome, of Dublin, are modeled after the Egan type of Union pipes and are quite as complete and well finished.

WILLIAM ROWSOME,
Dublin Piper and Pipe Maker.

The set on which he is represented as playing in the picture is one of his own make.

A phenomenal piper and mechanic named William Taylor, a native of Drogheda, County Louth, emigrated to Philadelphia in the sixties, and finding that the tones of the bagpipes of his day were too puny to meet the requirements of an American hall or theatre, he invented a more substantial instrument of powerful tone and concert pitch, which has become the standard in this country. So supreme was he among musicians of his class that the most ambitious and expert made no pretense of rivalry. Like many another genius, poverty pursued him through life, and though there was neither widow nor offspring to suffer bereavement, his death was sincerely lamented by a multitude of admirers. To the pipers, it was a catastrophe, for no one was left who had the technical skill to make or repair their instruments like the great and only "Billy" Taylor.

A study of the illustrations in this work will give the reader more general information on certain features of the subject than pages of printed description could convey.

"Loved pipe of the simple peasant still
    Where'er extend the Gael's domains,
Thou cheer'st the heart from vale to hill
    With thy enlivening strains.

And in the far and distant west,
    From prairie wide to woodland bower,
Thou sooth'st the drooping exile's breast
    Through many a lonely hour."

APPENDIX A

One of the causes enumerated by the writer for the decline of music and its cultivation in Ireland in the late centuries, was the absence of an established system of instruction. Although Irish pipers were still numerous after the extinction of the harpers, and yet exist in diminished numbers even in our day, the first attempt at systematic instructions on the Irish or Union pipes was that formulated by O'Farrell, the renowned piper elsewhere mentioned. Following is the full title:

O'Farrell's
Collection of NATIONAL IRISH MUSIC for the
UNION PIPES
Comprising a variety of the
Most Favorite Slow and Sprightly
TUNES SET in proper STILE & TASTE
with Variations and Adapted Likewise
for the GERMAN FLUTE, VIOLIN, FLAGELET
PIANO & HARP with a SELECTION
of Favorite Scotch Tunes
Also a Treatise with the most
Perfect Instructions ever yet Published for the
PIPES

Entd. at Stats. Hall.
To be had at Mr. Gaw's, 31 Carnaby Street, Golden Square, & Mr. O'Farrell's 65 Swallow Street, London,

Where Gentlemen may likewise be accommodated with Real-Toned Irish Pipes.

The work, although undated, was published about 1797-1800. Years of search and inquiry for this extremely rare volume, with the assistance of Irish and English book agencies, proved futile, and it was eventually through the never-failing kindness and courtesy of W. H. Grattan Flood, Mus. Doc., Organist of Enniscorthy Cathedral; author of "A History of Irish Music" and "The Story of the Harp," that we have come into possession of a literal transcript of O'Farrell's Treatise, etc.; from the original copy in Trinity College Library; and which is said to be the only one in Ireland.

Perhaps not for its rarity and novelty, so much as for its practical value, will it be appreciated by those for whom it will fill a long felt want; nor will it, we trust, be found devoid of interest to the many who still cherish at least a sentimental regard for the Folk Music of the Olden Time.

THE UNION PIPES

Being an instrument now so much improved as renders it able to play any kind of Music, and with the additional accompanyments which belong to it produce a variety of pleasing Harmony which forms as it were a little Band in itself.

Gentlemen often expressing a desire to learn the Pipes have been prevented by not meeting with a proper Book of Instructions, which has induced the Author to write the following Treatise, which it is presumed with the favorite Collection of Tunes added thereto will be acceptable to the Lovers of Ancient and Pastoral Music.

The first thing to be observ'd in learning this Instrument is the fixing it to the Body, so as to give it wind, which is done as follows. There is a small Pipe fasten'd to the Bag, the top of which is to be fix'd in the Mouth of the Bellows, so as to convey the wind freely to the Bag; there are also two ribbans or strings fastened to the bellows, the longest of which is tyed round the Body so as to keep the bellows steady: the other ribband is brought over the arm and fasten'd to the small end of the bellows. When done the Learner may begin to blow by moving the arm to which the bellows is fixed up and down easy and regular, untill the Bag is full of wind, which must then be fixed under the opposite Arm, and press'd so as to produce the tone. The Learner may at the same time stop the upper part of the Chanter with that hand where the Bag rests, by placing the tops of the fingers on the holes, keeping the bag well secured with one arm, and blowing constant and steady with the other, which when the Learner finds he can continue to do with ease for a few minutes, he may then proceed to stop the lower part of the chanter. But not with the tops of the fingers as the upper hand, it must be done by placing the little finger on the lower hole and the middle part of the other three fingers on the next holes, keeping the thumb behind to support the chanter. The Drones are not to be kept over the hand, but under so as to rest near the Body.

The Learner then setting as upright as possible, having all the holes stopt begins to sound the first note D—which will produce a soft full tone as often as the chanter is well stopt. When Master of blowing and stoping the pipes you may proceed to the following Scale. At the same time I would advise the Learner to stop all the Drones for some days untill he can play a tune or two.

APPENDIX A

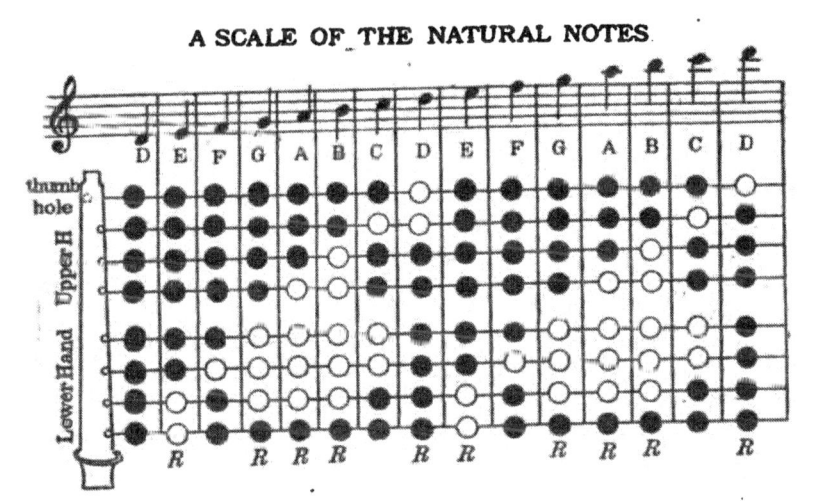

A SCALE OF THE NATURAL NOTES

The first thing to be observ'd in the above Scale is that the Notes of Music are placed on five parrelel Lines call'd a Stave. Each Note distinguished by its proper Name. Secondly the next table which has eight lines, on each of which there are a number of black and white dots, the black signifying such fingers as are to be stopt, and the white dots such as are to be raised.

The high Notes or what are call'd pinch'd Notes on the pipes begin in E over which there is a mark thus *x* to signify that the Bag must be pressed somewhat more than in sounding the other Notes.

The Letter R is like wise fixed under the eight lines, to signify that the chanter must there rest on the knee, and for that purpose it would be requisite to provide a small piece of white leather to place on the knee, under the chanter as nothing else will stop the wind so well.

The Learner may then begin to make the first note D by having all the holes perfectly stopt as may be seen by observing so many black Dots on the Lines representing the eight holes of the chanter. The next Note is E which is mark'd in the table with two white dots on the two lower lines, to signify that the two lower fingers are to be rais'd together, while the chanter rests on the Knee.

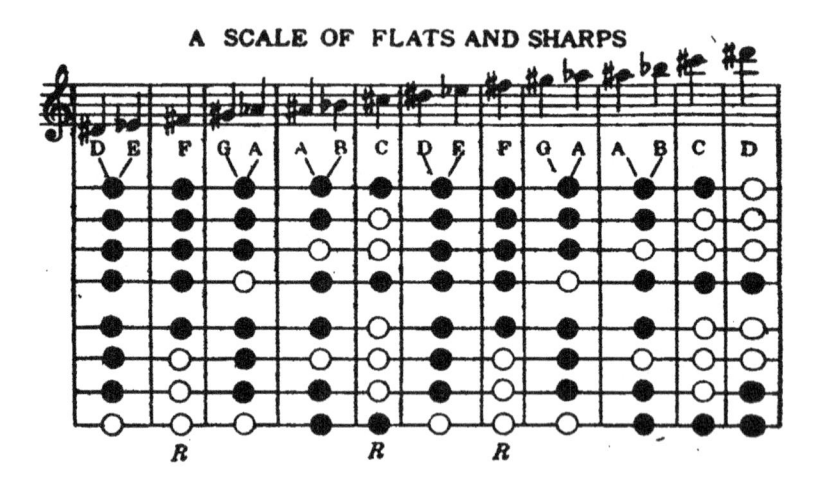

A SCALE OF FLATS AND SHARPS

EXPLANATION OF THE PRECEDING SCALE

It is to be observed in this Scale that the Sharp of one Note is the Flat of the next above it for Example D Sharp and E Flat in the beginning of this Scale are both performed in the same manner, likewise G Sharp and A Flat and so of the rest.

When Flats or Sharps are placed at the beginning of the Stave all the Notes on the Lines on which they are fixed are to be play'd Sharp or Flat unless contradicted by a Natural.

A Sharp, mark'd thus ♯ before any Note, makes it half a tone Sharper or higher. A Flat, mark'd thus ♭ makes it half a tone lower, and a Natural mark'd thus ♮ reduces any Note made Flat or Sharp to its primitive state.

APPENDIX A 325

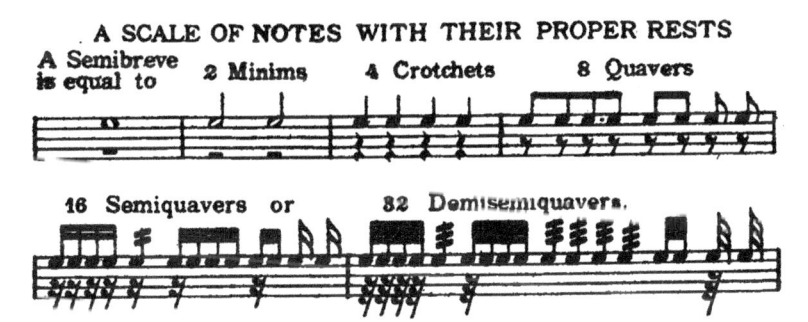

A SCALE OF NOTES WITH THEIR PROPER RESTS
A Semibreve is equal to   2 Minims   4 Crotchets   8 Quavers

16 Semiquavers or   32 Demisemiquavers.

When ever Rests occur they imply silence for the length of the note they severally correspond. As for Example the Rest in the beginning of this Scale is equal in time to a Semibreve or four Crotchets and the next to the time of a Minim &c.

OF TIME

There are two sorts of Time, viz.: Common and Triple. Common Time is known by any one of these Characters, call'd Time Moods **C C** or $\frac{2}{4}$. The two first marks contain the value of a Semibreve or four Crotchets in each Bar, but $\frac{2}{4}$ contains only a Minim or two Crotchets in a Bar. Likewise the first mark denotes the slowest sort of Common Time, the next a degree quicker, & last a brisk movement. Triple Time is known by any of the following figures $\frac{3}{2}$, $\frac{3}{4}$, $\frac{3}{8}$, $\frac{12}{8}$, $\frac{9}{8}$, $\frac{6}{4}$, or $\frac{6}{8}$, $\frac{9}{8}$, and are all moods of Triple Time, the first denoting a Grave movement, the two next marks are usually prefixt to slow Airs and Minuets, and all the rest adapted for Jigg tunes and brisk Music.

A SAMPLE OF COMMON AND TRIPLE TIME.
Common Time   Simple Triple Time

COMPOUND TRIPLE TIME.

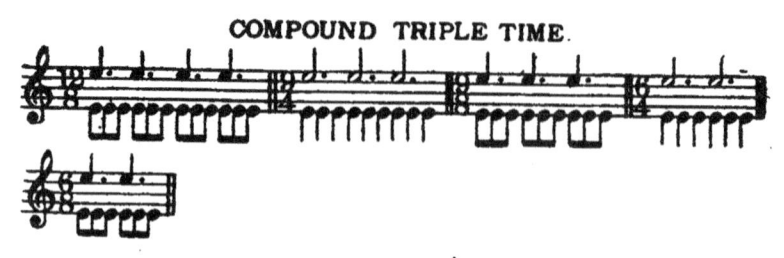

A dot following any Note thus 𝅗𝅥. 𝅘𝅥. 𝅘𝅥𝅮. 𝅘𝅥𝅯. makes it half as long again, that is a dotted Minim is equal to three Crotchets, a dotted Crotchet to three Quavers, and so of the others, a dot following a Rest lengthens it in the same manner.

EXAMPLE

EXPLANATION OF VARIOUS MARKS

A Single stroke or Bar thus ≡ drawn across the five lines divides the measure, and distinguishes one Bar from another. A Double Bar | | divides the Airs and Songs into longer parts, and is always put at the End of a movement. A Repeat 𝄇 or 𝄋 Signifies that such a part is to be play'd twice over.

A Slur ⌢ drawn over or under any number of Notes, signifies that the sound is to be continued from one note to the other. A figure 3 placed over or under any three Notes, imports they are to be play'd in the time of two. A figure 6 placed in the same manner signifies that they are to be play'd in the time of four. A Dot with a circular

APPENDIX A

stroke thus ⌢ signifies a pause or Rest on the Note over or under which it is placed. A Direct, thus ∿ is put at the end of a Stave to shew what Note begins the following.

OF GRACES

A Shake is an agitation or mixture of two sounds together, which is performed by a quick motion of the finger, and is commonly mark'd thus *tr* over the Note that is to be shook. The first shake on this instrument is made on E, and as this shake is occasionally done two different ways on the same Note, I would advise the learner to be acquainted with both, it is sometimes done with the chanter resting on the Knee, having every finger stopt except the two lower ones, and at the same time beating quick with the first finger of the Lower hand—it may also be done with the chanter rais'd off the knee having every finger stopt except the one next the lower finger then by a quick beating of the first finger of the lower hand it is performed. All the rest of the Shakes are done by a quick motion of the finger above the Note required to be shook, for Example if G is to be shaken the Note A above it must beat quick, as may be seen in the following Example.

Mark'd   Play'd   Mark'd   Play'd

Apogiaturas ♩ ♪ are little notes which borrow their time from the Notes before which they are placed, for Example

Mark'd Play'd Mark'd Play'd

OF TIPPING OR POPPING THE NOTES ON THE PIPES

A knowledge of this is very necessary to every person who is desirous of playing the Instrument perfect, so it ought to be studied as soon as the Pupil is well acquainted with the Gamut, and can blow and stop the chanter well.

What is meant by Tipping, is making every Note Staccato or distinct and is done by having the Chanter close on the knee with all the holes stopt, then by a quick rising of any one or more fingers up and down together the Tipping is performed.

In Tipping low D you must have all the holes stopt, then rising the Chanter quick off the knee and down again it is done, which you may repeat as often as you please. In Tipping some other Notes on the Pipes, you rise two or three fingers at a time, which must go up and down the same as if there was but one.

The following will shew such Notes as require Tipping, and likewise how many fingers are to be rais'd together, the Chanter must rest on the knee while the Tipping is performing.

A SCALE OF SUCH NOTES AS REQUIRE TIPPING

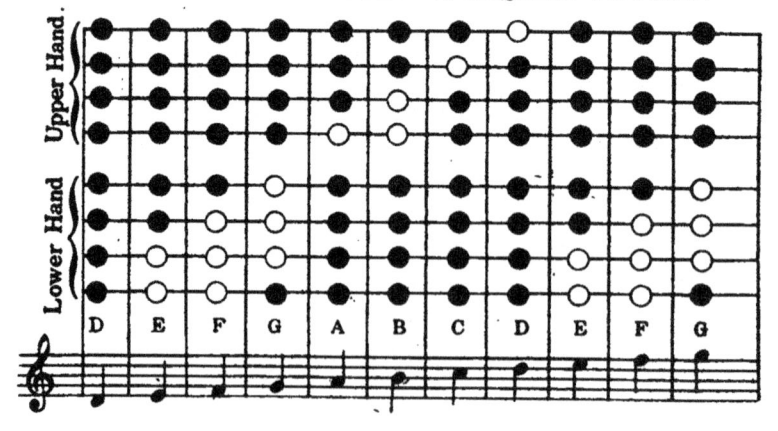

APPENDIX A 329

When the Pupil finds he can make all the above Notes distinct he can proceed to the following Example, where the notes are double tipt and make the two first by raising the thumb of the upper hand quick up and down twice, and so of the rest.

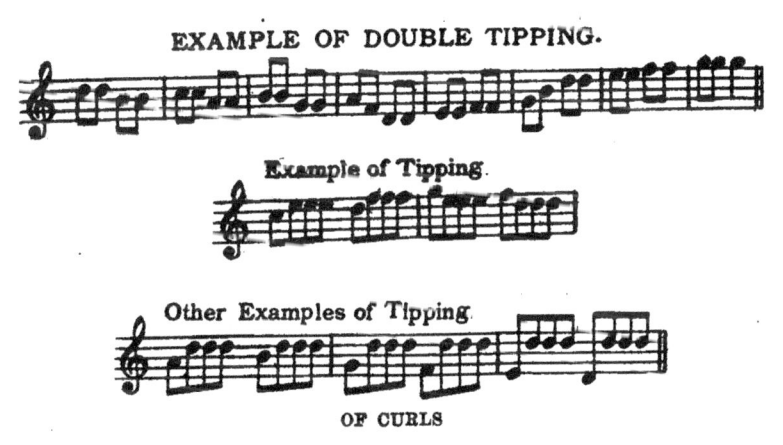

EXAMPLE OF DOUBLE TIPPING.

Example of Tipping.

Other Examples of Tipping.

OF CURLS

Curls are frequently introduced in Jigg tunes and Reels, and have a very pleasing effect in giving double harmony and Spirit to the Music, and therefore ought to be practised at leisure. In the following Example may be seen some useful and popular Curls much practised.

Example I   Example II   Example III

The Curl in the first Example being a principle one on the Pipes is perform'd by sounding the Note D, by a sudden patt of the lower finger of the upper hand, then slurring the other Notes quick and finishing the last Note by another patt of the lower finger of the upper hand. The

Curls in the second Example are easily done, as it is made while sounding the second Note of each of the three tyed quavers, by a sudden patt of the same lower finger of the upper hand and answers for two Notes. In the third Example the Curls are done in the same manner by patt of the finger while sounding the second Note of each of the tyed Quavers.

OF OTHER CURLS

Example IV.   Example V.   Example VI.

In the fourth Example the Curl is made by a patt of the same finger while sounding the second Note of the tyed Quavers, Example the fifth by a patt of the same finger while sounding D, slurring the next Note and finishing the last by another patt of the same finger. Example the sixth, the Curl is made by two quick patts of the upper finger of the lower hand while sounding the first Note F and finishing the next note D by a patt of the same finger. The third Note E in the same Example begins by two patts of the upper finger of the lower hand and finishes the next note D, with one patt of the lower finger of the upper hand.

OF TUNING THE DRONES OR BASS

Most good performers at this time have only two Drones going at once, which are the two large ones. The large Drone must be stopt, then sounding lower A to the smaller Drone it may be screwed inward or outward till the sound is equal to A, then sounding the large Drone it may be screwed in the same manner till the sound of it is an exact Octave to the rest.

OF THE USE OF THE REGULATOR

The Regulator being one of the principle accompaniments to the Chanter, is used by most performers on this instrument and when managed with Judgment produces a very pleasing harmony, but I would not advise the learner to practise the Regulator untill he could play a few tunes well.

There are generally four Keys fixt to the Regulator—the lower of which is F, and must sound the same Note as low F Sharp on the Chanter. The next key is G and must be exactly in tune with low G on the Chanter. The next Key above that is A and is tuned to low A on the Chanter. The upper key of the four is B & is likewise tuned to B on the Chanter. The following Example will shew what Notes on the Chanter that each key of the Regulator will agree with.

EXAMPLE OF THE CHANTER AND REGULATOR.

Chanter

Regulator

lower key

It must be observed that it is with the wrist or Heel of the lower hand that each Key is touch'd, and care must be taken not to touch two keys at the same time. I would advise the pupil to begin the use of the Regulator by first sounding the Note low D, on the Chanter, to the low key F on the Regulator, which after a little practise will lead to a knowledge of the other Keys.

APPENDIX B

HINTS TO AMATEUR PIPERS

BY PATRICK J. TOUHEY.
The Celebrated American Performer on the Irish Pipes

THERE is probably no musical instrument in existence today that is so difficult to master as the Irish or Union bagpipe, and for that reason the percentage of proficient performers is much less than on any other instrument. The lack of competent teachers is also an important drawback, particularly because on no instrument is an instructor so necessary to the success of the learner, as on the Union pipes, unless perhaps it be on the Scotch or Highland pipes, on account of the shriller tones.

In the hands of a capable performer, no instrument gives to Irish melody, especially dance music, such true traditional expression as the loved instrument of the Irish peasantry.

To acquire any reasonable degree of expertness on this most complicated and highly developed bagpipe, the learner instead of attempting too much, should be content to commence at the bottom, as he would in any other line of studies, and not undertake to play haphazard, as too many often do.

Fired by ambition on hearing the performance of some good piper, the music lover ordinarily having more or less acquaintance with some other wind instrument, obtains possession of a set of Irish pipes, out of tune and repair from disuse, and starts in to be a piper, without a teacher, and depending altogether on practice based probably on his previous fingering of the flute. He expects to accomplish in six months what may be took the piper whose playing inspired him, twenty years to acquire; the consequence being, of course, one more name added to the list of bad or indifferent pipers.

It is well to remember at the start that the fluter, Highland piper, or clarinet player, has also much to unlearn, if success is to be attained on the Irish or Union pipes.

Before attempting to play or practice on a full set, the learner should procure the best bag, bellows and chanter obtainable. With the bag under the left arm, strap the bellows under the right arm, and let the end of the chanter rest on the right knee. Hold the bag securely when inflating it with the bellows, and with the left hand uppermost, place the fingers so as to evenly cover the holes of the chanter; the first joint of the left thumb covering the D hole at the back of the chanter, which should be held as loosely as possible. It would be too tedious and confusing to describe in detail the manner of holding each individual finger, with the names of each hole, which, by the way, are the same as in the flute, excepting the low and high D. The amateur must, however, be particular to hold the fingers straight across the chanter, using the second joints of the second and third fingers of each hand to cover the holes. Neither shall the fingers be crooked or bent, or the tips thereof used instead of the flat joint for that purpose.

Assuming that the learner has already some rudimentary musical training, he will understand that with all eight holes stopped evenly the tone of low D is produced, that being the lowest note on the Irish chanter. Differing from other instruments, the end of the chanter rests on the knee, except when low D is being sounded. The player automatically lifts the chanter in playing that note.

To get the hard sound of low D, the note must be helped by a short snap of the A finger. After this trick has been learned, the E will be sounded by lifting the two lowest fingers—that is, the little and third finger of the right hand; F sharp, by lifting the middle finger; and G, the middle and forefinger of the right hand. Then follows A, which is sounded by lifting the third finger; B, the third and middle finger; C sharp, the forefinger; and high D in the first octave, the thumb of the left hand. To make each tone clear or staccato, the finger or fingers producing each note must be closed as the succeeding notes are being opened.

When the first eight notes or octave has been mastered, the learner may start the second octave by blowing stronger on the bellows, with a corresponding increase of pressure on the bag, and lifting the same fingers as before for E, F sharp, G, A and B. The C sharp, in the second octave, is produced by lifting the third and forefinger of the left hand, all others being closed. The tone of high D in the second octave is made by lifting the top or forefinger of the left hand and the three lowest fingers of the right hand, with all other holes closed.

Three months is not an unreasonable length of time for a beginner to practice reading and playing the scale in the key of D, that being the scale in which the Irish chanter is pitched. After he has practiced the scale in two octaves, until he can sound it up and down lively and without any after sounds between the notes, he may attempt some simple exercises, but above all things he must avoid playing for dancing or playing dance music even, except very slowly, for at least six months. Once the amateur starts to playing for dancing, and playing too fast, he can seldom or never learn to play slow or proper time.

Every beginner should first practice the scale of D, because he gets that scale with the fingers only, without the use of keys. After D, he should take the scale of G, with only F sharp, the C being natural and fingered with the key on the back of the chanter. With the proper fundamental knowledge, all the rest will come with practice.

One of the graces essential,—it might be called indispensable—to effective pipe-playing, is the "turn" or "curl." Without graces of this nature, the performance of even the best player is too formal and bare. It is done as follows: Sound first the note to be "turned," then the note above it, the note itself again, next the note below it, and lastly the note to be "turned." For example, if G is the note to be "turned" sound G, A, G, F, G in quick succession (the five notes to be made in two eighths or triplet time), otherwise the proper effect will be lost.

Another embellishment in pipe-playing is the "roll" or "cran," as it was termed by most of the old time players. This is accomplished on the low E and the low D by quickly snapping A, G, F, at the same time keeping the E or the D note open, both being similarly rolled. In other words, snapping the notes A, E, G, E, F, E or A, D, G, D, F, D in three-eighths time.

The "turn" and the "roll," I believe, are the two great embellishments of pipe-playing when done neatly.

Another embellishment is the triplet with the top hand. For instance, if B is the note to be taken for a foundation, the triplet consists of B, C, B, B played quickly. If it is A, the notes are A, C, A, A. This combination is very essential in jig, reel and hornpipe playing, or in fact any quick or lively music.

When the amateur has mastered the scales of D and G, and acquired dexterity in the "turns," "rolls" and triplets above mentioned, he is ready to start to play any kind of music on a full set of pipes. The experience acquired so far in practicing on the bag, bellows and chanter, will enable the advanced learner to keep wind to the full set without much inconvenience.

THE DRONES

The next step is tuning the drones, one of the most important features in connection with the instrument and an art in which some so-called pipers are lacking. Commence by tuning the smallest or tenor drone to A on the chanter. If the latter is properly fitted with a reed, it will tune also to low D and high D. Then tune the second drone to the tenor, and lastly the bass drone to the second. In some old style pipes there are four drones, but the same rule holds good in all cases. No piper worthy of the name will play in public when his instrument is out of tune.

THE REGULATORS

An instrument equipped with three drones and three regulators is considered a full set. Few made in this generation have more or less. The regulators are arranged as follows: First the G bass on the outside (furthest from the player) with four notes in the following order, G, A, B, C, and corresponding to the same notes on the chanter but an octave lower. Then comes the first treble regulator with D, F sharp, G, A, corresponding to the same notes on the first octave of the chanter. Next comes the second treble regulator with F sharp, G, A, B, C, in unison with the same notes on the first octave on the chanter. Should there be a fourth regulator or D bass, it is generally placed on the inside or nearest the performer's body. It has three notes, viz., D, E, F sharp, an octave lower than the same notes on the chanter, being in fact a continuation or complement of the G bass.

Across the bottom of the three outside regulators, we have G on the bass, D on the first and G on the second treble regulators, making the chord of G—first, fifth and octave of the chord. We also get first, third, and fifth, of the chord of G by sounding G on bass, D on first, and B on second treble regulators, which is the form of G chord most commonly used on the Irish or Union pipes. A form of the chord of D is obtained by sounding the notes D on the D bass, F sharp on the second, and D on the first treble, and A on the G bass regulators, the full chord of D being D, F sharp, A and D. The chords of D and G are most frequently used and the only ones that can be made correctly on the limited compass of the regulators.

A good accompaniment for lively music in the key of G can be made by the wrist on first and second treble regulators, using G on the first and B on the second, as changes in the tune require, the ear being the guide in changing the chord.

TUNING THE REGULATORS

The lowest note G on the bass can be tuned to G on the chanter and D on the first treble to G on the bass. G on the second treble can be tuned also to G on the chanter. All other notes on the regulators may be tuned to their corresponding notes on the chanter.

To amateur pipers endowed with special aptitude, tireless persistence, and unlimited patience, the foregoing suggestions will, it is hoped, prove both helpful and instructive.

APPENDIX C.

As illustrating the extent to which time, taste, and development have varied. Irish Folk Music, or traditional melodies, the following typical examples are submitted for comparison.

MY LODGING IT IS ON THE COLD GROUND.

From – *Vocal Music or The Songster's Companion* – London 1775.

Nº 1. *N.B.* This is the air of Moore's "Believe me if all those endearing Young Charms."

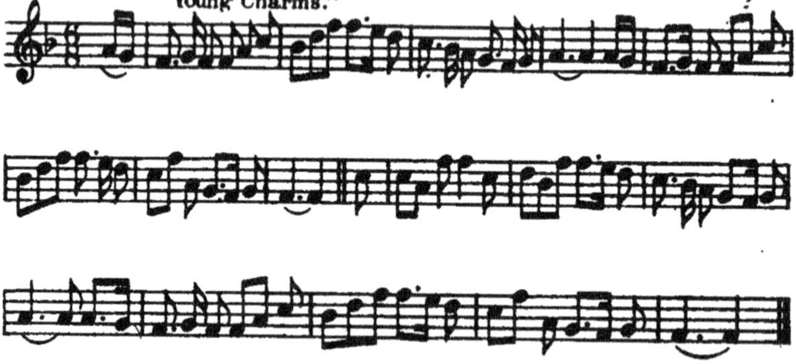

MY LODGING IS ON THE COLD GROUND.

From – Aird's *Selection of Scotch, English, Irish, and Foreign Airs, Vol.1.*, Glasgow 1782.

Nº 2.

MY LODGING IS ON THE COLD GROUND.
From — *O'Neill's Music of Ireland* — Chicago, 1908

No 3.

No 1.   TOBY PEYTON'S PLANGSTY
Composed by the Bard, O'CAROLAN Born 1670 Died 1738.
Bunting's Version procured from Higgins the Harper in 1792.

No 2. TRADITIONAL MUNSTER VERSION.

No 3. FLORID SETTING.

By Sergt. James O'Neill, as played by his father,
a native of County Down.

Nº 1. THE HUMORS OF BANDON.
A LONG DANCE.
THE HUMORS OF LISTIVAIN – Irish.
From – Aird's *Selection of Scotch, English, Irish and Foreign Airs. Vol 3.*
Glasgow, 1788.

Nº 2. THE MERRY OLD WOMAN.
From – *The Complete Petrie Collection*
(Compiled early in the 19th Century.)

Nº 3. THE HUMORS OF BANDON.
From – *Levey's Dance Music of Ireland.* – London, 1858.

Nº 4. THE HUMORS OF BANDON.

From – *O'Neill's Dance Music of Ireland*, – Chicago, 1907.

Nº 1. THE BLACKBIRD.

A traditional air, Set by Sergt. James O'Neill as played by his father in County Down.

From – *O'Neill's Music of Ireland* – Chicago, 1908.

Nº 2. LONG DANCE. SETTING.
By Sergt. James O'Neill.

From — *O'Neill's Dance Music of Ireland* — Chicago, 1907.

Nº 3. BUNTING'S ARRANGEMENT.
Procured from D. O'Donnell — County Mayo — 1803.

Remarks — Very ancient — Author and date unknown.

INDEX.

A

Absent-minded Man, The, 158.
Absent-minded Woman, The, 35.
Ace and Deuce of Pipering, 40, 123.
A Country Wake—Comedy, 170.
Adair, Patrick, 166.
Adam's *Musical Repository*, 135.
Agreeable Surprise—Opera, 239, 240.
A Handefull of Pleasant Delites, 188, 231.
Aird's *Selection of Scotch, English, Irish and Foreign Airs*, 90, 92, 93, 94, 103, 110, 111, 116, 120, 131, 136, 138, 139, 140, 149, 154, 157, 161, 171, 174, 176, 185, 189, 191, 197, 199, 201, 234, 239, 259, 338, 341.
A Jig to the Irish Cry, 140.
Alas, My Bright Lady, 129.
Alday's *A Pocket Volume of Airs, Duets, etc.*, 99, 116, 143, 144, 166, 189, 199, 201, 203, 260.
Alexander's *Flowers of the Emerald Isle*, 248.
Alexander's *Select Beauties for the Flute*, 261.
Alexander's *Miscellaneous Beauties*, 261.
A Little Hour Before Day, 70.
All Covered with Moss, 88.
Allen, John, 121, 122.
Ally Croker, 179.
American Anthology, 90.
A Mug of Brown Ale, 96.
An Cailin deas Cruidte na m-bo, 202.
An Onoicin Fraoich, 150.
Andy the Fiddler, 209.
A New Book of Tabliture, 233.
An Gaedhaine Fiadhaine, 194.
An Gearan Buidhe, 152.
A Night in Ireland, 222.
An Peacthach 'sa Bas, 78.
An Rogaire Dubh, 133.
An Seanduine, 72, 112, 171, 172.
Aonach Bearna Gaoithe, 138.
Apollo's Banquet—Opera, 173.
Appeal—Revival of Pastimes, 286.
Apples in Winter, 93.
Arethusa, The, 183.

A Rose Tree in Full Bearing, 131.
As Down by Banna's Banks, 235.
Ask My Father, 37.
A Soft, Mild Morning, 241.
At Past 12 O'Clock, 201.
Auld Robin Gray, 136.
Ayle House, Clare, 122.

B

Baal-tigh-abhoran, 198.
Baal tinne, 198.
Bagpipes—Various kinds, 308 to 319.
Baker's Island, 16.
Balfe, Michael W., 16, 80, 289, 290.
Balfe's Compositions, 80.
Balinamona, oro, 192.
Balin a Mone, 192, 237.
Ball the—*A Glance at Almack's* 299-307.
Ballet, William—*Lute Book*, 233.
Baltiorum, 198.
Banish Misfortune, 88.
Bank of Ireland, 49.
Banks of Banna, 235.
Banks of Claudy, 26.
Banks of the Ilen, 117.
Bannocks of Barley Meal, 137.
Bantry Bay, 145.
Bantry Bay Boys, 145.
Bantry Boys, 145.
Bantry Bay, hornpipe, 19, 145.
Bantry Hornpipe, 120, 145.
Bards—See Irish Bards.
Bark Is on the Swelling Shore, 134.
Barley Grain, 73.
Barndoor Jig, 140.
Barony Jig, 125.
Dathe, William—*A Brief Introduction to the Art of Music*, 231.
Battle of Killicrankie, 124.
Baulthy Oura, 199.
Beamish, Abram S., 98, 102.
Bean a Tigh ar Lar, 111.
Bean Dubh an Gleanna, 68.
Beardless Boy, 134.
Beatty, John K., 25, 26, 50.
Bee, The, 21, 139, 190, 198, 239, 247.
Be Easy, You Rogue, 94.

INDEX

Beethoven—Irish Melodies, 52, 247.
Beggar's Wedding—Opera, 165, 170, 201, 236.
Beg, van Ella gum, 203.
Beidmaoid Ag ol, 79.
Belfast Harp Meeting. 241, 269.
Belfast Harp Society, 269.
Believe Me It All, etc., 179, 184.
Belles of Liscarroll, 102.
Beranger, French traveler, 112.
Bessy Murphy, 37, 89.
Biddy Maloney, 93.
Bigger, Frances Joseph, 43.
Big or Little, 131.
"Big Pat's" Reel, 19.
Billy Byrne of Ballymanus, 75.
Billy O'Rourke is the Bouchal, 138, 139.
Black-backed Cow, 190.
Blackbird, The, 75, 169. 342, 343.
Black Burke, 107.
Black But Lovely, 191.
Black-eyed Susan, 185.
Black-haired Little Rose, 153.
Black-headed Dearie, 190.
Black Rock, 107.
Black Rogue, 133.
Black Rosebud, 153.
Blacksmith's Hornpipe, 144.
Blackthorn Stick, 125.
Blanchard's Hornpipe, 116, 144.
Bland and Weller's Country Dances, 199.
Blind Mary, 83.
Blood-red Rose, 154.
Blooming Meadows, 105.
Blossom of the Raspberry, 241.
Bodach an Drantain, 101.
Bothar o Huaid.
Bonaparte Crossing the Rhine, 146.
Bonaparte's Defeat, 146.
Bonaparte's Retreat, 125, 146, 147.
Boney Highlander, 132.
Bonny Cuckoo, 241.
Bowlan, Tom, 28, 213.
Boy from the Mountain, 102.
Boys of Ballinamore, 41.
Boys of Blue Hill, 41.
Boys of the Lough, 97.
Box About the Fireplace, 141.
Breestheen, Mira, 97.
Bremner's *Scots Reels and Country Dances*, 171.
Bridget O'Neill, 132.
Bright Black Rose, 154.
Bright Love of My Heart, 151.
Brighton Camp, 177, 178.
Bright Pulse of My Heart, 148, 151.
Brigid of the Fair Hair, 133.
Brisk Irish Lad, 21.
Brisk Young Lad, 21.
British Musical Biography, 71, 250, 259.

Broderick, Thomas, 16, 17, 139.
Brogue Hornpipe, 114.
Brown, Dr., *Poetry and Music*, 278.
Brysson's *Curious Selection of Irish Airs*, 149, 180, 240.
Buachaillin Ban, 98.
Buckley, James (piper), 150, 157.
Bucky Highlander, 133.
"Bugga Fee Hoosa," 108.
Bully for You, 133.
Bumper Squire Jones, 191.
Bunch of Green Rushes, 134.
Bung Your Eye, 21.
Bunker Hill Reel, 98.
Bunting Edward, 12, 56, 57, 66, 69, 70, 74, 83, 84, 89, 93, 94, 99, 103, 109, 118, 120, 132, 140, 150, 153, 154, 155, 159, 184, 194, 195, 198, 200, 231, 235, (241,) 243, 268, 269, 281, 282.
Bunting's *Collection of the Ancient Irish Music*, 82, 134, 152, 161, 165, 194, 199, 240, 241, 247, 294.
Bunting's *Collection of the Ancient Music of Ireland*, 134, 153, 156, 241, 247, 294.
Bunting's *The Ancient Music of Ireland*, 90, 129, 139, 147, 150, 155, 157, 191, 197, 239, 241, 242, 248, 282, 294, 298, 339, 343.
Burns, Robert, on Irish Airs, 169, 257.

C

Cahill, Sergt. James, 30, 42.
Cahirciveen, 73.
Cailin Beag mo Chroidhe, 68.
Cailin Deas Donn, 102.
Cailin og a Stuire me, 188
Cailleach on Airgid, 89.
Ca Ira, 123.
Caledonian Muse, 155, 176, 278, 298.
Calen o Custure me, 188, 232.
Calino Custurame, 188.
Caitilin ni Uallachain, 169.
Calleen oge Asthore, 188.
Calliope or Musical Miscellany, 176, 259.
Cambrian Minstrelsie, 184.
Campbell's *Albyn's Anthology*, 260.
Campbells Are Coming, 72, 112, 171, 172.
Campbell's *Philosophical Survey*, 103, 280.
Cant, Joseph, 28, 101, 102.
Cantwell MSS., 51.
Captivating Youth, 241.
Capt. McGreal of Connemara, 131.
Capt. Oakhain, 194.

INDEX

Capt. O'Kane, or the Wounded Hussar, 194.
Cara Ceann Dilis, 190.
Carbray, James, 66, 95, 156.
Carbray's Frolics, 95.
"Carberry Piper," 115, 126.
Carey, John, 35, 87, 146, 157.
Carleton, William, 9, 122, 220.
Carllone—A Favorite Irish Tune, 193.
Carolan's Cap, 156.
Caroline O'Neill's Hornpipe, 120.
Carroll, Rev. John J., 47.
Carter, C. F., the "Milesian," 183.
Carter, Timothy, 183.
Cash, John—Wicklow Piper, 228.
Cashmere Shawl, 34.
Cassey's Jig, 139.
Castle Donovan, 12.
Castle Hyde, 81.
Castle of Andalusia, opera, 240.
Castletown, Conners, 87.
Cead Mile Failte, origin, 167.
Ceann Dubh Dileas, 190, 191.
Cecelia O'Gara, 180.
Chami ma Chattie, 200.
Change in Musical Taste, 267, 285, 286.
Chappell's Old English Popular Music. 177, 178, 179, 180, 185, 188, 233, 257, 286, 299.
Charmer With the Fair Locks, 130.
Cherish the Ladies, 94.
Chief O'Neill's Favorite, 114.
Child of My Heart, 37.
Chiling O guiry, 189, 237.
Chorus Jig, 102, 103, 155, 298.
Chorus Reel, 34, 156.
Church Hill Reel, 102.
Cianach Mor, 12.
Citizen Magazine, 82, 107, 249.
Clashmore House, 121, 224.
Clergymen Pipers, 272, 273.
Cliffs of Moher, 19.
Clinton's Gems of Ireland, 21, 83, 113, 139, 157, 190, 193, 198, 249.
Clinton's 200 Irish Melodies, 248.
Clancy, "Rick," 223.
Clive, Kitty, 164.
Cloone Hornpipe, 114.
Cobbler's Jig, 298.
Cockle Shells, 176.
Coleman, Jas T., 306.
Colleen Rue, 69.
College Grove, reel, 37, 110.
College Hornpipe, 144, 160.
Col. O'Gara, 131.
Colomane Cross, 14.
Col. Rodney, reel, 34.
Come Ashore Jolly Tar, 120.
Come Under My Plaids, 133.
Complainte of Scotland, 302.
Compleat Tutor for the Guitar, 136, 238.
Conneely, "Paddy"—Galway Piper, 50, 130, 239.

Conners, John—Chicago Piper, 19, 20, 209, 210, 211, 283.
Conran, Michael, National Music of Ireland, 198, 283.
Conway, James, 121, 122.
Conway, Neill, 22.
Cooke's Selection of Favorite Irish Airs, 240.
Cook in the Kitchen, jig, 89.
Coolin, The, 64.
Copey's Jig, 21, 139.
Cork Pipers' Club, 289.
Cormac na Paidireacha, 13.
Country Dances. See 296 to 307.
County Limerick Buck Hunt, 179.
County Mayo—Air, 74, 75.
Courtney's Favorite, 95.
Courtney—Kerry Fiddler, 95, 156.
Cover the Buckle, 300, 301.
Cows Are a Milking, 111.
Craig, Adam—A Collection of the Choicest Scots Tunes, 170.
Creedan—Cork Cobbler, 126.
Creigh, Pierce—Clare poet, 179.
Criticism by Cork Cleric, 55, 56, 57.
Croker, Crofton, 179.
Cronin, Edward, 44, 45, 53, 61, 66, 70, 78, 83, 87, 88, 89, 90, 98, 104, 110, 114, 120, 123, 124, 125, 136, 141, 145, 146, 180, 223.
Crooghan a Venee, 196.
Croppy Tailor, The, 77.
Crosby's Irish Musical Repository, 57, 134, 140, 147, 199, 202, 203, 244.
Crouch's Specimens, 260.
Crouch, Frederick Nicholls, 248.
Crouch's Celebrated Songs of Ireland, 249.
Cruachan na Feinne, 196.
Cuckoo's Nest, 120, 121.
Cudgell, The, 139.
Cuisle Geal mo Chroidhe, 148, 151.
Cuisle mo Chroidhe, 148.
Cumberland's Crew, 73.
Cup of Tea, 34.
Curri Koun Dilich, 237.
Cushlamachree, 148.

D

Dainty Besom Maker, 131.
Daly, Jerry, 116.
Da Mihi Manum, 237.
Dance Revival a Success, 226, 271.
Dances—Ancient and Obsolete, 296 to 307.
Dandy Denny Cronin, 98.
Dandy O, The, 148, 149, 180, 240.
Dangling of the Irish Bearns, 193, 237.
Daniel of the Sun, 132.
Dan the Cobbler, 87.
Dark Maiden of the Valley, 68.
Dark Woman of the Glen, 60.

INDEX

Daughter of the Rock, 206.
Davey on *English Music*, 286.
Davidson's *Irish Melodies*, 253.
Davis, Thomas, 290.
Dawning of the Day, 154.
Dawson, Baron, 192.
Day I Married Susan, 138.
Death and the Sinner, 78.
Delaney, Bernard, 20, 30, 31, 32, 49, 53, 66, 96, 97, 101, 108, 109, 111, 119, 209, 210, 211, 222, 223.
Denis Delaney, jig, 244.
Denis Don't Be Threatening, 180.
Derrick's *Image of Ireland*, 314.
Devil Among the Tailors, 116.
Devil's Dream, 115, 116.
DeWier's Hornpipe, 118.
Dillon's Fancy, 102.
Dillon, Timothy, 42, 43, 102, 155.
Dissipated Youth, 134.
Dobbin's Flowery Vale, 76, 130.
Doctor O'Neill, jig, 88.
Doggett, Thomas (actor), 170.
Dogs Among the Bushes, 37.
Doherty's Fancy, 92.
Dollard, Rev. Father Wm., 47, 48.
Domhnall na Greine, 132.
"Donegal Piper," 84, 119.
Downfall of Paris, 123.
Downing, Miss Jane, 15.
Downing, Timothy, 15, 105.
Downing, Timothy A., 15.
Down With the Tithes, 105.
Doyle, John, 109.
Doyle, Johnny, 225.
Doyle, Michael, 225.
Doyle's Opinion of Killarney, 225, 226.
Dribbles of Brandy, 139.
Drimen Duff, 190, 237.
Drimendoo, 190.
Drive the Cows Home, 101.
Drogheda Lasses, 34.
Dromfionn Dubh, 190.
Drops of Brandy, 139.
Drunken Sailor, 118.
Dublin Monthly Magazine, 36, 249.
Dublin University Magazine, 8.
Duenna, The, opera, 235, 240.
Duffet, William, 181.
Dungan, James—Copenhagen, 268.
Duke of Buccleugh's Tune, 173.
Dunn, Pat., MSS., 63.
Dunning, I. S., 52, 71, 77.
Dunphy's Hornpipe, 115.
D'Urfey's Pills to Purge Melancholy, 258.

E

Eamonn an Chnuic, 189.
Early, Sergt. James, 30, 36, 38, 49, 53, 66, 88, 89, 90, 96, 99, 100, 101, 102, 108, 110, 111, 113, 114, 118, 211, 223.

Early, Sergt.'s, Hospitality, 89.
Edinburgh Musical Miscellany, 165, 176.
Edinburgh Musical Museum, 259.
Egan, John, Musical Instruments, 316, 317.
Egan's *National Lyrics*, 248.
Egg Hornpipe, 144.
Eibhlin a Ruin, 164, 165, 166, 167.
Eileen Aroon, 164, 165, 166, 167, 168, 237.
Ella Rosenberg, 104.
Emerald Wreath, 257.
Emmett, Dan—Minstrel, 290.
Emon, O. Knuck, 189.
English Music, first printed, 231, 232, 236.
Ennis, John, 37, 38, 53, 89, 107, 110, 160, 211.
Ennis, Tom, 38.
Enright, Michael G., 70.
Enterprise and Boxer, 112.
Ettrick Shepherd, 176.
Erin go Braugh, 135.
Eveleen's Bower, 149, 180, 240.
Evenings at O'Neill's, 91.
Ewe Reel, 34.
Exile of Erin, 135.

F

Faddy, The, 302.
Fading, The, 302.
Fag an Baile, 204.
Fag an bealach, 204.
Fague an ballach, 204.
Faugh a balleach, 204.
Fair at Dungarvan, 129.
Fair-haired Boy, 98.
Fair-haired Little Child, 199.
Fair Maid of Cavan, 43.
Fair Mary Mulholland, 70.
Fair of Windgap, 138.
Fair-skinned, Black-haired Rose, 153.
Fanning, Charles (harper), 229, 235.
Farewell to Lochaber, 180, 181.
Farewell Ye Groves, 135.
Fare You Well, 67.
Fare You Well, Killeavy, 131.
Far From Home, 16.
Farmer Hayes, 69.
Father Dollard's Hornpipe, 48.
Father Fielding's Favorite, 104.
Father Jack Walsh, 138.
Father O'Flynn, 137.
Father Walsh's Hornpipe, 63.
Feakle's Patriotism, 224.
Feudal System Demoralized, 266.
Fidlers, Morris, 173.
Field, John—composer, 289.
Fielding, Rev. James K., 47, 49, 50, 115, 142, 223, 224.
Fingalian's Dance, 193, 237.
Finucane, Michael, 23.
Fire on the Mountain, 99.

INDEX

Fisherman's Widow, 19.
Fisher's Hornpipe, 144.
Fitz Gerald Adair—*Stories of Famous Songs*, 112, 163, 165, 168, 170, 172, 174, 176, 178, 182, 232.
Fitzgerald's *Old Songs of Old Ireland*, 250.
Fitzmaurice—Pipers' Tunes, 244.
Fitzsimon's *Irish Minstrelsy*, 81, 247.
Flood, Grattan — *A History of Irish Music*, 45, 82, 112, 117, 124, 168, 170, 171, 174, 176, 188, 190, 195, 232, 236, 239, 289, 294, 317.
Flotow's Opera, *Martha*, 291.
Flower of the Flock, 18.
Foggy Dew, 150.
Fontainbleau, opera, 188, 240.
Foot of the Mountain, 87.
Forde, MSS., 119, 129, 131, 151, 156, 255.
Forde's *Encyclopedia of Melody*, 80, 82, 134, 138, 140, 144, 161, 185, 190, 191, 192, 198, 261, 262.
Fordyce, Rev., *Sermons*, 267.
Forgive the Muse that Slumbered, 131.
Forrester, Ike, 17.
Foster, Stephen Collins, 290.
Four Courts, reel, 160.
Fox Chase, The, 38.
Fraser, Alex. Duncan—*Some Reminiscences and the Bagpipe*, 271, 309.
Fraser's *Highland Airs*, 260.
Friar's Hill, 69.
Frieze Breeches, jig, 97.
From the Court to the Cottage, 133.
Frost Is All Over, jig and hornpipe, 137, 156.
Fun at Donnybrook, 40, 68.

G

Gaelic League Influence, 222, 224, 284.
Gage, Fane, 194, 195.
Galilei—*Dialogue on Ancient and Modern Music*, 264, 313.
Gallagher's Frolic, 97.
Galway, Tom, 90.
Gamba ora, 196.
Ga mba ora, 196.
Gandsey—Lord Headley's Piper, 39, 40, 230.
Garden of Daisies, 38, 40.
Garryowen, 23, 234, 247.
Gaudry's *Masonic Songs*, 240.
Geese in the Bog, 91.
Gen. Monroe's Lament, 71.
Gentleman's Magazine, 182, 304, 315.
Gubbins' Delight, 80.

Get Up Early, 139.
Get Up Old Woman and Shake Yourself, 99, 143.
Gillan, John, 50, 51, 93, 94, 119.
Gillan, Miss Nellie, 95, 119.
Gillan, na drover, 101, 194.
Gillan's Apples, 93.
Gilmore, Patrick Sarsfield, 290.
Gimlet, The, 131.
Geraldus Cambrensis, 264, 279, 310.
Girl I Left Behind Me, 177, 178, 179.
Girls of the West, 133.
God Bless the Grey Mountain, 134.
God Save Ireland, 285.
Go Home to Your Rest, 149.
Gold Ring, The, 89.
Goodman, Rev. Canon, 256, 273.
Goodman's *School and Home Song Book*, 256.
Gosson's *Short Apologie, etc.*, 266.
Go to the Devil and Shake Yourself, 99, 143.
Gow's *Collection*, 131, 135.
Gradh gan Fios, 195.
Gradh Geal Mo Chroidhe, 151.
Graga-nish, 195, 196.
Graham, Ferquhar, 110, 169, 176, 181, 232, 241, 258.
Graine, Uaile, 169.
Gramachree, 235.
Graves, Alfred Perceval, 137, 196, 206, 253, 256, 282, 284.
Graves' *Irish Folk Songs*, 256.
Graves' *Irish Song Book*, 75, 195, 204, 256, 284.
Graves' *Irish Songs and Ballads*, 256.
Graves' *Song of Erin*, 205, 256.
Graves' *Songs of Old Ireland*, 256.
Graves, Rev. Charles, D.D., 253.
Greencastle Hornpipe, 18.
Green Garters, 84.
Green Jacket, 110.
Green Sleeves, 87, 157.
Green Woods of Truicha, 131.
Griffin, Gerald, 132.
Grogan, Lawrence, 179.
Groves' *Dictionary of Music and Musicians*, 164.
Groves, The (hornpipe), 23, 118.
Groves of Blarney, 81, 291.
Grumbling Rustic, 101.
Gudgeon of Maurice's Car, 20, 211.
Gubbins, George, 80.
Guiry's Favorite, 87.
Guernsey, Wellington—*Songs of Ireland*, 253.

H

Had I a Heart for Falsehood Framed, 235.

INDEX

Hag and Her Praskeen, 105.
Hagerty, Peter, 13, 14.
Hag With the Money, 90.
Hall's *Ireland*, 208.
Handel's *Messiah*, 285.
Happy Days of Youth, 19.
Happy to Meet and Sorry to Part, 101.
Hardiman's *Irish Minstrelsy*, 76, 82, 124, 130, 161, 162, 165, 166, 168, 169, 170, 192, 231.
Hare in the Corn, 157, 158, 159.
Harlequin Amulet, opera, 234.
Harp Revival Attempted, 268, 269, 270.
Harp School Financed From India, 270.
Harpers Ordered Hanged, 265.
Harp That Once, etc., 234.
Hartigan's Fancy, 87, 157.
Hartnett, Sergt. Michael, 38, 40, 68, 73, 79, 123, 125, 146.
Haverty's *300 Irish Airs*, 38, 40, 57, 68, 73, 79, 99, 119, 123, 125, 134, 144, 146, 191, 192, 193, 199, 255.
Hawaiian Islands, 16.
Health to King Philip, 190.
He Asked Me Name the Day, 75.
Heffernan (famous harper), 229.
Hempson, Denis (famous harper), 165, 166, 229, 241, 279.
Henderson's *Flowers of Irish Melody*, 257.
Henebry, Rev. Rich., Ph.D., 30, 40, 43, 68, 113.
Henebry's Work on Irish Music, 47, 48.
Henebry On Chicago Musicians, 48, 49.
Henebry On Touhey's Pipe Playing, 113, 114.
Hennessy Brothers, Dancers, 223, 306.
Herbert, Victor, 289.
Herd's *Ancient and Modern Scottish Songs*, 235.
Herd's *Collection of Scottish Songs*, 169.
Hibernian Catch Book, 239.
Hibernian Muse, 104, 111, 138, 184, 189, 190, 191, 193, 197, 199, 201, 203, 240, 247, 277.
Hicks, John (piper), 21, 22, 23, 24, 30, 66, 91, 93, 118.
Hicks' Hornpipe, 23.
High Cauled Cap, 175, 176, 177.
Highland Laddie, 176.
Hills of Glenorchy, 87.
Hime's *Collection of Country Dances*, 244.
Hime's *Selection of the Most Admired Irish Airs*, 244.
Hinchy, Tom (Clare fiddler), 104, 224.
Hinchy's Delight, 104.
Hob or Nob, 171.

Hoffman's *Selections from Petrie*, 255, 294.
Hogg, James (Scotch poet), 149.
Holden, Smollett, 242, 244, 282.
Holden's *Favorite Irish Airs*, 248.
Holden's *Masonic Songs*, 138.
Holden's *Old Established Irish Tunes*, 133, 135, 195, 198, 244.
Holden's *Periodical Irish Melodies*, 131, 244.
Holland Is a Fine Place, 72.
Horncastle's *Music of Ireland*, 250.
Horrigan, Dan, 215.
Houlihan, Michael, 212, 213.
House of Clonelphin, 87.
House on the Corner, 158.
How Are You Now, My Maid? 125.
How Dear to Me the Hour, 161.
Hudson, Henry, MSS., 63, 249.
Hudson, Dr. Wm. Elliott, 36, 50, 82, 105, 107, 249, 250.
Hugar ma fean, 237.
Hughes' *Collection of Irish Airs*, 253.
Hugh O'Neill's Lament, 72.
Humors of Bandon, 136, 341, 342.
Humors of Bantry, 99.
Humors of Castle Lyons, 105.
Humors of Donnybrook Fair, 134.
Humors of Listivain, 136, 341.
Humors of Milltown, 105.
Humors of Scariff, 122.
Humors of Schull, 98.
Hurry the Jug, 126.
Hyde, Dr. Douglas, 82, 222, 223, 224, 228.
Hyland, Edward Keating, 39.

I

I'm Asleep and Don't Waken Me, 199, 241.
I Am Sleeping, 199.
I Buried My Wife, etc., 97.
I'd Mourn the Hopes, etc., 131, 155.
Idiotic Order of E. Z. Marks, 23.
If All the Young Maidens, 74.
I Gave to My Nelly, 133.
I Have a Wife of My Own, 15.
I Know What You Like, 90.
I'll Follow My Own Figary O, 149.
I'll Hang My Harp on a Willow Tree, 258.
In Comes Great Bonaparte, 146.
Inishowen, 134.
"Inquest Committee," 54.
In This Village Dwells a Maid, 147.
I Rambled Once, 126.
Irish Bards High Rank, 265.
Irish Bards Persecuted, 265.
Irish Brigade at Fontenoy, 174.

Irish Choral Society, 51, 282, 285.
Irish Chroniclers Negligent, 163, 164, 232.
Irish Composers' Work Accredited to England, 290.
Irish Cry, air, 140, 237.
Irish Dance Music Neglected by Collectors, 61, 253, 294.
Irish Dance Music Played too Fast, 291, 292.
Irish Fairs—Destitute of Music, 288.
Irish Folk Song Society of London, 140, 284.
Irish Gillicranky, 124.
Irish and Scots Harps, 71.
Irish Harpers in Scotland, 165, 182, 235.
Irish Jigs, Description of, 106, 107.
Irish Lady, The, 134.
Irish Lass, The, 134.
Irish Lilt, The, 131, 138.
Irish Literary Society of London, 252.
Irish Mad Song, 184.
Irish Melodies, Estimated Total, 293, 294, 295.
Irish Music Appropriated, 234, 235, 257, 258, 290, 291.
Irish Music Club, 47, 64, 209.
Irish Music Club Organized, 58.
Irish Music Club Demoralized, 59.
Irish Music Described, 277, 279.
Irish Music Lauded by Ancient Writers, 264, 265, 279, 280, 296.
Irish Music Fountain of Scotland and Wales, 278-280.
Irish Music First Printed, 236.
Irish Music Decadence, 62, 73, 98, 112, 122, 252, 267, 268, 270, 274, 284, 287, 288.
Irish Music Revival, 60, 227, 271, 277.
Irish Music, Variants Originated, 110, 242, 281.
Irish Musicians Dying in Poorhouses, 14-15.
Irish Musicians Not Appreciated at Home, 58, 289.
Irish Musicians' Professional Jealousy, 208, 209, 219, 220, 268, 275, 276.
Irish Musicians, Many Blind, 101, 121, 280.
Irish Musicians Often Selfish and Secretive, 33, 66, 97, 126, 275, 276.
Irish Musicians Imprisoned, 45, 270.
Irish or Union Bagpipes, 308-319.
Irish or Union Bagpipes, O'Farrell's Instructions, 320-331.
Irish or Union Bagpipes, Touhey's Instructions, 332-337.
Irish Ragg, The, 193, 207.
Irish Washerwoman, 140.

Irish Wedding, 149.
Irishwoman, 140.
I Saw From the Beach, 135.
Is Maith an Duine tu, 206.
Is the Big Man Within? 125.
Italian Music Introduced, 267.
I've Come Into My Home Again, 132.
Ivy Leaf, 31.
I Will Have Another Wife, 203.
I Would Not Give My Irish Wife, 92.

J

Jackey Tar, 121.
Jackson, "Piper," 92, 103, 118, 139, 230, 238, 290.
Jackson's Bonner Bougher, 92, 201.
Jackson's *Celebrated Irish Tunes*, 92, 208.
Jackson's Delight, 140.
Jackson's Morning Brush, 238, 239.
Jack's the Lad, 160.
Jacobite Relics, 176.
Jennie Pippin, 87.
Jenny Picking Cockles, 21.
Jerry Daly's Hornpipe, 116, 151.
Jigg to the Irish Cry, 237.
Jim Moore's Fancy, 18.
Jimmy O'Brien's Jig, 21, 189.
Job of Journeywork, 161.
Jockey at the Fair, 126.
John Doe, 157.
Johnny Allen's Reel, 122.
Johnny McGill, 133.
John O'Dwyer of the Glens, 70, 125.
John Roy Stewart, 139.
Johnson's *Choice Collection of Two Hundred Favorite Country Dances*, 192.
Johnson's *Two Hundred Country Dances*, 136.
Johnson's *Scots Musical Museum*, 259.
Jolly Corkonian, 87.
Jolly Old Man, 21.
Jones, Thomas Morris, 191.
Joyce, Dr. P. W., 12, 45, 53, 66, 97, 100, 103, 105, 111, 119, 126, 129, 135, 144, 150, 153, 155, 206, 242, 256, 293, 294, 295.
Joyce, Dr., *Ancient Irish Music*, 61, 72, 76, 105, 130, 146, 150, 154, 157, 161, 255.
Joyce, Dr., *Irish Local Names*, 205.
Joyce, Dr., *Irish Music and Song*, 255.
Joyce, Dr., *Old Irish Folk Music and Songs*, 69, 76, 80, 81, 87, 88, 92, 94, 99, 105, 108, 111, 113, 117, 118, 123, 124, 125, 131, 151, 152, 154, 155, 156, 157, 161, 255, 293, 295.

INDEX

Joyce, Dr., Estimates Questioned, 293, 294, 295.
Joyce, Eddie, Piper, 31.
Joy of My Life, 101.

K

Kanaka Musician, 16.
Kate Kearney, 134, 135.
Kate Martin, 134.
Kathleen Mavourneen, 54, 249.
Katie's Fancy, 94, 95.
Keane, James, 77.
Keating, Michael, 19.
Kelly, Blind Piper, 32.
Kelly, Michael, Composer, 289, 290.
Kelly, Bannow Piper, 209.
Kennedy, James, 34, 36, 41, 66, 91, 92, 102, 110, 156, 160.
Kennedy, Nellie, 34, 81, 160.
Kennedy, Peter, 94.
Kenny, Mrs., Dublin Violinist, 115.
Kerwin, Sergt. James, 42, 43.
Kerwin's Hospitality, 43, 44, 47, 58.
Kid on the Mountain, 108.
Kildare Fancy, 37.
Kildroughalt Fair, 131, 132.
Killarney, Air, 48, 54, 80.
Killarney, Michael Doyle's Opinion, 225, 226.
Killeavy, 131.
King James' March to Ireland, 181.
King of the Pipers, 88.
Kinloch's *One Hundred Irish Airs*, 247.
Kinnegad Slashers, 136, 137.
Kiss the Maid Behind the Barrel, 34.
Kit O'Mahony's Hornpipe, 117.
Kitty Losty's Reel, 37.
Kitty of Ballinamore, 138.
Kitty's Rambles, 87.
Kneebuckle Jig, 98.

L

Lacy, Tim, "the Fiddler," 209.
Ladies of Carrick, 34.
Ladies' Pantalettes, 25.
Ladies' Triumph, 88.
Lady Aberdeen's Irish Village, 119.
Lady Behind the Boat, 102.
Lady Carbury's Reel, 111.
Lady Mary Ramsey, 19.
Lady Morgan, 134, 316.
Laing David, 169.
Lament for Kilcash, 129.
Land of Sweet Erin, 136.
Langolee, New, 201.
Langolee, Old, 201.
Lannigan's Ball, 139.

Lark, The, 165.
Lark in the Morning, 95, 156.
Lass from the County Mayo, 74.
Last Rose of Summer, 291.
Leaves So Green, 249.
Ledwich, Rev. Dr., *Antiquities of Ireland,* 239, 313, 314.
Leinster Feis, 113, 228.
Let Us Be Drinking, 79.
Levey's *Dance Music of Ireland,* 53, 62, 117, 254, 341.
Life Is All Checkered, 133.
Ligrum Cus, 201.
Limerick Lamentation, 180, 181, 182.
Link About, 103.
Little and Great Mountain, 241.
Little Black Rosebud, 153.
Little Bunch of Rushes, 134.
Little Girl of My Heart, 68.
Little Heathy Hill, 150.
Little House Under the Hill, 103.
Little Katie Kearney, 19.
Little Mary Cullenan, 130, 154.
Little Red Lark of the Mountain, 78.
Liverpool Hornpipe, 116.
Lochaber No More, 180, 181.
Loch Hela, 205.
Lock and Key, Opera, 183.
Lock, Mathew, 185.
Locke On Education, 307.
Lodge Road, Long Dance, 125.
Logan's *Scottish Gael,* 303, 304, 316.
Londonderry Clog, 119, 120.
London Minstrel, 261.
Long Dance, Description, 297-306.
Long Strand, 102.
Loobeens, 74.
Lord Howe's Hornpipe, 144.
Lord Kames on Music, 280.
Lord Ronald, 181.
Lough, Allen, Reel, 141.
Lough, Sheeling, 141.
Love in a Camp, Opera, 240.
Love in a Riddle, Opera, 179.
Love in a Village, Opera, 234, 298.
Love in Secret, 195.
Lover's *Poems of Ireland,* 121, 181, 247.
Love's Young Dream, 151.
Lowlands of Holland, 72.
Ludwig, Dublin Baritone, 38.
Luggelaw, 205.
Luinigs, 74.
Lynch's *Melodies of Ireland,* 88, 119, 132, 138, 149, 197, 251.
Lyons, Cornelius, Harper, 229.

Mc

McCrimmons, Famous Pipers, 311, 312, 313.
McAdam, John, 270.
McCabe, Highland Piper, 213.
McCarthy, Henry, 290.

INDEX 353

McCormick, William, Piper, 223.
McCullagh, Tommy, 200.
McCullagh's *Collection of Irish Airs*, 190, 198, 248.
McDermott, Roe, 183, 184.
McDonald, John, 215, 216.
McDonald's *Collection of Highland Airs*, 259
McDonnell, Piper, 103, 155.
McDonnell, Dr., 269.
McFadden, John, 34, 36, 38, 44, 49, 53, 66, 83, 84, 89, 90, 99, 101, 102, 107, 108, 111, 113, 114, 115, 116, 118, 211, 217, 223.
McFadyen, John, Glasgow, 93, 259.
McGaffey, Ernest, 158.
McGibbon's *Collection of Scots Tunes*, 234.
McGlashan's *Scots Measures*, 183.
McGoun's *Repository of Scots and Irish Airs*, 63, 90, 93, 101, 103, 125, 140, 171, 191, 193, 194, 260.
McGrath, Andrew, 172.
McIntosh, *Collection of Irish Airs*, 260.
McKenna's Dream, 69.
McLean's *Selection of Original Irish Airs*, 165, 238.
McLean, William, Highland Piper, 28, 101.
McMahon, Teig, 130.
McNamara, John E., 306.
McNamara Music MSS., 50.
McNeill, Hector, 133, 200.
McNulty, Rev. Father, 271.
McNurney, Alderman Michael, 30, 213.
McSwiney, Turlogh, 84, 119.

M

Mackenzie, Shelton, *Bits of Blarney*, 9, 300, 301.
Macklin, Rev. Charles, 273.
Mack, "Paddy," 121, 122, 224.
Madam Bonaparte, Long Dance, 146.
Maggy Laidir, Air, 168, 170.
Maiden, The, 68, 170.
Maid in Bedlam, 235.
Maid of Derby, 149
Maid of Feakle, 122.
Maid of Templenoe, 130.
Maids of Ballinacarty, 87.
Mairin ni Chiullionain, 130, 154, 169.
Major, The, 237.
Mallow, Town of, 136.
Maloney, Denis, 20.
Maloney Family, 20.
Malonys, Bagpipe Makers, 318.
Malowney's Wife, 89.
Mansion House Reception, 228.
Manson's *Highland Bagpipe*, 312.

Manuscript Collections, 232, 233, 262.
Man in the Moon, 90.
Man Who Died and Rose Again, 105.
Market Stake, The, 193.
Martin's One-horned Cow, 87.
Mary Grace, 21.
Mason's Apron, 111.
Mason's Cap, 111.
Masson Laddie, 111.
Maureen from Gibberland, 131.
Mavourneen na Gruaige Baine, 76, 130.
Mehauleen Cuis na Thinna, 224.
Merry Old Woman, 100, 136.
Merry Wives of Windsor, Opera, 157.
Michael Malloy, 134.
Miller of Glanmire, 41.
Miller's Frolic, 113.
Milliner's Daughter, 109.
Millstream, The, 141.
Miners of Wicklow, 90.
Miniature Museum, 176.
Miss Corbett's Reel, 110.
Miss Dawson's Hornpipe, 298.
Miss Hope's Favorite, 111.
Miss McLeod's Reel, 112, 140, 227.
Miss Molly, My Love, I'll Go, 135.
Miss Monaghan, Reel, 37.
Miss Redmond's Hornpipe, 117.
Miss Wallace, Reel, 19.
Mist of Clonmel, 137.
Moffat, Alfred, 124, 133, 135, 136, 137, 164, 171, 177, 183, 187, 193, 200, 201, 234.
Moffat's *Minstrelsy of Ireland*, 124, 132, 140, 148, 149, 152, 164, 173, 180, 184, 192, 195, 199, 204, 232, 237, 244, 250.
Moffat's *Minstrelsy of Scotland*, 124, 164, 173, 176.
Moggy Lauder, Air, 168, 170.
Moirin ni Chuillionain, 130, 154, 169.
Molecatcher's Daughter, 135.
Molloy's *Songs of Ireland*, 255.
Molly My Treasure, 235.
Molly St. George, 237.
Mo Muirnin na Gruaige Baine, 76, 130.
Monaghan Jig, 94.
Mona's Melodies, 261.
Moneymusk, The, 204.
Mooncoin Reel, 48.
Mooney Rose, Harper, 229
Mooney's *History of Ireland*, 84, 104, 118, 278.
Moore, Harper and Violinist, 192.
Moore, James, 17.
Moore, Thomas, Poet, 133, 140, 149, 155, 161, 164, 232, 244.
Moore's *Irish Melodies*, 51, 54, 61, 64, 131, 132, 135, 148, 151, 179, 180, 184, 195, 196, 197, 201, 204, 205, 206, 208, 243, 244,

245, 246, 247, 248, 251, 255, 282, 291.
Moore Indebted to Bunting, 242, 281.
Morgan Rattler, 92.
Mor no Beag, 131.
Mountain Dew, 121.
Mountain Lark, 34, 160.
Mrs. Casey, 138.
Mrs. Martin's Favorite, 87.
Mr. William Clark's Favorite, 125.
Mug of Brown Ale, 96.
Muiris MacDaibhi Dubh MacGerailt, 173.
Mulhollan's *Ancient Irish Airs*, 244.
Mulnollan's *Irish and Scots Tunes*, 131, 244.
Mulligan, Edward Howard, 52.
Mulvihill, John, 98.
Munster Fews, 70, 112, 226, 288.
Murnihan, Frank, 20.
Munster Gimlet, 108.
Murphy, Blind Piper, 24, 211, 212, 213, 214, 215.
Murphy, Charley, Piper, 13.
Murphy, Coachman Piper, 24.
Murphy, Delaney, 140, 237.
Murphy, Harper, 229.
Murphy's *Irish Airs and Jigys*, 134, 135, 244, 315.
Musical Repository of Scotch, English and Irish Songs, 260.
Music for Allan Ramsay's Collection of Scotch Songs, 200, 254.
My Brother Tom, 34.
My Darling Asleep, 98.
My Darling, I Am Fond of You, 69.
My Fair-haired Darling, 76, 130.
My Former Wife, 96.
My Heart's Delight, 235.
My Lodging Is Uncertain, 132.
My Lodging Is on the Cold Ground, 184, 185, 338, 339.
My Love Is a Bandboy, 69.
My Love Is Fair and Handsome, 17, 139.
My Name Is Moll Mackey, 69.
My Nannie O, 237.
My Old Kentucky Home, 290.

N

Nancy Dawson, 298.
Nancy Hynes, Jig, 89.
National Melodies of England and Ireland, 260.
Nature and Melody, 134.
Neale, John and William, 236, 262.
Neale's *A Book of Irish Tunes*, 232.
Neale's *A Collection of Irish and Scotch Tunes*, 232.
Ned of the Hill, 131, 189.
Nell Flaherty's Drake, 99.
Nelly, My Love, and Me, 129.

New Demesne, Reel, 34, 110.
New Poems and Songs, etc., 181.
New Policeman, 18.
News from Scotland, 299.
Nolan, the Soldier, 17.
No, Not More Welcome, 205.
Noonan, Patrick, 28.
Nora an Oiste, 197.
Nora Chreena, 228.
Noran Kitsa, 197.
Nora with the Cake, 197.
Noreen Keesta, 198.
Norickystie, 197.
Northern Road, 102.

O

O! An Irishman's Heart, 137.
O, an Ye Were Dead Guid Man, 173.
O'Brien, Arthur, *Old Songs of Ireland*, 253.
O'Brien, Jimmy, Mayo Piper, 21, 66, 111.
O'Brien MSS., 262.
O'Cahan Rory Dall, 71, 229.
O'Callaghan's *Collection of Irish Airs*, 248.
O'Carolan, Turlogh, 82, 83, 93, 154, 180, 183, 191, 192, 193, 202, 221, 229, 249, 268.
O'Carolan's *A Favorite Collection of Irish Tunes*, 238.
O'Carolan's Farewell, 84.
O'Carolan's Farewell to Music, 84, 85.
O'Carolan's Receipt, etc., 193.
O'Connellan, Thomas, Harper, 124, 154, 182, 229, 249.
O'Connell's Welcome to Clare, 249.
O'Conor, Charles, Field Dance, 303.
O'Curry, Prof. Eugene, *Manners and Customs of the Ancient Irish*, 152, 274, 297, 298, 309.
O'Daly Carol, 166.
O'Daly's *Donogh Mor*, 166.
O'Daly, Gerald, 164, 229.
O'Daly's *Poets and Poetry of Munster*, 70, 72, 112, 132, 150, 153, 154, 155, 164, 171, 173, 175, 189, 251.
O'Donnell, D. K., 290.
O'Donovan, Bernie, 115, 126.
O'Dwyer's Hornpipe, 118.
O'Farrell's *Instructions for the Irish or Union Pipes*, 320-331.
O'Farrell's *Collection of National Irish Music*, etc., 92, 135, 243.
O'Farrell's *Pocket Companion for the Irish or Union Pipes*, 90, 102, 104, 132, 134, 137, 149, 175, 180, 184, 197, 199, 201, 203.
Off to California, 16.
O'Flannagan's *Collection*, 244.
O'Gallagher's Frolics, 97.

INDEX

Ogden's *Gems from Ould Ireland*, 253.
Oh, Arranmore, Loved Arranmore, 131.
Oh, 'Tis Sweet to Think, 132.
O'Kearin, Dancing-master, 306.
O'Keeffe and O'Brien, *A Handbook of Irish Dance*, 70, 177, 236, 287, 299, 300.
O'Keeffe, John, Dramatist, 130, 192.
Old Eileen a Roon, 165.
Old Folks at Home, 290.
Old Grey Goose, 91, 92.
Old Lee Rigg, 131.
"Old Man" Dillon, 100.
"Old Man" Quinn, 114.
Old Man, The, 72, 112, 171, 172.
Old Molly Ahern, 142.
Old Plaid Shawl, 75.
Old Truicha, 132.
Old Woman, The, 151.
Old Woman Tossed Up in a Blanket, 89.
O'Leary, Prof. Denis, 318.
O'Mahony, Conor, 289.
O'Mahony, Patrick, 18, 19, 212, 213.
O'Malley, Eccentric Fiddler, 42.
O! Merry am I, 137.
O! My Dear Judy, 132.
On a Monday Morning, 137.
O Nanny, Wilt Thou Gang With Me? 182, 183.
O'Neachtan, John, 168, 170.
O'Neale, John and William, 191. (See 236, 262.)
One Evening in June, 130.
O'Neill, Arthur, harper, 178, 184, 200, 229, 269, 281.
O'Neill, Arthur, Harp School, 269, 270.
O'Neill, Capt. Francis, 48, 49, 222, 224.
O'Neill's *Music of Ireland*, 23, 25, 38, 43, 55, 57, 61, 62, 63, 64, 68, 72, 73, 75, 76, 77, 80, 81, 84, 95, 99, 113, 115, 117, 118, 120, 124, 125, 130, 136, 143, 148, 150, 151, 152, 153, 154, 155, 156, 157, 160, 161, 171, 293, 295, 339, 342.
O'Neill's *Dance Music of Ireland*, 62, 67, 70, 76, 89, 99, 102, 106, 113, 115, 118, 124, 125, 126, 129, 143, 155, 222, 224, 293, 295, 318, 342, 343.
O'Neill's *Irish Music for Piano or Violin*, 63, 64, 101, 118, 130, 141, 194.
O'Neill's Rumored Assassination, 216, 217.
O'Neill, Sergt. James, 29, 33, 35, 37, 44, 51, 52, 53, 61, 66, 70, 71, 72, 75, 77, 78, 84, 90, 91, 92, 93, 96, 97, 114, 115, 119, 125, 126, 136, 146, 148, 153, 154, 160, 216, 217, 223, 340, 342, 343.
O'Neill, John, fluter, 15.
O'Neill, Lane, *English-Irish Dictionary*, 197.
O'Neill Pipers of Armagh, 43.
O'Neill, Miss Selena A., 60.
On the Deck of Patrick Lynch's Boat, 74, 75.
Open the Door for Three, 15.
Operas Named in *Hibernian Muse*, 240.
O! Pleasant Was the Moon, 134.
Orangeman, The, 124.
Orange Rogue, 124.
O'Reilly's *Irish-English Dictionary*, 82.
O'Reilly, Philip J., MSS., 50.
O'Rourke's Feast, 193.
Orpheus Caledonius, 234.
O'Scanlan Teig Rua, 306.
O'Shaughnessy, Richard Michael, 254.
Oscar and Malvina, Opera, 243.
O! Southern Breeze, 241.
O'Sullivan's March, 88, 89.
Oswald's *Caledonian Pocket Companion*, 131, 165, 171, 173, 234, 258.
O'Tuomy, John, poet, 130.
Out of My Sight, etc., 180.
Out on the Ocean, 19.
Over the Bridge to Peggy, 37.
Oh! Weep for the Hour, 149.
Owen Roe O'Neill Lament, 82.
Owenson, Miss, *Hibernian Melodies*, 244.
Owenson, Miss, *Patriotic Sketches*, 316, 317.

P

Paddeen O'Rafardie, 94.
Paddy Digging for Goold, 137.
Paddy in London, 23, 218.
Paddy Mack's Hornpipe, 122.
Paddy McFadden, 139.
Paddy O'Rafferty, 93.
Paddy's Trip from Dublin, 140.
Paistin Fionn, 199.
Parson in His Boots, 140.
Past One o'Clock, 200, 237.
Pat and Kate, 149.
Patheen a Fuen, 199.
Patrons, Ancient, Described, 271, 272.
Pearl of the White Breast, 152.
Peggy of Darby, etc., 150.
Penniless Traveler, 143.
"Peter Bawn." (See Hagerty.)
Peter Kennedy's Fancy, 35.
Peter Street, reel, 112.
Petrie, George, 12, 45, 56, 57, 66, 69, 79, 84, 89, 90, 92, 94, 99, 103, 118, 120, 139, 141, 151, 152, 153, 156, 157, 161, 188,

INDEX

198, 205, 206, 232, 241, 242, 251, 253, 254, 282.
Petrie, *Collection of the Ancient Music of Ireland*, 56, 61, 106, 141, 152, 154, 252, 283, 294.
Petrie, *Complete Collection of Irish Music*, 23, 38, 77, 102, 104, 107, 111, 113, 117, 124, 129, 130, 135, 136, 137, 141, 147, 150, 153, 154, 188, 196, 294, 341.
Petrie, On Variants, 56, 110.
Phair, Alderman William, Cork, 289.
Pharroh or War March, 89.
Pigot Music MSS., 156, 161, 255.
Pipe on the Hob, 87.
Pipers and Fiddlers in London, 266.
Pipers and Fiddlers Suppressed, 266.
Piper's Lass, The, 142.
Piper's Picnic, 90.
Planks of Connaught, 237.
Planxty, Meaning of the Term, 82, 202.
Planxty Davis, 124.
Planxty Dobbins, 83.
Planxty O'Rourke, 193.
Planxty Reilly, 83.
Planxty Toby Peyton, 83, 339, 340.
Playford, John, 173, 233, 282.
Playford's Dancing Master, 190, 233, 258, 298.
Playford's Collection of Original Scotch Tunes, 233.
Playford's Music's Handmaid, 233.
Playford's Wit and Mirth, etc., 258.
Plumstead's *Beauties of Melody*, 261.
Plumptre, Mrs., *Narrative, etc.*, 205, 272, 305.
Polly, Opera, 236.
Poor Old Woman, 117, 151.
Poor Soldier, Opera, 104, 130, 135, 180, 192, 240.
Popular Songs and Melodies of Scotland, 183.
Power's *Musical Cabinet*, 137, 244.
Powers of Whiskey, 137.
Praises of Limerick, 69.
"Praties" Are Dug, etc., 137, 156.
Pretty Girl Milking Her Cow, 202.
Pretty Girl of Derby O, 149.
Priest in His Boots, 140, 237, 298.
Priest with the Collar, 94.
Prime's Hornpipe, 118.
Princess Royal, 183.
Pringle's *Reels and Jigs*, 149.
Professional Jealousy, 208, 209, 219, 220, 268, 275, 276.
Proposal, The, 75.
Pulse of My Heart, 148.
Punch for the Ladies, 87.
Purcell, Henry, 289.

Q

Quaker's Opera, 170.
Queen of the Fair, 90.
Queen Elizabeth, 265, 270.
Queen's County Lasses, 117.
Queen's Shilling, 19.
Quinn, David, Piper, 36, 37, 83, 100, 105, 110, 111, 114, 115.

R

Rakes of Clonmel, 97.
Rakes of Kildare, 139, 140.
Rakes of Kinsale, 92.
Rakes of London, 136.
Rakes of Mallow, 135, 237.
Rakes of Marlow, 136.
Rakes of Newcastle West, 100.
Rakes of Westmeath, 237.
Raking Paudeen Rue, 43, 69.
Rambles of Kitty, 87.
Ramsay, Allan, *Tea Table Miscellany*, 181.
Ranting Highlander, 174.
Rathkeale Hunt, 142.
Reel of Bogie, 37.
Reel of Mullinavat, 84.
Reillaghan, Munster piper, 105, 220, 221.
Remains of Nithsdale and Galloway Songs, 176.
Rickett's Hornpipe, 160.
Rights of Man Hornpipe, 115, 227.
Ring or Rinka Dance, 302.
Rinnce Fada, 254, 297, 302, 303, 305.
Robin Adair, 164, 166.
Robin Hood Opera, 149, 240.
Rocking a Baby that's None of My Own, 81.
Rocking the Cradle, 80.
Rocks of Cashel, 103, 155.
Rocky Road to Dublin, 107.
Rodney's Glory, 69.
Rogers, Daniel, 104, 210.
Roger the Weaver, 88.
Roisin Dubh, 153.
Rois Geal Dubh, 153, 154.
Rollicking Irishman, 138.
Rolling on the Ryegrass, 141, 142.
Ronayne's Jig, 87.
Rory Dall's Sister's Lament, 71.
Rose Connolly, 129.
Rose Tree, The, 130, 155.
Rosetree of Paddy's Land, 131.
Rosina Opera, 240.
Rough Little Heathy Hill, 67, 150.
Rowan James, 22.
Rowsome, William, piper, 228, 318.
Royal Irish Jig, 158.

INDEX

Royal Society of Antiquaries, 284, 293.
Rutherford's *200 Country Dances*, 171, 234, 259.
Rutherford's *Ladies' Pocket Guide for the Guitar*, 237.
Ryan, Dan, 223, 306.
Ryan, John, 306.
Ryan, John P., 42, 43.
Ryan, Rev. Father Abram J., 290.

S

Saddle the Pony, 90.
Sailor's Hornpipe, 160, 161, 301.
Saint Patrick's Day in the Morning, 174, 234, 247.
Sally's New Answer, 170.
Sarsfield's Lamentation, 182.
Sault's Own Hornpipe, 119.
Savourneen Deelish, 135.
Sawyer, Charles Carroll, 290.
Scariff, Experience at, 224.
Scatter the Mud, 90.
School for Scandal, Opera, 240.
Scolding Wife, 156.
Scotch Music derived from Ireland, 280.
Scotch Music first printed, 233, 236.
Scotch Patriotism, etc., 275, 283.
Scots Musical Museum, 169, 259.
Scott, John and Henry, harpers, 229.
Sean bhean bhocht, 117, 151.
Seanduine. See *An Seanduine*.
Sean O Duibhir An Gleanna, 70.
Semple, Francis, 169.
Sergeant Early's Dream, 90.
Shamrock, The, 179.
Shanavest and Caravath, 156.
Shandon Bells, 87.
Shannon Breeze, 142.
Shaskan Reel, 113.
Shea, Insp. John D., 25, 216.
Shea, John Gilmary, 317.
Sheehan, Margaret, 71, 72.
Sheela na Guira, 169, 190.
Sheela ni Gara, 189.
She is the Girl that can do it, 133.
Sighile ni Gadhra, 189.
Silver Tip, 34.
Since Coelia is my Foe, 181.
Sinner's Lament, 67.
Sín sios agus suas liom, 197.
Sios agus sios liom, 196.
Sir Archibald Grant of Moniemusk, 204.
Sir Muddin dum da man, 206.
Sit Down Beside Me, 196.
Six Mile Bridge, 117.
Skene Manuscripts, 233.
Skibbereen Lassies, 98.
Skiver the Quilt, 102.
Slainte Righ Pilib, 190.
Slaunt Ri Piulib, 190, 237.
Sligo Chorus, 37.

Smah Dunna hoo, 206.
Smith's *Irish Minstrel*, 57, 81, 133, 150, 185, 195, 196, 248.
Snowy-breasted Pearl, 152.
Soaped fiddle strings, 216.
Society for the Preservation and the Publication of the Melodies of Ireland, 152, 252, 283.
Songster's Companion, 185.
Songs of Uladh, 256.
Song to the Irish Tune, 181.
Spailpin Fanach, 177.
Spence, Bob, fiddler, 101.
Staca an Margaidh, 198.
Stack in Virgo, 193.
Stack, Sergt. Garrett, 42.
Stadh a Rogaire, Stadh, 194.
Stagger the Buck, 90.
Stanford, Sir Villiers, 179, 180, 253.
Stark, Sergt. Gerald, 42.
Star of Munster, 21.
Steam Packet, 160.
Stephenson, Kerry piper.
Stevenson, Sir John, 39, 164, 243, 250.
Stirling, "Parson," piper, 230, 238, 290.
Stolen Heart, The, 206.
Stolen Purse, 98.
Straloch Manuscripts, 233.
Stratagem, The, 206.
Such Beauties in View, 239.
Sullivan, Daniel, Boston violinist, 68.
Sullivan, Dan, composer, 68.
Sullivan Family, Palos, Ills., 142.
Sullivan, Cork piper, 105, 220, 221.
Sullivan, Johnny—the Poet, 71, 72.
Sullivan, Richard, dancer, 223.
Sullivan, Sir Arthur, 223, 289.
Sunny Dan, 132.
Surenne's *Songs of Ireland*, 129, 130, 149, 251.
Surrender of Calais, Opera, 135.
Sweet Peter Street, 113.
Swift from the Covert, 140.
Sword Dance, 304.

T

Tailor's Wedding, 102.
Talbot, William, piper, 230, 317, 318.
Ta me i mo Codhladh, etc., 199.
Ta na La, 135.
Taste in Music, 267, 285, 286.
Tatter Jack Walsh, 138, 227.
Taylor, William, piper, 33, 319.
Teige *Maire's* Daughter, 69.
Templehouse Jig, 88.
Tenpenny Bit, 34, 102.
Thady, You Gander, 132.
Thama Hulla, 199.
Thamama Hulla, 199.
Thanksgiving—Air, 71.

There are Few Good Fellows, etc., 76.
There Came to the Beach, 135.
There'll Never be Peace, etc., 76.
There's an End to My Sorrow, 76.
There is a Beech Tree Grove, 129.
This is the Ranting Season O, 149.
Thomas Burk—Air, 237.
Thomas McJudge—Air, 83.
Thomaus a Moumpus, 203.
Thompson's *Country Dances,* 197, 201, 235, 239, 259.
Thompson's *Compleat Collection of Favorite Hornpipes,* 140, 237, 298.
Thomson's *Select Collection, Original Irish Airs,* 52, 57, 131, 147, 187, 190, 247.
Thomson's *Select Melodies of Scotland,* 169, 235.
Three Captains, 125.
Three Halfpence a Day, 15.
Three Little Drummers, 103.
Three Sea Captains, 125.
Thrush, The, 261.
Thumoth Burk—*Twelve Scotch and Twelve Irish Airs,* 140, 166, 189, 191, 193, 201, 237, 247.
Thumoth Burk—*Twelve English and Twelve Irish Airs,* 136, 189, 191, 192, 193, 237.
Thunder Hornpipe, 19.
Thy Fair Bosom, 132.
Tie the Bonnet, 98.
"Tightwad Club," 22.
'Tis a Bit of a Thing, 134.
'Tis Gone and Forever, 135.
Tobin, Adam, 34, 44, 49, 221, 222
Tobin's Gallantry, 221, 222.
Toby Peyton's Piangsty, 83, 339, 340.
To Cashel I'm Going, 138.
To Drink with the Devil, 138.
To Ladies' Eyes, 204.
Tom Judge, 83.
Tom Linton, 135.
Top of Cork Road, 137.
Top the Candle, 34.
Toss the Feathers, 37.
Touch Me if You Dare, 35, 160.
Tow, Row, Row, 135.
Tralibane Bridge, 13, 77, 78.
Tramp, Tramp, the Boys are Marching, 285.
Trim the Velvet, 37.
Trip It Along, 105.
Trotter, John Bernard, 76.
Tubridy, John, 113, 122.
Touhey, "Darby Simon," 121.
Touhey, Michael, 121, 122.
Touhey's *Hints to Amateur Pipers,* 332 to 337.
Touhey, Patrick J., 23, 32, 38, 96, 105, 108, 111, 113, 118.
Twisting of the Rope, 161.
Twopenny Jig, 50.

V

Vandaleur, Col., 318.
Vocal "Chestnuts," 282.
Vocalists' Pretensions, 291.
Vocal Magazine, 259.
Vocal Miscellany, 236.
Vocal Music or Songster's Companion, 185, 338.

W

Walker, Joseph C. M.—M. R. I. A. *Historical Memoir of the Irish Bards,* 239, 266, 267, 277.
Wallace, Vincent, 289, 290.
Walls of Enniscorthy, 100.
Walls of Liscarroll, 87.
Walsh's *Compleat Country Dancing Master,* 173, 185.
Walsh's *Merry Musician,* 258.
Walsh, John, J. P., 122.
Walsh, Paddy, piper, 161.
Walsh, Rev. Father J. T., 63.
Walsh, William, piper, 42, 43, 154, 175, 219.
Wanderer's Return, 132.
Ward, Mary, 142.
Wayland, John Smithwick, 227, 289.
Wedding of Ballinamona, 193.
Wedding of Ballyporeen, 192.
Wedding Ring, The, 80.
We'll All Take a Coach and Trip It Away, 92.
Wellington's Advance, 92.
Were You ever in Sweet Tipperary? 129.
West, George, 41, 42.
What Sounds Can Compare? 134.
What Would You Do if You Married a Soldier? 137.
When a Man's in Love, etc., 75.
When You are Sick, is it Tea You Want? 143.
Where Have You Been All Day? 176.
White-backed Black Cow, 190.
White Bread and Butter, 77.
White Cockade, The, 173, 174, 175.
Why Should not Poor Folk? 241.
Wicklow Hornpipe, 37.
Wild Geese, The, 194.
Wild Irish Boy, 249.
Wild Irishman, 197.
Will You Come Down to Limerick? 37, 107.
Will You Go to Flanders? 234, 235.
Will You List Young Man? 175
Wilson's *Companion to the Ballroom,* 93, 106, 116, 121, 123, 141, 144, 176, 261.
Winter Apples, 142.
Within this Village Dwells a Maid, 147.

Woman of the House, 21, 111.
Woodcock, The, 102.
Woods of Kilmurry, 66.
Wood's *Songs of Scotland*, 56, 73, 110, 169, 176, 181, 232, 241, 258.
Wreathe the Bowl, 197.
Wright's *Aria di Camera*, 182, 193, 197, 236.
Wright's *Country Dances*, 183.

Y

Ye Banks and Braes o' Bonnie Doon, 56.
Ye Friendly Stars that Rule the Night, 196.

Yellow Garron, 152, 153.
Yemon o nock, 189, 237.
Yogh hone, O hone, 203.
Yorkshire Lasses, 137.
Youghal Harbor, 81, 82, 118, 119.
You Know I'm Your Priest, 192.
You May Talk as You Please, 133.
Young May Moon, 149, 180, 240.
Young Tom Ennis, 37.
You Rogue, You Dar'n't Meddle Me, 160.
Youth in Bloom, 130.

Z

Zampa Opa, 206.